HONG KONG, APPOINTMENT WITH CHINA

TO LOUIS AND MAY CHA

HONG KONG
Appointment with China

Steve Tsang

I.B.Tauris
London · New York

Published in 1997 by
I.B.Tauris & Co. Ltd
Victoria House
Bloomsbury Square
London WC1B 4DZ

In the United States of America and Canada distributed by
St Martin's Press
175 Fifth Avenue
New York
NY 10010

A full CIP record for this book is available from the British Library
A full CIP record for this book is available from the Library of Congress

ISBN 1–86064–311–6
Library of Congress Catalog card number available

Copy-edited and laser-set by Oxford Publishing Services, Oxford
Printed and bound in Great Britain by WBC Ltd, Bridgend, Mid Glamorgan

Contents

Abbreviations

BAAG	British Army Aid Group
BBC	British Broadcasting Corporation
BLCC	Basic Law Consultative Committee
BLDC	Basic Law Drafting Committee
CAB	Cabinet Office
CO	Colonial Office
CPC	Communist Party of China
DEFE	Ministry of Defence
FO	Foreign Office
FRUS	Foreign Relations of the United States
GOC	General Officer Commanding
HK	Hong Kong
HKMAO	Hong Kong and Macao Affairs Office
HMS	His/Her Majesty's Ship
HS	Special Operations Executive
JIC	Joint Intelligence Committee
JLG	Joint Liaison Group
LegCo	Legislative Council
MACHIN	Military Attaché China
NPC	National People's Congress
NSC	National Security Council
OAG	Officer Administering the Government
PADS	Port and Airport Development Strategy
PLA	People's Liberation Army
PRC	People's Republic of China
PWC	preliminary working committee
ROC	Republic of China
SAR	Special Administrative Region
SOE	Special Operations Executive
SWB	Summary of World Broadcasts

Acknowledgements

Although this volume was written over the last five months, research for it was carried out over a period of about ten years. Much of the basic research was done in conjunction with other projects or in preparation for a modern history of Hong Kong. For a few years I had entertained the idea of putting a volume like this together before the transfer of sovereignty over Hong Kong to the People's Republic of China, but decided against it for various reasons. Dr Lester Crook at I.B.Tauris was largely instrumental in persuading me to embark on this endeavour around Christmas last year. Without his encouragement and unfailing efforts in expediting the editorial and production work, this volume would not have been attempted and would have taken much longer to see the light of day. Mrs Selina Cohen, who did the copy-editing, also deserves a note of gratitude for her splendid work under immense pressure of time.

Since this book was completed during a period when my normal academic duties were reinforced by the administrative responsibilities as Dean at my College, much of the writing was in fact done late in the evenings. What inspired and sustained me through the long nights were the great novels about Chinese knights errant by my good friend Professor Louis Cha, or Jin Rong as he is known for his novels. Rereading the gripping stories in between draft paragraphs has proved to be most uplifting for the spirit and refreshing for the mind. To him and his wife, May, who has a heart of gold and is an esteemed friend herself, I dedicate this volume.

In undertaking research that directly affected the preparation of this volume, I would like to thank Miss Carmen Tsang for her assistance in checking various sources in Hong Kong at the last minute. I am grateful to Lieutenant-General Fu Ying-chuan for special access to the Ministry of Defence archives of the Republic of China, and to the Foreign Ministry for access to its papers in Taipei. I am also obliged to the keepers of the Butler Library (Columbia University), the Eisenhower Library (Abilene, Kansas), the Hung On-to Memorial Library (Hong Kong University), the Public Record Office (Kew), Rhodes House Library (Oxford) and the Truman Library (Independence, Missouri) for access to and permission to cite from archival material in their care.

Over the last decade, while director of the Oxford University Hong Kong Project, I benefited greatly from more than 40 in-depth interviews. These were with former members of the Hong Kong government, the British diplomatic service, the Executive and Legislative Councils of Hong Kong, and the Basic Law Drafting Committee. The interviews were conducted on a confidential basis. The oral records and the tens of thousands of pages of transcript are lodged at the Rhodes House Library and are still closed to public access. I have made no use of this vast source because of the need to honour the pledge of confidence. But the many intensive hours of historical discourse clearly influenced the perspective I have adopted in this volume. To all the contributors to the Hong Kong Project — whom I shall not name — I owe a debt of gratitude.

Finally, I would like to thank the trustees of Columbia University and the *Journal of International Affairs* for their kind permission to reproduce, substantially in Chapters 7 and 10, a number of paragraphs from my article 'Maximum Flexibility, Rigid Framework: China's Policy Towards Hong Kong and its Implications' from issue 49(2) of the journal. Where they occur they are identified by their references.

Preface

Hong Kong has always mesmerized me, not least because I was born there. It is a place about which hardly any visitor or resident feels indifferent. They either love it or hate it. Needless to say, I adore it.

This book is about the origins, evolution and eventual resolution of Hong Kong's '1997' problem. It tells a fascinating story of how imperial expansion a century ago ironically introduced a legal requirement that eventually led to the end of Hong Kong as the last dazzling jewel in the British imperial crown. When the British acquired the New Territories in 1898, they also unwittingly made an appointment with China over the future of Hong Kong as a whole. This appointment has survived a republican revolution and the rise of nationalism in China, war and invasion, a temporary Japanese occupation of Hong Kong and near scramble between Britain and China to liberate it, the Chinese communist revolution and the Cold War. Negotiations have now finally determined Hong Kong's future and the original appointment is being kept.

More than half this book is devoted to a description of how Sino–British negotiations over the last two decades have determined the fate of Hong Kong's six million people in a territory of just over 400 square miles. The ironies, spectacular achievements, tragedies and accidents of history that have unfolded in Hong Kong over the last century make gripping reading. This is the background to how, on 1 July 1997, Hong Kong — the world's eighth largest trading economy — came to change its status from a British Crown colony to a Chinese Special Administrative Region.

This is not the history of a remote country and alien people of a bygone age. As a native of Hong Kong and deeply interested in its future, I have written the story of a place and people I know intimately and love dearly. Since events are still unfolding, a correct understanding of the forces for change may help policy makers and other actors shape the future of Hong Kong. My long and intimate experience of Hong Kong has given me certain insights into the thinking of the various actors involved in recent events. This also, however, may have influenced my judgement as a historian. Objectivity based on detachment from the events cannot be taken for granted in this situation, yet it is needed more than ever. For this I have to rely on the strict disciplinary training in British imperial history I received at Oxford many years ago. I also constantly need to remind myself that Hong Kong's interests will not be served by anything less than a completely fair, judicious and dispassionate account.

In this book, I have tried to reconstruct the discussions, debates and arguments that have taken place between and within China and Britain over Hong Kong and its New Territories. I have also presented Hong Kong's own perspective and, in so doing, have dealt with the question of democratization, or the lack of democratic progress.

For the British and Hong Kong side of the story, most of the relevant archives are available up until the first half of the 1960s, and have been used for the historical reconstruction. The same degree of access to Chinese archives is not possible, though I have made extensive use of published documents. I have supplemented these with what little was available in the Republic of China archives, and with Chinese and US private papers in the USA. For more recent events, I have had to rely on published documents, memoirs, media reports and, where possible, personal contacts to verify the authenticity of my sources.

While I have tried to ensure the highest degree of accuracy and objectivity, there is always a possibility of misinformation and indeed misinterpretation of the more recent events. Nevertheless, my objective has been to explain and analyse as clearly, simply and objectively as possible, the forces that have affected the status of Hong Kong in the past. In this process, I have tried to provide pointers with which to assess what the future may hold.

During the decade I have spent working on modern Chinese history and politics, I have learned one important lesson. To understand the forces behind political change or policy making, it is necessary to look beyond the documentary sources. This applies more to China than to the study of a Western country. One needs to develop a feel for the way certain Chinese policy makers think, particularly PRC leaders on an important matter like Chinese sovereignty over Hong Kong. For this reason, I have put the PRC's Hong Kong policy into an analytical structure best summed up as exercising maximum flexibility within a rigid framework.

This book is as much for general readers as for specialists. General readers should ignore the fairly large number of notes, which give specialists the exact references with which to check on the authenticity and reliability of sources. Because I have tried to disperse a number of widely popularized misconceptions or even myths about Hong Kong's recent history, I have decided against dispensing with a list of references. General readers may not wish to enter into scholarly debates, but specialists may like to have the opportunity to trace the sources for their own scholarly pursuits.

Readers are advised that in China the surname precedes the given names. In Hong Kong most ethnic Chinese follow the same rule, but not everyone does so. In the case of those who have put their names in the English way, their preference is respected. In the transliteration of names and Chinese terms, the *pinyin* system adopted in the People's Republic has been followed except for personal or place names in Hong Kong, where their usual form is used.

Steve Tsang
May 1997

1. Beginning of the End: 1898

With the Treaty of Nanking (1843) and the Convention of Peking (1860), imperial China ceded Hong Kong and the tip of the Kowloon peninsula in perpetuity to Britain. The British Empire was at its most powerful, serene and self-confident. For the next half-century of Britain's 156-year rule in Hong Kong, the end of British sovereignty seemed quite out of the question.

In 1898, however, a fundamental change occurred. Through Western expansion and imperial rivalry, Britain acquired territory north of the colony of Hong Kong and south of the Shenzhen River: this was Kowloon, better known as the New Territories. Under the terms of the Convention of Peking, the lease was to run for 99 years and would expire at the end of June 1997. It increased the size of the colony tenfold and applied, strictly speaking, only to the New Territories. Subsequent events, however, linked the New Territories to the rest of the colony and laid the ground for questioning its future status.

This lit the slow-burning and long fuse that would lead to the 'appointment with China'. The imperial expansion of 1898 marked the beginning of the end of Hong Kong as a British territory. By 1997, Britain as an imperial power had, of course, long left the international stage. With the roles of Britain and China by then reversed, perhaps historians will detect in the events leading up to the handing back of Hong Kong a poignant echo of Sino–British imperial history.

Imperial Expansion

In the nineteenth century, Britain's fundamental interest in

China was trade, not territorial expansion. For this reason, when Hong Kong became a colony at the end of the first Anglo–Chinese war (1839–43), it was as a free port to promote international trade in the broadest sense. Such an approach served British interests well, for Britain was the premier trading nation in the world and dominated the China trade. Victorian Britain's leaders 'stood firmly for free trade' and 'strongly preferred influence to political possession as a means to national prosperity and world power'.[1] Keeping the door to trade with China open to all without discrimination meant British domination. Consequently, when the colony was extended in 1860 — after another war had been fought to put Sino–British relations on a more satisfactory footing for the British — London hesitated before acting on its military advisers' advice to expand the colony for its better defence. The British government instructed its plenipotentiary, Lord Elgin, to acquire the tip of the Kowloon peninsula only if it would not 'lead to other demands injurious to China and unfavourable to British interests'.[2] London had no wish to set an example for other European powers to seek territorial cession from China. Territorial expansion on its own had little appeal to London. Indeed, the British government did not want another India and 'consistently refused to extend colonial rule' in the mid-Victorian era.[3]

Although the British government had little territorial ambition in China, one could not say the same of its colonists in Hong Kong. Even though founded as a free port, Hong Kong also became a major outpost of the British Empire in the East. In the nineteenth century it was a significant naval station. As long as the fleet was in harbour, Hong Kong was deemed to be unassailable. However, it was defended only very lightly in the absence of the China Squadron.[4] Major-General Sir Charles van Straubenzee, who commanded the British forces in China and was responsible for the colony's defence, had suggested the 1860 expansion. Local agitation for further expansion quickly followed. In 1863, for example, some people advised building a battery on land that still belonged to China on the northern shore of the harbour's eastern approach.[5] In the 1880s and 1890s, successive commanders of the local garrison urged the War Office to acquire the entire peninsula of Kowloon for military purposes. Sir Paul Chater, a leading local advocate for expansion, summed up the thinking behind this decision: 'The same arguments that prevailed in 1860 must prevail now. We want now only what we wanted then: what is essential to the safety of the Colony. What was enough then, has become from the changes in weapons and the alterations in modes of warfare wholly insufficient now, and we must have more.'[6]

Sir William Robinson, who was governor from 1891 to 1898, shared Chater's views. With Victoria Harbour's northern shore and entrances in Chinese hands, he felt 'the position of this Colony in the event of any war must . . . be very insecure from a defensive point of view'.[7] China was clearly in no position to pose a military threat to this British colony, but local advocates for expansion nevertheless laid heavy emphasis on hypothetical defensive requirements.

There were other grounds for local agitation for expansion. Most were utterly trivial, such as a need for more land and open space on which to exercise troops, or for cemeteries and barracks. A real driving force, apart from the security consideration, was the land speculators' urge to make profits. The British minister to China, Sir Claude MacDonald, observed in 1898 that '[m]any of the Colonists have been for years past buying up ground on the Kowloon promontory and adjacent islands as a speculation on the chance of our getting what we are now more or less on the point of getting'.[8] Chater and members of the local Navy League were among the most vocal advocates of expansion. This was no coincidence, for Chater was a leading land developer and several of the local Navy League's most prominent members were speculators. They had vested interests in lobbying for extension.

Until the beginning of 1898, London resisted the local Hong Kong campaign for expansion on the grounds that it worked against Britain's basic interest in China, which was economic. Although only 1.5 per cent of its exports that year went to China, Britain's share of China's trade was larger than that of the rest of the world combined.[9] Almost 62 per cent of China's external trade was with Britain. It was therefore in Britain's best interests to keep China as a whole open to free trade. This would prevent European powers dividing it into imperial possessions or spheres of influence, as had happened in Africa. It thus becomes understandable why, as late as January 1898, the British government stressed that the 'integrity and independence of China ... may be considered to be the cardinal base of our policy. ... We are opposed to the alienation of any portion of Chinese territory, or the sacrifice of any part of Chinese independence'.[10] Britain also generally carried great weight with China's Manchu government, so keeping an 'open door' in China best served its interests.

Within a matter of a few months, however, Britain modified its policy to maintain China's absolute territorial integrity. It secured for itself two additional pieces of land from the Chinese — Weihaiwei (now Weihai) in north China and the New Territories in the south. This resulted from changes the British were powerless to stop in the international arena.

The chain of events started with the exposure of the true extent of the Chinese Empire's weakness when Japan defeated China in a war over Korea, a Chinese vassal, between 1894 and 1895. Unlike the European great powers, Japan was an oriental country. It was forced open to the West by US Commodore Matthew Perry's 'black ships' only in 1853. Many were therefore surprised by China's inability to hold its own against Japan. It tempted various European powers with imperialist pretensions to turn their attentions to China. The aggressiveness of the Japanese demand for large territorial cessions under the Treaty of Simonoseki (1895), including Taiwan, the Pescadores islands and the Liaodong peninsula in southern Manchuria, prompted Russia, Germany and France to interfere. They forced the Japanese to return Liaodong (with its ice-free ports that Russia coveted) to China in exchange for vastly increased reparations paid by the Chinese. Behind their protestations of friendship and support, these powers were seeking to establish territorial bases in China at a time of its weakness.[11] Their actions also set an example to other powers. From 1898 to 1899, various countries joined in the scramble for concessions from China. They were afraid of being excluded in the event of the Chinese Empire facing the same fate as Africa.

At first, the British government responded to this rising tide of imperialism by declaring what the Chancellor of the Exchequer, Sir Michael Hicks Beach, described as a 'Monroe Doctrine for China'. This meant that the British government did 'not regard China as a place for conquest or acquisition by any European Power'. Instead, it looked 'upon it as a place, the most hopeful place, of the future of the commerce of' Britain 'and the commerce of the world at large'.[12] Despite various attempts to dissuade it, including Britain's offer of an alliance, Germany pursued its territorial ambition.[13] It used the killing of two German missionaries in November 1897 as a pretext to occupy Jiaozhou (now part of Qingdao) on the southern side of the Shandong promontory in north China. By March 1898, the Germans had imposed a treaty on the hapless Chinese and leased Jiaozhou for 99 years. Britain was equally unsuccessful in preventing Russia from taking over the ice-free ports of Lushun (Port Arthur) and Dalien in the Liaodong peninsula. Russia sent its navy to occupy the ports in December 1897 and followed the German example over Jiaozhou. In March 1898, the Russians then forced the Chinese to sign a treaty that leased the two ports for 25 years. British diplomacy's attempt to uphold the 'open door' in China in this period had only two tangible results. These were to guarantee equal trading rights for everyone in all foreign-controlled Chinese ports and to substitute outright annexation for long leases.

Unable to prevent Russia and Germany from pursuing their territorial ambitions, Britain tried to counter their presence and increased influence in north China by leasing the port of

Weihaiwei from China for as long as Russia occupied Lushun.[14] Britain chose Weihaiwei because it was the only port of any significance remaining on the coast of north China whose occupation could be seen as a counterpoise to restore British prestige and pre-eminence.[15] It is on the north side of the Shandong promontory, directly opposite Lushun and Dalien across the Gulf of Chihli (now the Gulf of Bohai) and to the northeast of Jiaozhou. This turn of events marked a major adaptation of the policy to uphold China's territorial integrity. The British government still insisted that it 'desired neither territorial acquisition in China nor even the extension of British influence in the Chinese government beyond such extensions and such influences as may be necessary for the protection and maintenance of [its] commercial position in China'. Nonetheless, it accepted the existence in China of foreign, including British, 'spheres of interest'.[16] As Foreign Office Under-Secretary George Curzon put it, this change was to 'preserve in an age of competition what we had gained in an age of monopoly'.[17]

The change in British policy also ended London's resistance to the colonists' demands to extend Hong Kong. The French acquisition, again by a 99-year lease, of Guangzhou Wan (now Zhanjiang), a mere 210 miles southwest of Hong Kong, provided an immediate reason to expand.[18] The French also tried to get the Chinese to agree not to alienate certain provinces to other powers, including that of Guangdong, of which Hong Kong was originally a part. This alarmed the British.[19] The old hypothetical arguments about defence suddenly seemed relevant, for the French could turn out to be an enemy of a completely different sort from the Chinese. Britain's response to the French competition was to seek to extend Hong Kong.

Though defence was the only argument the British put forward for the extension, the defensive requirements remained more potential or hypothetical than real. The long established enmity towards (and imperial competition with) France helped the expansionists' cause. At the turn of the century, neither France nor any other power posed a military threat to Hong Kong. Indeed, after the British secured the lease of the New Territories in June, they failed to take possession until the middle of April the following year. Also, the British forces in Hong Kong built no significant fortifications in the New Territories in the decade that followed. The acquisition was a purely imperial expansion.

A Diplomatic Solution: Convention of Peking

The minister in Beijing, Sir Claude MacDonald, represented Britain in the negotiations with the Chinese office for foreign affairs, the Zongli Yamen, for the extension of Hong Kong. Veteran diplomat and reformer Li Hongzhang led the Chinese team. MacDonald was anxious not to hasten the dismemberment of China and saw it in Britain's interest to ask for only enough to cover the defence of Hong Kong.[20] Once the negotiations opened in early April 1898, the parties quickly reached an agreement in principle. The whole process took only two months. The Chinese were in no position to resist. For them it was a matter of minimizing the losses China had to concede. They formally signed the Convention of Peking on 9 June and it came into effect on 1 July.

Negotiators from both sides shared an important common ground. They all wanted to prevent other powers seizing on the extension of Hong Kong to demand further territorial concessions from China. Thus, while the negotiations were tough, given the circumstances, they took place in a remarkable atmosphere of cooperation. Both sides proceeded expeditiously.

Although the Chinese fought their corner hard against all major British demands, they yielded almost immediately to the basic principle of Hong Kong's extension. What they tried to secure for China were above all the non-permanent cession of any territory and the retention of the symbol of Chinese sovereignty.[21] The Chinese negotiators were influenced by the emergence of nationalism as a political force, which, in turn, was a response to the imperialist encroachments on Chinese sovereignty. A significant component of this new nationalist approach was 'a willingness to make heavy financial sacrifices in order to curtail even theoretical infringements on Chinese sovereignty'.[22] The Chinese manifested this by insisting on the New Territories being leased for a specific period only. They also insisted that China retain the fort of Kowloon near its southern tip and that Chinese officials keep their right of free access to the fort. Though the question of paying rental arose, the negotiators later dropped it because the Chinese wanted to avoid being accused of selling off their country's sacred territories.[23] The Chinese also wanted to protect their customs revenues, but did not insist on retaining customs collection houses in the New Territories. Mistakenly, they relied instead on a British promise not to use the territory to the detriment of Chinese interests.[24] As it turned out, though the Hong Kong government subsequently took measures to increase China's customs revenue, it also prevented the Chinese maritime customs from operating within the New Territories. The increase in revenue was offset by the additional costs involved in the Chinese customs having to patrol much longer borders. From fewer than three miles, the land borders had increased to more than 60 miles, and the sea borders from 20 to 80 miles.[25] However, the Chinese negotiators' main endeavours were basically successful.

The Chinese managed to minimize their losses partly because the British were keen to wrap up the negotiations quickly. It was also because MacDonald and, to a lesser extent, his government were so confident of British supremacy in China that they signed the agreement before tying up all the loose ends. In an important sense, the British saw the preservation of various Chinese rights merely as a matter of detail.

The British fairly readily accepted the Chinese position that the instrument for transferring the New Territories should be a 99-year lease. MacDonald, the chief negotiator, agreed to it because he deemed it a permanent cession in disguise.[26] From its point of view, London accepted a lease 'so as to follow the example of Germany and Russia, and to avoid accusations of going one better and beginning the break up of China'.[27] The negotiations did not properly consider the long-term future status of the colony and the implications for British jurisdiction. Indeed, when the question of jurisdiction came up later, the Secretary of State for the Colonies, Joseph Chamberlain, simply pronounced that the New Territories should 'be treated as an integral part of the colony'.[28] He did not take seriously the prospect that China might reform itself sufficiently to build up the necessary strength to enforce the lease and recover the territory in due course. This was notwithstanding the observation that Chater, the leading local expansionist, made in 1894. He warned that in a few decades China might turn itself into 'a powerful nation fully armed and with the skill and knowledge that [would] enable her to make use of her vast strength' to pose a threat to the British position in Hong Kong.[29] Chater spoke before an oriental country had defeated China. In the era of Rule Britannia, when China was on the verge of being carved up, Britain dismissed the idea that it could ever pose a challenge to the might of the British Empire — too readily in retrospect.

Other important provisions the Chinese insisted on including in the agreement concerned the fort of Kowloon and the right of access by Chinese officials. The fort had a population of 744, of whom 544 were serving military personnel under the command of a colonel. The remaining civilians were either in the employ of the Chinese government or were dependent on the military.[30] It was not a city in any real sense. However, as a result of poor translation, it has since generally become known as the 'walled city of Kowloon'. The 1898 Convention of Peking states that 'the Chinese officials now stationed there shall continue to exercise jurisdiction except so far as may be inconsistent with the military requirements for the defence of Hong Kong'. It also states that

'Chinese officials and people shall be allowed as heretofore to use the road from Kowloon to Hsinan [Xinan]'.[31] It was absurd that Britain should extend the colony of Hong Kong to improve its defence but permit the Chinese to maintain a fort in the New Territories. The Chinese had built the fort in 1846/7 specifically to counter the British presence in Hong Kong.[32] It was equally ridiculous for the Convention to provide 'that the existing landing-place near Kowloon city shall be reserved for the convenience of Chinese men-of-war, merchant and passenger vessels, which may come and go and lie there at their pleasure'. It also stated that 'Chinese vessels of war, whether neutral or otherwise, shall retain the right to use' Deep Bay and Mirs Bay, which the Chinese also leased to the British.[33]

At that time, the British obviously did not regard these Chinese reservations as major problems. Hong Kong's colonial secretary, James Stewart Lockhart, who conducted a survey of the territory prior to the British takeover, considered the fort an issue that would resolve itself. He believed that the functions of the fort lay primarily in keeping public order in its vicinity and expected the garrison to be 'disbanded or transferred elsewhere'. The troops would no longer be required and, once that happened, the 'residence, therefore, of the Colonel Commanding' would become 'entirely unnecessary'.[34] In a similar vein, MacDonald urged London to tolerate Chinese retention of the fort. This was because he thought it was 'not to be supposed that the city of Kowloon will remain outside British jurisdiction with the surrounding district subject to it'.[35] Lockhart, too, expected the removal of the garrison and its commander if they would not voluntarily withdraw. He saw their permanent presence as 'inconsistent with the military requirements for the defence of Hong Kong'[36] and did not regard the right of movement of Chinese officials as a key problem. MacDonald was of the opinion that if the Hong Kong authorities could not keep the remaining Chinese officials in the fort under control they would have to be a 'thundering poor lot'.[37] He took an off-handed view about the Chinese navy's right of access to the jetties adjacent to the fort, to Deep Bay and to Mirs Bay.[38] With regard to the exact boundary of the New Territories, MacDonald and the British government were content that they be 'fixed when proper surveys have been made by officials appointed by the two governments'.[39] MacDonald and London were so confident of British preponderance that they were certain such an arrangement would not be to the detriment of British interests.

Although the Convention forms the basis of the leasehold, the authority for the extension of British jurisdiction comes from a different instrument, the Royal Order in Council of 20 October 1898. By this order, Queen Victoria decreed that the New Territories be deemed 'part and parcel of Her Majesty's Colony of Hong Kong in like manner and for all intents and purposes as if they had originally formed part of the said Colony'.[40] The duration of this extension of jurisdiction was, however, limited to the period 'during the continuance of the said lease'.[41] Under British law, British jurisdiction over the New Territories would expire by midnight on 30 June 1997, unless and until this stipulation were superseded. The British formally took possession of and exercised jurisdiction in the New Territories on 16 April 1899.

In the short term, the Convention was a diplomatic triumph for MacDonald. It gave Britain what it wanted at no cost and did not damage its relations with China or the other powers. MacDonald negotiated it with a somewhat cavalier attitude. He initiated the negotiations without an up-to-date map of the territory concerned and was happy to proceed with only a general idea of the extent of the territory he demanded for his government.[42] He did not give due consideration to the long-term or legal implications involved — perhaps because of his background, which was more military than diplomatic. His experiences as an army officer subduing Egyptians in the preceding decade seemed to have influenced his attitude towards the Chinese. He bared his soul in a private letter he wrote in early 1899, by saying: 'To my mind the whole Chinese question boils down to this — give me an army at Peking (not a Chinese one) but such as one as was encamped in and around Cairo [in] September 1882 and I (or anybody else) will fix up the Chinese question within a year.'[43] The arrogance of MacDonald and of the empire he served characterized Britain's handling of the negotiations. In the long term and in retrospect, the Convention must be seen as a major blunder for British diplomacy in the modern era. As a treaty, it had left far too many important issues with significant implications unresolved. In time, they would haunt the British and raise questions about the long-term future of even the original colony of Hong Kong.

An Appointment with China

Whatever assumptions MacDonald and his colleagues in London and Hong Kong might have made about the 99-year lease, by signing the Convention they had made an appointment with China. Like other appointments, it could be overtaken by events, nullified, ignored, cancelled, altered, forgotten, or kept.

One way or another, all the leases on the other territories extracted from China at around the same time ended before their expiry dates. The First World War nullified the German lease on Jiaozhou and the Washington Conference of 1922 then formally returned the territory to China. The Japanese took over Russia's lease on Lushun and Dalien when Japan defeated Russia in a war in 1905. After its own defeat in the Second World War in 1945, Japan returned the two ports to China, though they later became available to the Soviet Union under a new treaty. The French returned the port of Guangzhou Wan the same year. Even the British lease on Weihaiwei, which was to last for as long as Russia held Lushun and Dalien, came up for review in 1905. In the end, the British ignored this particular treaty obligation. They still wished to use it to check the Germans in Jiaozhou and the Japanese were keen to see them stay.[44] The Chinese Empire was so weak at that time that the British merely informed it to regard 'Britain's continued occupation of the leasehold as a protection against the other powers'. The Chinese could, however, hope 'that rendition might be possible at some later date'.[45] Both parties simply took the legality of the leasehold for granted and the British stayed for another quarter of a century.

By 1928 China had been a republic for 16 years. It had seen its central authority collapsed for over a decade and the country nominally reunified by force under the leadership of Chiang Kai-shek. Chiang was the leader of a nationalist party, the Kuomintang, and actively engaged in state building after establishing a national government in Nanjing. By this time, the international situation had also changed. Weihaiwei no longer served any strategic purpose for the British. Britain decided to leave it because 'the leasehold was becoming ever more of a burden to the British who derived little benefit from it but were responsible for its administration and security'.[46] Instead of incurring the wrath of rising Chinese nationalism for no tangible gains, the British restored Weihaiwei to Chinese jurisdiction in October 1930. This was on the basis of new negotiations that seemed to fail to take into account the fact that the original lease should have expired 25 years earlier.[47] Of all the appointments the great powers made with China in 1898, the only one that is being kept is over the New Territories.

There are two reasons why the lease on the New Territories has proved to be the exception in this sense. To begin with, unlike Weihaiwei, which, apart from its strategic value, was of practically no worth to the British, the New Territories came to play an increasingly important role in the development and prosperity of the thriving colony of Hong Kong. Even before the massive industrial developments of the postwar era, major developments had gradually but steadily been taking place there, and these were vital to Hong Kong's survival. They included the construction of large reservoirs and an airport. As

the economic and general lives of the people in the old colony
and the New Territories became increasingly integrated, the
idea of separating the two and giving the latter back to China
became less and less acceptable. As time went by, the crucial
issue about the lease was that it was not long or secure enough
to benefit Hong Kong as a whole.

Furthermore, the balance of power between Britain and
China slowly changed as the twentieth century progressed. By
the time the appointed date eventually approached, the two
countries' relative power over Hong Kong had been reversed.
When Britain lost its dominance in China, it also lost its ability
to attempt to resolve the New Territories' problem with a
1905-type Weihaiwei solution. Thus, instead of resorting to
imperial expediency based on superior power, the traditionally
legal minded British decided to take a legalistic view of the
lease. As British power continued to decline and Chinese
power ascended, the British hung on to the lease, however
limited its duration, to retain their security of tenure over the
New Territories in international law. This was still the position
in September 1982 when, in Beijing, Prime Minister Margaret
Thatcher opened negotiations with the Chinese over Hong
Kong.

It is a great irony that it was the very success of the British
administration and the residents of Hong Kong that integrated
the New Territories into the colony proper. They did this so
tightly that, when the time came to examine the issue of future
status in earnest, it had become impossible even to consider
separating the two. Given their quest to wipe out China's
humiliations at the hands of the West, the Chinese nationalists
would in any event have linked the futures of the New
Territories and Hong Kong proper. If the British government
and people of Hong Kong had deemed Hong Kong viable
without the New Territories, they could have dealt with their
respective futures separately at some stage during the last
century. As it turned out, although they gave considerable
thought to the matter at different times, they never made any

real attempt to solve the problem. Ironically, the New Territories, acquired to bolster the security of the old colony of Hong Kong, in the end prevented the old colony from being able to remain British. The signing of the Convention of Peking in 1898 therefore marked the beginning of the long process leading to the end of British rule in Hong Kong.

The Chinese attitude to the lease changed over the century. It started as a means of minimizing losses and protecting Chinese sovereignty. When the country re-emerged with a meaningful central government under Chiang Kai-shek, in a rising tide of nationalism Chiang and his colleagues wanted to recover both the original colony of Hong Kong and the New Territories. Chiang and his government, however, had made a general commitment to abide by international law and the rules of the international community. The Nanjing government accepted the lease as valid, but used the fact that it would expire as a lever with which to negotiate the retrocession of Hong Kong in its entirety.

The coming to power of the Mao Zedong-led Communist Party in 1949 marked a major change. Mao did not feel the People's Republic of China (PRC) had to conform to the conventions of the international community.[48] He preferred to define the conditions for conducting relations with the outside world himself. He also wanted to destroy all remnants of imperialism in the country.[49] His government deemed the Sino–British treaties over Hong Kong unequal and therefore invalid. However, he accepted that the British were in Hong Kong and regarded the issue as a legacy from history. He decided to defer its seizure because of its 'value to China'.[50] Beijing thus kept its options open. By entering into negotiations with Britain in 1982, the PRC had by its action implied that the 'unequal treaties' were not meaningless. The choice of 1 July 1997 as the date for the PRC to recover Hong Kong from Britain was without question based on the New Territories' lease.

In the end, both parties honoured the expiry date on the lease. They kept this particular appointment in history because

Beijing deemed it to its advantage and London felt it had no better option.

2. Emergence of a Hong Kong Problem: 1925–42

The twentieth century marked a new beginning for China. The rise of modern nationalism as a powerful political force coincided with the emergence of the future Hong Kong problem. The 1898 Convention of Peking proved to be a difficult treaty from the beginning. The one complication that emerged quickly and returned to haunt the British time and again concerned the Chinese retention of the fort of Kowloon. There was considerable disquiet about this arrangement in Hong Kong and London even at that time.[1] The British only tolerated the existence of the fort and its garrison to expedite the conclusion of the treaty without overt use of threats. Shortly after signing the Convention, the British authorities decided that 'the continued existence of a Chinese garrison in British territory would be out of the question'.[2] The British commander in China and Hong Kong, Major-General W. J. Gascoigne, provided an excuse to act in 1899 when some local residents attempted to resist the British takeover in the New Territories. He expressed his professional military opinion that 'the presence of a Chinese city in the midst of British territory is and must always be a source of danger'.[3] It met a stipulation in the Convention that allowed for the revocation of Chinese jurisdiction in the fort if it proved 'inconsistent with the military requirements for the defence of Hong Kong'. The Convention contained no guidelines on how this could or should take place, but Chinese resistance provided the excuse for seizure.

In May 1899, British forces occupied the fort and, without

bloodshed, evicted the Chinese garrison.[4] At the same time, the British also occupied Shenzhen, north of the new border, and informed the Chinese of their decision and actions. The British later restored Shenzhen to China, but stood firm over the fort. The Chinese demanded that the British at least pay for Chinese government properties in the fort. However, the British rejected their demand on the grounds that the costs incurred in dealing with the resistance had exceeded the value of the properties concerned. The following December, the British enacted a Royal Order in Council. This duly revoked the Kowloon clause in the 1898 order and extended British jurisdiction over the old fort.

The Chinese refused to accept the legality of Britain's unilateral actions and tried to persuade the British to reverse course.[5] Such attempts stopped after early 1900. Within the year China descended into the chaos of the xenophobic Boxer uprising, which led the central government to declare war simultaneously on eight powers, including Britain. The issue of the Kowloon fort did not get back on the diplomatic agenda. After the collapse of the empire and the installation of a republican government in 1912, all successive Chinese governments took the same view over the fort. They acknowledged the British occupation, but refused to recognize its legality. No Chinese government has ever formally admitted to having lost sovereignty over the old fort. Differences over the legality of Britain's actions caused disputes between the two countries in the 1930s, 1940s and 1960s. Once nationalism became a potent force in Chinese politics and the balance of power between the two countries shifted, the Convention's unsatisfactory treatment of the old fort of Kowloon came back to torment British policy makers.

The problems of the old fort were only mild headaches, however, compared with those of the lease for the New Territories as a whole. The same basic factors that made the old fort an issue were also eventually responsible for turning the lease into a nightmare for the colony of Hong Kong. However, although related, the disputes over the Kowloon fort were different from the problems of the lease. It is important not to confuse the two. The lease only became a 'Hong Kong problem' after the colony fell under Japanese occupation at the end of 1941.

Early Warnings

The twentieth century began with the anti-foreign Boxer uprising. It was a landmark event. It led to the emergence of nationalism as a force in Chinese politics and affected China's handling of relations with the outside world. Although the Boxer movement 'stood as a dramatic example of ordinary Chinese peasants rising up to rid China of the hated foreign presence', it 'was really an instance of mass shamanism', or xenophobic ecstasy.[6] The great powers 'forced on China a polar choice: national extinction or wholesale transformation'.[7] They dramatically suppressed the uprising and humiliated the Chinese nation. Thus, in its aftermath, it brought a sharp reaction against imperialism. There emerged a national mission — to recover sovereign rights lost.[8] Even the reactionary empress dowager, who staged a coup against Emperor Guangxu to stop his 'Hundred Days Reform' in 1898, turned to introducing major reforms herself. More importantly, the revolutionary movement led by Sun Yat-sen, which advocated nationalism above all, picked up steam. By 1912 it had brought down the empire.

Although the empire crumbled and gave way to a republic quickly, the revolutionaries failed to produce the necessary vision, leadership, organization and resources to revitalize the country. Despite nationalism continuing to develop, power politics pre-empted national consolidation. The central government that emerged under Yuan Shikai attempted to crush its opponents by both political and military means. It, too, failed and central authority collapsed in 1916. China disintegrated into regions run by military men, commonly known as warlords. It was not until 1928 that Chiang Kai-shek managed to reunify the country nominally and set up a meaningful national government in Nanjing. In the meantime, nationalism developed into a potent political force. Indeed, Chiang was the military leader of the Kuomintang, the nationalist party that developed out of Sun Yat-sen's revolutionary movement. Chiang rode to power at the head of his party army on a rising tide of nationalism. Nation building was at the top of the Kuomintang's agenda. Domestically, this meant wiping out the remnants of warlordism and consolidating the power of the central government. Externally, it meant recovering sovereign rights lost.

As the paramount foreign power in China, Britain occupied a special position in the minds of the Chinese nationalists. Interestingly, for the first two decades of the century, it did not become a focal point of anti-imperialist nationalism in China. Britain's prestige as a leader of the advanced, industrialized and democratic world, and its might and record as an empire, put it above other powers. A generation of Chinese intellectuals, some of whom joined the revolution led by Sun, looked to Britain for inspiration and support, though their anti-imperialist sentiments also generated resentment towards the British. The aggressiveness of the Japanese in the 1910s directed the wrath of Chinese nationalism away from the British. In 1915, when the First World War was preoccupying Britain and the Western powers, the Japanese presented their infamous 'Twenty-one Demands' to China. They asked for control over Manchuria, Inner Mongolia, Shandong, the southeast coastal region and the Yangtze valley. They also 'intended to deprive the Chinese government of virtually any effective control over its own domestic affairs'.[9] The Chinese government, then under Yuan Shikai, managed to avoid capitulating to all the Japanese demands by skilfully leaking them. This led other powers to make representations to Japan and created strong and widespread public outrage and protest in China. Japan became the focus of China's anti-imperialist nationalism until the early 1920s. In this period, as a leading world power wielding great influence, some Chinese nationalist writers saw Britain as a potential partner to check Japanese aggression in China.[10] As late as 1923, Sun Yat-sen himself, as leader of the Kuomintang, still looked to Britain for aid.[11]

The Washington Conference (1921/2), which was convened to resolve Far Eastern questions after the First World War, forced the Japanese to put aside their ambitious expansionism in China.[12] They were made to return to China the German concessions they had seized during the war in Shandong (including Jiaozhou). When, as a result, anti-Japanese sentiments subsided in the country, the Chinese nationalists turned their attentions to the leading imperialist power in their land, Britain. This development was particularly noticeable in the southern Chinese province of Guangdong, adjacent to the Crown colony of Hong Kong. This was where Sun and his Kuomintang followers established a government after the collapse of Yuan Shikai's central government.[13] It was also the regional base from which Chiang Kai-shek led his army to reunify the country after Sun's death in the spring of 1925. The same year also saw the Kuomintang regime in Canton (Guangzhou) openly challenging the British hold over Hong Kong as part of a nationalist movement.

On 30 May 1925, there was a demonstration by students and workers in the International Settlement of Shanghai. This was a protest over a worker being killed during a labour dispute in a Japanese-owned mill. It set off a chain of events that challenged the British presence in China, including Hong Kong.[14] A British officer of the Shanghai Municipal Police ordered his men to open fire on the demonstrators when scuffles broke out in front of a police station. This sparked off an anti-British movement in Shanghai, which quickly escalated and spread to many other cities. At that time, campaigns against two regional militarists were preoccupying the Kuomintang regime in Canton. However, once this situation was out of the way, the Kuomintang joined the communists in a united front.

Together, in June, they organized a general strike in the British-dominated foreign concession of Shameen (Shamian), Canton. The communists also staged a major strike in Hong Kong to 'struggle against imperialism and capitalism'.[15] During a large demonstration in Shameen on 23 June, the demonstrators and the Anglo-French concession police exchanged shots. There were fatalities on both sides, though the majority were Chinese. The Kuomintang leadership wanted to contain the impact of this incident, but its own left-wing, which was under the influence of the communists and Chiang Kai-shek, then a high-ranking military officer, challenged the leadership's caution.[16] At that time, Chiang was trying to consolidate his position in the Kuomintang and took the public stand that 'there was no room for compromise with Britain'.[17] Canton was set on a course of confrontation with Hong Kong, the bastion of British power in south China.

With support and directions from the communist dominated steering committee in Canton, the strike in Hong Kong escalated into as complete a boycott as had ever been attempted in the colony. The committee induced Chinese workers in Hong Kong to leave their jobs and return to Canton, where provisions were made for their maintenance. By July some 250,000 workers and their families (out of a total population of 725,100) had left the colony. For 15 months, an embargo was imposed on all trade between Hong Kong and Guangdong and this caused immense damage to the economic life of the colony.[18] The strike-cum-boycott did not end until October 1926. By then, Chiang had emerged as the most powerful leader in the Kuomintang.

At this time, Chiang's party–army was in the midst of clearing the country of warlords in an operation that became known as the Northern Expedition. After sweeping north with great success, in September Chiang's numerically inferior forces, without any siege guns, were stopped in the strongly defended central Chinese city of Wuchang.[19] This happened a few days after the British, who were trying to break the

deadlock with a negotiated settlement, had mounted a demonstration of their naval power in the harbour of Canton. At this
point, the 'fate of the expedition and even the Revolutionary
Base truly hung in the balance'.[20] Wishing to secure his rear,
and in any event preparing to break with the communists in
the Kuomintang, Chiang ordered an end to the boycott. He was
obeyed.

Hong Kong emerged victorious from the first Chinese
nationalist challenge, but the strike-cum-boycott left its mark.
The question of Hong Kong's long-term security, particularly
with respect to the New Territories' lease, became more serious
than ever before. Sir Cecil Clementi took the initiative. He
had become governor of Hong Kong during the strike-cum-
boycott in November 1925 and was partly responsible for
bringing it to an end almost a year later. He first raised the
issue in January 1926, but London overruled him.[21] A year
later, after the strike-cum-boycott ended and important
developments were happening in Sino–British relations, he
returned to the charge. By then Britain had worked out a new
China policy, which recognized the existence of a powerful
nationalist movement in China and sought to meet it 'with
sympathy and understanding'.[22] In January 1927, a nationalist
outburst in the Kuomintang-controlled city of Hankou resulted
in a Chinese mob overrunning, and thereby recovering, the
British Concession there without bloodshed.[23] At this point,
Clementi again urged London to review the New Territories'
lease and turn the region into 'a permanent part of the
colony'.[24] He recommended that Britain either consider using
the return of Weihaiwei or 'the very generous Treaty revision
at present under contemplation by His Majesty's Government,
to be treated as a quid pro quo for the cession of the leased
area'.[25]

Clementi was not the first British policy maker to raise the
issue. Sir Frederick Lugard, governor from 1907 to 1912, had
earlier suggested making the permanent cession of the New
Territories a condition for Weihaiwei's return to China.[26] His

successor, Sir Francis May, who as captain superintendent of police in 1898 had personally dealt with Chinese resistance in the New Territories, also recommended 'seizing the first opportunity to convert the 99-year lease ... into a cession in perpetuity'.[27] The British government in London considered the matter prior to the Paris peace conference of 1919 and again before the Washington Conference of 1922. On both occasions the possibility of surrendering the New Territories was raised during discussions about the German lease of Shandong and, on both occasions, it was dismissed as out of the question.[28] Although, like his predecessors, Clementi failed to secure London's support, he put in a strong marker. He was persistent and raised the issue again and again until 1929, the year before his transfer to Malaya.

Clementi's differences with London arose because the colony and Britain had different interests and concerns, and assessed Chinese reactions differently. With his deep knowledge of the Chinese and his experience of handling the strike-cum-boycott, Clementi was alive to the forces and trends of Chinese nationalism. He persisted in his recommendation because he believed that the 'handing back of the New Territories would be fatal to' Hong Kong.[29] Unless Britain took action while China was divided or weak, China's rising nationalism and military power would eventually rule out such an option. The urgency that was self-evident to the person on the spot was not to a government half the globe away. The picture looked different from London.

As explained above, by adopting a new China policy in December 1926, the British had already shown a willingness to deal sympathetically with the rising tide of Chinese nationalism. They based this on realism, not altruism, but it was a realism that did not conform to Clementi's assessment. Essentially, London did not consider that 'any responsible Chinese authority could be induced in present circumstances to enter into any agreement which provided for a cession of territory to a foreign Power'.[30] Raising the issue would merely indicate British anxiety over the lease. It would also 'expose a weakness, which they would not be slow to exploit, and might well lead to [a] campaign for the rendition'.[31] There was no meeting of minds on this issue between Hong Kong and London.

In the 1930s, all the successive governors of Hong Kong raised the issue at least once during their terms of office, but none did so as forcefully as Clementi. In London, the Foreign Office responded to Clementi's persistence with internal deliberations that went on for so long that they outlasted him. The Foreign Office gradually moved to a position of expecting the Chinese to raise the question of the lease well before the expiry date. It also surmised that Britain should prepare itself to lose exclusive control over Hong Kong.[32] This view developed from an idea put forward by Sir John Pratt, an old China hand. Pratt argued that London should let 'in a certain amount of Chinese control in Hong Kong in return for being allowed to continue to exercise a certain amount of British control in the New Territories'.[33] In setting out this view, the Foreign Office was merely exploring options and generally preparing itself. Pratt's view did not become British government policy and was in any event kept confidential.

As far as the British government was concerned, prior to the Pacific war, which began in 1941, there was no 'Hong Kong question' — whether based on the New Territories' lease or not. Nevertheless, the idea that Hong Kong and the New Territories stood or fell together came to be accepted.[34] By implication, Britain realized that the long-term future of Hong Kong would be tied to the lease for the New Territories.

War and Negotiations

When the Japanese attacks on Pearl Harbor and Hong Kong started the Pacific war in early December 1941, China had been resisting full-scale Japanese invasions for over four years with neither side declaring war.[35] The invasion, which started in July 1937, involved the deployment in China proper, almost throughout the entire conflict, of 1.2 million Japanese troops and 500 aircraft.[36] China was still essentially an agricultural country, and in the first year of the war it lost most of its industrial base, which was in the coastal regions, to the Japanese. To sustain its war efforts, China had to secure as much equipment and strategic material as possible from the outside. The bulk of supplies China eventually obtained in the early war years came from the Soviet Union and, to a lesser extent, Germany and Italy. Despite this, the Chinese government looked to Britain and the USA for support.[37] Overland deliveries were possible from the Soviet Union. However, because the Japanese navy controlled the China coast, supplies from other countries had to come through Hong Kong or over China's border with British Burma or French Indo-China. British support was therefore very important to China, but the mighty British Empire in the Far East rested ultimately on bluff.

By the late 1930s, Britain was no longer in a position to defend its empire in the East.[38] In the years when China desperately needed its support, Britain was preoccupied with the Nazi threat in Europe and, on several occasions, was forced to appease Japan. The British government repeatedly turned down China's requests for British pilots to serve as advisers in the Chinese air force. It also, for example, refused the Chinese permission to set up a secret aeroplane assembly depot in Hong Kong.[39] Even worse, in July 1940 the British succumbed to Japanese pressure and temporarily closed the Burma Road. Since October 1938, when Canton and its vicinity fell to the Japanese, this supply route had become particularly important to China; its closure significantly reduced the flow of materials through Hong Kong. Britain's demonstrations of weakness in the face of Japanese aggression greatly damaged its standing in China.[40]

Before the Japanese attacked Hong Kong and other British positions in Southeast Asia in 1941, London reluctantly considered Hong Kong expendable in the event of war.[41]

Although staunchly against giving up any British territory, Prime Minister Winston Churchill accepted that Hong Kong would fall to the Japanese and that the peace conference would deal with its future.[42] To minimize losses there, he even wanted to reduce the garrison to a nominal size. He later agreed to reinforce it when, in the autumn of 1941, Canada showed its willingness to provide two battalions. The main considerations were that such a move might deter the Japanese, would certainly encourage Chinese resistance, and would be good for British prestige and morale in Asia.[43] At this point, the British reached an understanding with the Chinese government and the two powers agreed to coordinate their respective military operations in the event of a Japanese attack on Hong Kong.[44]

The British also explored the possibility of cooperating with the Chinese communist guerrillas, who operated in the vicinity of Hong Kong.[45] On the day the Japanese attacked Hong Kong and Pearl Harbor, Chiang declared war on Japan. On the following day, he ordered three corps under the command of General Yu Hanmou to march towards Hong Kong.[46] To relieve the Hong Kong garrison, he planned to launch a New Year's Day attack on the Japanese in the Canton region. Under the resolute leadership of Governor Sir Mark Young, Hong Kong was defended differently from Malaya or Singapore. Its defenders followed Churchill's order to resist with utmost stubbornness 'in spirit and to the letter'.[47] They put up a gallant fight for 17 days and earned, in Churchill's words, the 'lasting honour' that was their due. However, on Christmas Day, before the Chinese infantry could get into position to attack, the Japanese shattered Hong Kong's defences and forced its garrison to capitulate.

The defenders of Hong Kong's valour could not hide the fact that their resistance was ineffective. In any event, the fall of Singapore, the symbol of British imperial power in the East, in February 1942, greatly overshadowed the battle of Hong Kong.

The Japanese not only called the bluff of the British Empire, but also humiliated it and, in the process, destroyed the myth of the superiority of the white race. The prestige of the British Empire hit rock bottom. As a result, even long-time supporters of the empire at that time, such as Secretary of State for India Leo Amery, lost heart. He admitted that 'we were on the eve of very great changes in the relation of Asia to Europe' and it is doubtful 'whether in the future empires like our Asiatic empire' could subsist.[48]

Hong Kong's geographical location meant that it lay inside the Allied powers' China theatre, which covered the whole of China, Indo-China and Thailand.[49] On US President Franklin Roosevelt's initiative, Chiang Kai-shek became supreme commander of this theatre in January 1942.[50] This arrangement was primarily a gesture to Chiang and at this stage was largely academic with regard to Hong Kong. Indeed, it was not clarified whether Hong Kong, as a British territory, was within the remit of Chiang's command. Nevertheless, Chiang was justified in considering Hong Kong within his theatre. A shadow was cast on its long-term future as a British territory.

As the shock of the rapid collapse of the Allied defences in Southeast Asia sank in, responsible officials in both the British and Chinese governments began to think about Hong Kong's future. An important parallel that occurred was that both sides accepted that it was impossible to separate the futures of Hong Kong and the New Territories. However, when they negotiated earnestly on this subject towards the end of the year, neither side raised the future of Hong Kong as such. They scrupulously restricted themselves to the lease for the New Territories, but neither party had any illusion about what was really at stake.[51]

To understand the Chinese attitude to Hong Kong, it is necessary to set it in the wider context of what the Pacific war and China's resistance to Japan meant to them. The outbreak of the Pacific war was greeted with elation in China's wartime capital of Chongqing, partly because it meant that China would no longer be fighting alone.[52] It was also of great significance in a wider sense. From the Chinese point of view, at long last their country had become an ally of the great powers and a major player in the global conflict. Chiang harboured a Confucian yearning to see China behave in a way that befitted a great power, which meant China taking 'a leading role' in the war in the East.[53] He therefore immediately ordered the Chinese army to go to Hong Kong's rescue and organized a new army for operations in Burma.[54] The military consideration that it was necessary to secure these two vital supply links to the outside world was undoubtedly also relevant.

If he had acted on military considerations alone, he would have waited until the new situation became clearer. He issued his orders even although Japan had also launched a major assault against the Chinese in Changsha in central south China. Three corps totalling 100,000 men constituted the new army for operations in Burma and it was formed on 16 December, more than a month before the British felt they needed help in Burma.[55] They were 'the last of the crack fighting units from China's strategic reserves' and were earmarked for Burma before the outcome of the battle for Changsha was known.[56] Responding to his nationalist instincts, he expected to use the wider war to end, as soon as possible, the 'unequal treaties' to which China had been subjected since the 1840s. About this time, Chiang instructed the Chinese ambassador to Britain, Wellington Koo (Gu Weijun), to explore the British attitude to Hong Kong.[57] He intended to build on China's role as an Allied power to strengthen his position in negotiating Hong Kong's future with Britain.

In London, the Colonial Office was the first to reflect on — and recognize the implications of — Britain's failure to defend Hong Kong for any length of time.[58] While Britain had no illusions about the difficulty of defending the colony successfully, it had expected the garrison to 'hold out on the fortified island for a good many weeks, possibly for several months'.[59] Its rapid fall was a major blow. When David

MacDougall, an administrative officer of the Hong Kong government, joined the Colonial Office after a daring escape to China on the day the colony fell, he immediately warned about Hong Kong. He reported that all Chinese government officials he met in China, up to the vice-ministerial level, assumed that Hong Kong would be returned to China after the war.[60] The Colonial Office accepted that 'the arrangements existing before the Japanese occupation would not be restored'.[61]

The question of Hong Kong's future became the subject of an intense internal debate within the British government in June 1942, which was when the Foreign Office took an active interest. The head of the Foreign Office's Far Eastern Department, Ashley Clarke, who had initiated the debate, visited the USA where he engaged in lengthy discussions with State Department officials. His US colleagues, particularly Stanley Hornbeck, expressed strong pro-China and anti-British Empire sentiments. This troubled Clarke deeply,[62] for he believed that the USA would reject the restoration of the *status quo ante* in Hong Kong. He thus urged the British government to prepare itself to give up Hong Kong (and even Malaya if necessary) 'in order to maintain the really important things'.[63] The Colonial Office officials, led by Gerald (later Sir Edward) Gent, considered Clarke's view 'defeatist'.[64]

With the help of MacDougall and the blessings of his senior colleagues, Gent proceeded to produce a policy paper on Hong Kong. This was to pre-empt an unacceptable one being put forward by Clarke.[65] The Secretary of State for the Colonies, Lord Cranborne, strongly supported Gent and MacDougall in their attempts to resist Foreign Office pressure.[66] The issue was eventually referred to the War Cabinet, which preferred to avoid giving up Hong Kong. Churchill felt that 'questions of territorial adjustment could not be considered now and must be left to be raised at the peace conference'.[67]

While the British government carried on its internal debates, Chinese diplomats assessed Britain and the USA's true attitude to a Chinese proposal to abolish the extraterritorial and other privileges these powers enjoyed in China. They based their assessment on Chiang's earlier initiative to instruct his foreign minister, Guo Taiqi, to test the US government's attitude while he was on a visit to that country in April 1941.[68] Although both Britain and the USA had publicly announced their intention to comply with China's demands at the end of the war, Chiang pushed for an early agreement. Both countries entered into parallel negotiations with the Chinese government in October 1942.

In the course of the Sino–British negotiations being conducted in Chongqing, the Chinese asked Britain to return the New Territories to their jurisdiction, along with various British concessions in China.[69] As Foreign Minister T. V. Soong (Song Ziwen) explained to the chief British negotiator, Ambassador Sir Horace Seymour, the Chinese made no distinction between foreign concessions and leased territories such as the New Territories.[70] The general view was that only a treaty that covered the latter would meet Chinese expectations. Soong intended to push the British as far as he could, but not at the expense of the proposed new treaty.[71] Chiang, by contrast, was adamant over the New Territories and Soong was unable to move him.

In London, despite ongoing internal debates over Hong Kong, the British government did not expect the issue to be raised in connection with the extraterritoriality negotiations.[72] In their minds, the negotiations were about ending British privileges in Chinese, not British, territories.[73] The Foreign Office had tended to compromise with the Chinese, but Foreign Secretary Anthony Eden toughened its stand. The most Eden would concede was a vague promise to discuss the New Territories after victory was won.[74] The War Cabinet adopted the same position.

Between the middle of November and the end of December, senior officials in both the Chinese and British governments tried very hard to work out a formula both sides would find acceptable. Wellington Koo, the ambassador to London, was in

Chongqing at the time and he provided the eventual solution. Soong asked him to persuade Chiang. A seasoned diplomat who understood Chiang's mentality, he persuaded Chiang to allow a degree of flexibility by explaining Britain's attitude in a language Chiang could understand.

He told Chiang that the British saw the ending of the privileges as a gesture of goodwill and had no idea that the New Territories would be involved when they started the negotiations.[75] He added that, though he agreed with Chiang that the British should deliver two gestures (the other being the New Territories), this was something the British would not understand. Koo gently argued that it would be to China's advantage to accept the first gesture right away. To reject it would antagonize the British and destroy the basis for a new treaty. He added that China could at the same time indicate to the British that it expected the second gesture in due course.[76] Chiang reflected further before reluctantly acceded to Koo's idea.[77]

Soong subsequently asked Han Liwu to test the Koo proposal informally on the British. He chose Han because he was well known for his Anglophile sentiments and for being particularly warmly disposed to Churchill's personal representative in Chongqing, Lieutenant-General Adrian Carton de Wiart.[78] Han offered the British a possible solution. The Chinese government would write to the British government saying that it recognized that the lease was outside the remit of the current negotiations, but that it wished to raise it later. The British government would then make an appropriate response.[79] This proved acceptable to both governments and an understanding was finally reached on 31 December 1942 that the issue would be deferred until after Japan's defeat.

After other outstanding issues were settled, on 11 January 1943 Britain and the USA signed two parallel treaties with China to end their privileges in that country. On the same day Soong wrote to Seymour: 'The early termination of the Treaty of June 9, 1898 . . . is one of the long cherished desires of the

Chinese people and ... I wish to inform you that the Chinese government reserves its right to propose it again for discussion at a later date.'[80] As agreed, Britain formally acknowledged the Chinese position.[81]

For the first time Britain accepted it had a 'Hong Kong problem' — a problem the Chinese could raise at any time after the victory over Japan. This was a fundamental change from the days before Japan humbled the British Empire, when the British wondered whether they should ask to convert the New Territories' lease into a permanent cession.[82]

3. British or Chinese Hong Kong? 1943–5

The Anglo–Chinese race to take over Hong Kong and the New Territories after the war, with the USA first supporting China and then Britain, ended in a British triumph. Even then, however, shrewd observers may have seen that Anglo–Chinese rivalry, rising Chinese nationalism and Britain's postwar weakness were leading inexorably to the eventual end of British rule. Also, US power reflected a sea change in world power politics. The exchange of letters in January 1943 over the future of the New Territories merely postponed the issue until after Japan's defeat. The Chinese and British governments continued to deliberate on the subject in preparation for raising it in due course. When the war ended in August 1945, a diplomatic dispute developed over whether Chinese or British forces should liberate Hong Kong. Both could dispatch powerful modern forces to recover it from Japanese occupation. This chapter is about the wartime preparations and the eventual scramble for liberation.

Planning in Chongqing

When China's war of resistance against Japan merged with the Pacific war, Chiang advanced a five-part set of objectives to restore what he saw as China's rightful place in the world. They were:

- to defeat Japan and expel it from the Asian mainland;
- to recover territories lost in the preceding century of 'humiliation';

- to end the 'unequal treaties';
- to get recognized as a great power; and
- to secure external support for China's unification and economic developments.[1]

Hong Kong was included among the territories to be recovered. Chiang demonstrated his strength of feeling in the course of the Sino–British negotiations at the end of 1942. Before a solution for the New Territories was found, Chiang considered the option of eventually using military force to oust the Japanese and reclaim the land.[2]

Unhappy with the failure to secure an agreement from the British to end the New Territories' lease, Chiang tried to enlist US support. He employed his US educated wife, then 'the prima donna in American favour', to charm the USA into supporting his cause.[3] Chiang asked her to test his idea about Hong Kong on President Roosevelt during her visit to Washington in early 1943.[4] Roosevelt responded positively. Chiang thus instructed Foreign Minister Soong to raise the issue formally with the President. Roosevelt told Soong that he believed the British would be reluctant to return Hong Kong, but he thought a compromise might be possible. This was that Britain return Hong Kong to China and that China turn it into a free port and protect the interests of British residents there.[5]

Inspired by Roosevelt, Chiang laid down the basic principle of a policy during a meeting in March of the Supreme Council for National Defence.[6] This was that once Britain had returned Hong Kong, the Chinese government would voluntarily declare it and the New Territories a free port.[7] Chiang was working on the basis that the territory to be returned was the whole of Hong Kong, not just the New Territories.[8] In line with his ambition to raise China to the status of a great power, Chiang was only willing to turn Hong Kong into a free port as a Chinese initiative, not as a condition for the British retrocession.

The *Waijiaobu* (Foreign Ministry) was primarily responsible for turning Chiang's guiding principle into policy. However, wartime exigencies upset its usual organization and were not conducive to working out a policy on Hong Kong. China's need for US supplies to sustain its war effort involved stationing Foreign Minister Soong in Washington as Chiang's personal representative to Roosevelt for most of the time until 1945. From Washington, Soong did not keep the ministry fully informed of his activities or thinking. He routinely communicated with Chiang directly on top secret matters without going through or informing the ministry.[9] K. C. Wu (Wu Guozhen), whom Chiang had chosen as vice-minister, was left in charge of the ministry in Chongqing. Soong showed a strong interest in the Hong Kong question and handled it personally during the Sino–British negotiations of late 1942. Wu took a hard line over the New Territories and was involved in the negotiations, but did not play an important role.[10] After 1942 he devoted little personal attention to the matter and left the working out of a detailed Hong Kong policy to Liang Long, head of the European Department.

Liang, who had been educated in England, was noted for his reluctance to take responsibility.[11] He subsequently achieved notoriety for his irresponsibility while ambassador to Czechoslovakia. In 1949, he secretly abandoned the embassy and its staff as soon as the Czechoslovakian government announced that it would switch recognition from the Kuomintang government to the Communist People's Republic of China. During the war in Chongqing, he did not enjoy the confidence of Vice-Minister Wu, who publicly ridiculed his incompetence. Since the Hong Kong issue was undoubtedly a thorny and difficult one, Liang took a decidedly passive approach — one that would avoid causing trouble or inviting reprimand. He made no attempt to encourage concerned parties from other departments or ministries to take an interest. Liang even discouraged the active participation of T. W. Kwok (Guo Dehua), the ministry's commissioner for Guangdong and Guangxi provinces with responsibility for Hong Kong, who on his own initiative had suggested working out a policy in September 1944.[12] Liang responded to Chiang's directive over Hong Kong in a bureaucratic and passive way.

The European Department under Liang did, however, produce a paper on Hong Kong. Its main proposal was that China should negotiate with Britain, explain the pros and cons and encourage Britain to do right by China.[13] In other words, China should ask the British to restore Hong Kong and the New Territories. In return, the Chinese government would make the necessary arrangements to protect all legitimate British interests in Hong Kong, protect and promote the legitimate interests of British investors and traders in China proper, and ensure that Hong Kong would not be used against British interests or security. When Hong Kong came up on the diplomatic agenda in August 1945, Liang's department revised and expanded the paper into two longer ones.

Essentially, the department argued that, since the original reasons for Britain's acquisition of the territories no longer applied, the territories should be returned to China.[14] The department felt that the New Territories and Hong Kong proper should be handled together because the British had deemed them inseparable. Large sections of both papers merely recounted the history of the cessions and the lease, and restated Chiang's views of 1943. The only new idea was in the suggestion that the Chinese government consult the British and US governments over whether this was a suitable subject to raise at a five-power conference scheduled later that month. In short, the European Department under Liang completely failed to work out the basis for a viable policy on either Hong Kong or the New Territories. China's diplomatic machine was thus unprepared to exercise the right it reserved to raise the issue of the New Territories with Britain at the end of the war.

Of the other branches of government in China, the army was the only one to make plans with significant implications for Hong Kong's future. In early 1945, the Chinese armed forces worked on several plans to launch a general counterattack against the Japanese in south China in order to recapture various seaports.[15] The most important and immediately relevant of these were the 'Icemen' and 'White Tower' plans, which aimed to recapture, among other places, the Canton–Hong Kong region.[16] They were devised with the help of Lieutenant-General Albert Wedemeyer, US Chief of Staff to Chiang. In the British assessment, Wedemeyer was 'personally opposed to any action by the British in China directed to the reoccupation of Hong Kong'.[17]

By March, Chiang had earmarked 13 corps or a total of 39 divisions for these operations.[18] Among them were the fully US trained and equipped elite divisions, which were the most combat effective in the Chinese army.[19] By June, the Chinese had already liberated Nanjing and were poised to strike against Guangzhou Wan. Wedemeyer planned to capture Guangzhou Wan first and then deploy the assault force to move east and attack Canton in November.[20] The vanguard was the New First Corps under the command of Lieutenant-General Sun Liren, which had distinguished itself in the Burma campaign of the preceding year. As it turned out, Japan surrendered just as the operational plans were being finalized.[21] However, it meant that the three divisions under Sun, which had already reached Wuzhou in August and were equipped with motor transport and tanks, were less than 300 miles away from Hong Kong.

It is unclear exactly what Chiang intended to do about Hong Kong in the event of his forces attacking and seizing it from the Japanese. In internal discussions in 1942, it was understood that even if China recovered the New Territories militarily, it would still negotiate with Britain over their future, for the 1898 lease was still legally binding.[22] Given Chiang's concern that China should behave like a great power, he would have been highly unlikely to have changed his mind over the need for a negotiated settlement in 1945. He had probably intended to use a Chinese military occupation of Hong Kong to enhance China's position in negotiations with the British. In any event, the Chinese army's counteroffensive provided him with the option, should he choose to exercise it, of racing against the British to take over Hong Kong at the time of the Japanese surrender.

Planning in London

British officialdom's handling of the Hong Kong question in the war period contrasted sharply with that of the Chinese Foreign Ministry's European department. In London, the Hong Kong question was examined carefully, particularly by the Colonial and Foreign Offices, which had primary respon-sibility. The defeatism Ashley Clarke and some of his colleagues in the Foreign Office showed in the summer of 1942 gradually gave way to a new attitude. This mainly happened after Britain successfully put off including the New Territories in the Sino–British negotiations at the end of that year. When Clarke stopped pushing to give up Hong Kong, Gerald Edward Gent, an assistant under-secretary in the Colonial Office, organized a counteroffensive in the bureaucratic battles over Hong Kong. Gent wanted to recover some of the lost ground. As the Allied powers' fortunes in the war changed, Gent tried to persuade others that Britain should give up neither Hong Kong nor, if possible, the New Territories.

At the end of 1942, Colonial Office thinking was that Britain must try to avoid giving up sovereignty over Hong Kong. Should that prove impossible, at the end of the war it would negotiate with China and treat Hong Kong as Britain's contribution to a general settlement for a new order in the Far East.[23] The Colonial Office insisted that, in such a situation, Britain's contribution must be matched (though in still undefined forms) by China and the USA.[24] Though official British government policy separated sovereignty over Hong Kong proper from that over the New Territories, officialdom dealt with the two together in internal deliberations.

In the summer of 1943, Gent launched his main counter-offensive in the bureaucratic battles by proposing an inter-departmental meeting to examine Hong Kong policy in detail.[25]

He undoubtedly expected support, or at least sympathy, for his position from the armed services, the Board of Trade and the Ministry of War Transport. The armed forces could be counted on to wish to avenge their humiliation of 1941, and the other ministries to value Hong Kong — a great port and trading centre. To counter the Foreign Office's dominant position in Whitehall, Gent had attempted to build up a coalition to buttress the relatively weaker Colonial Office in this debate.

Gent prepared a paper arguing that Britain should retain the New Territories or keep Hong Kong proper if it could not hold on to the New Territories.[26] In the event of the latter, he suggested Britain use the early end of the lease to negotiate with China for joint control over the airport, reservoirs and other parts of the infrastructure in the New Territories essential for Hong Kong's wellbeing. Gent proposed to examine the option of keeping the New Territories on practical grounds, not just on a technical legal basis as the British government had done in late 1942 during negotiations over the end of extraterritoriality. In his attempt, Gent had the support of his permanent secretary and the mild blessings of the secretary of state, Oliver Stanley.[27] This was the first time in internal discussions that British officials had seriously proposed to examine the possibility of keeping Hong Kong proper without the New Territories and its implications.

As it turned out, Gent's initiative failed because the Foreign Office refused to take part. Clarke declined to hold an interdepartmental meeting. He was still personally inclined to give up Hong Kong voluntarily in exchange for certain undefined benefits to Britain, but realized his idea was unacceptable within the government.[28] He had no wish to help Gent push for a course about which he disapproved. When Gent again pressed the issue, Clarke secured Foreign Secretary Anthony Eden's backing to reject a meeting, and the issue was therefore dropped.[29]

In the meantime, Gent made what arrangements he could within the authority of the Colonial Office to strength Britain's ability to recover Hong Kong. He proceeded to create a civil affairs staff for Hong Kong even before the armed forces were ready to accommodate such a unit in their organizations or, indeed, to plan an operation to recover the colony.[30] In the middle of 1943, a counteroffensive in the Far East was very low on their list of priorities. Thus, a Hong Kong Planning Unit was created under the wing of the Colonial Office. It was initially put under a recently retired colonial secretary of Hong Kong, Norman Smith. From 1944 onwards, it was headed by David MacDougall, the escapee from Hong Kong who had helped Gent defend Hong Kong in the bureaucratic battles of 1942. By setting up the Planning Unit at such an early date, Gent tried to build up an implied acceptance at the official level that Britain would return to Hong Kong at the end of the war.[31] It also provided Britain with the human resources, the core of a civil affairs staff, it needed to take over the administration of the colony as soon as it could be liberated.

The fortunes of war continued to affect Britain's attitude towards Hong Kong. In 1944, China suffered a major reverse when the Japanese made their last general offensive in the China theatre. During Japan's Operation Ichigo, which lasted from April to November, China lost vast territories and more than half a million troops.[32] In contrast, by the latter part of the year, the British counteroffensive in Burma, which was assisted by the Chinese, was making steady progress and a campaign to liberate Malaya was being planned. Britain's successes in the war and the prospect of instability and weakness in postwar China hardened its attitude towards Hong Kong. When the government prepared to make a policy statement over Malaya and Borneo, the Colonial Office insisted that Hong Kong be included lest it be seen to imply that the British government did not intend to recover it as well.[33] The Foreign Office raised no objection.

J. C. Sterndale-Bennett had by then replaced Clarke as head of the Far Eastern Department. He did not share Clarke's belief that it would be in Britain's interests to give up Hong Kong. In

November, the deputy prime minister and leader of the Labour Party, Clement Attlee, duly made a statement in the House of Commons that reaffirmed Britain's intention to return to Hong Kong.[34] The British government's attitude hardened further when US ambassador to China, Patrick Hurley, visited London in April 1945. In response to Hurley's suggestion that Britain should return Hong Kong to China, Prime Minister Churchill emphatically stated that it could only happen 'over my dead body'.[35] The Foreign Office was duly informed of the prime minister's strong stand.

There was no sense of urgency until the middle of 1945. The British officialdom had been busy preparing for an eventual return to Hong Kong and had been drafting a proposal for constitutional reform there.[36] The British were not informed that Wedemeyer had started planning an operation to liberate south China in the spring, including the Canton–Hong Kong region.[37] Until May, though a land operation directed by Wedemeyer was considered a possibility, the British worked on the assumption that Hong Kong would be recaptured by US or British forces operating from the sea.[38] British plans were based on the premise that 'nothing whatever has been settled' with regard to the manner of Hong Kong's liberation and 'no decision [was] likely for a considerable time'.[39] As a result of Wedemeyer's objection, the British even abandoned Operation Oblivion, which the Special Operations Executive (SOE) had been preparing since August 1944.[40]

Operation Oblivion was meant to introduce a specially trained British and Chinese Canadian unit into the vicinity of Hong Kong. Its purpose was to establish contact with the communist guerrillas, initiate subversive activities and have 'a British sponsored party available for any duties immediately after the liberation of the colony'.[41] In the meantime, the Colonial Office and the Hong Kong Planning Unit explored the possibility of getting the British Army Aid Group (BAAG) to provide and infiltrate a small number of British personnel into the colony. The aim of this exercise would be to re-establish

British authority in Hong Kong after its recapture.[42] The BAAG was a small unit in the Indian Army. It had been set up mainly by former citizens of Hong Kong to gather intelligence and to rescue prisoners and Allied pilots who had been shot down. Under Colonel Lindsay Ride's command, the BAAG declined the invitation because it would mean its end as an operational unit in China.[43]

In July 1945 a bombshell was dropped on the British. At the Potsdam Conference, the Americans told them that Wedemeyer was planning a land operation to liberate the Canton–Hong Kong region.[44] The prospect of the regular Chinese army reoccupying Hong Kong in the near future galvanized the British officials responsible for Hong Kong into action immediately. When the issues involved were examined at an interdepartmental meeting held shortly after the news broke, there was an unspoken understanding — Britain must be included in such an operation. The idea of launching a British military attack to liberate Hong Kong was considered, but dismissed because there were 'insufficient British forces available at present to oust the enemy'.[45] The consensus reached was that Britain should attach a civil affairs unit to the Chinese invasion force. In the event of Chinese irregular forces retaking Hong Kong, it was agreed that the SOE would send in a British civil affairs unit in a clandestine operation mounted outside China.[46] Such options were available thanks in no small part to Gent's earlier initiative to establish the Hong Kong Planning Unit. The Planning Unit was put on standby for incorporation into the armed forces as civil affairs staff. Its head, David MacDougall, was the first to be commissioned and he took the rank of brigadier.

The British felt they were working against great odds. They felt certain Wedemeyer was 'personally opposed to' their forces in China trying to recover Hong Kong.[47] This assessment was correct because 'Wedemeyer regarded British intentions and plans as incompatible with American policy in China'.[48] British hands were tied in other ways. The BAAG could not be used to infiltrate MacDougall's men into Hong Kong because it was 'watched and reported on by both local Americans and Chinese'.[49] Furthermore, the British ambassador and head of the military mission in Chongqing had pledged to inform Wedemeyer of all British military operations in China. Should Britain appeal over Wedemeyer's head? This would involve mobilizing the prime minister to ask US President Harry Truman directly to back a British proposal to be put to Chiang to attach MacDougall's unit to the invasion force.[50] However, Ernest Bevin, the new Labour Party foreign secretary who took over after a general election half way through the Potsdam Conference, vetoed such a high level approach.[51] He preferred to work through normal diplomatic channels.

In the meantime, the Colonial Office continued to explore every possible option to enhance the restoration of British sovereignty in Hong Kong. It arranged with the Admiralty and the Southeast Asian Command under Lord Mountbatten to set aside 'two or three suitable fast moving fleet units to be so placed, if Japanese capitulation looks possible, that they may steam at once for Hong Kong under sealed orders on given signal'.[52] The Colonial Office also instructed the BAAG to smuggle a message to Franklin Gimson (colonial secretary when Hong Kong fell), who was the most senior official interned in the colony. Gimson was instructed 'to restore British sovereignty and administration immediately' in the event of Japanese capitulation in Hong Kong.[53]

British officials in both London and Chongqing were driven by the common belief that the recovery of Hong Kong was very important for British 'prestige and future relations with China'.[54] There was also a feeling that, 'once in occupation [of Hong Kong], a Chinese force of whatever nature might prove difficult to extrude by ordinary diplomatic means'.[55] By then, the Foreign Office had come a long way from Ashley Clarke's 1942 position. In July, it modified and adopted as its own a position paper on Hong Kong that Gent had originally prepared in 1943. In the new circumstances, the Foreign Office sought to recover Hong Kong, including the New Territories, on three grounds.[56] These were:

- British enterprise and good government had built a barren island with a few thousand inhabitants into one of the world's great ports;
- with the removal of extraterritoriality and a probability of unsettled conditions in postwar China, Hong Kong was more important than ever as a base for British merchants and industrialists operating in China; and
- having lost the colony to the Japanese, it was 'a point of national honour . . . to recover it, and restore it to its normal state of order and prosperity'.[57]

Scramble for Liberation

On 14 August 1945, Emperor Hirohito announced that Japan would accept the terms laid down by the Allied powers in the Potsdam Declaration and surrender unconditionally. The war was coming to an end. The question of Hong Kong's liberation became a live issue that required urgent attention.

The British found themselves in a very awkward situation. When the prospect of a military campaign to liberate Hong Kong loomed earlier, they had already accepted that it was 'within the operational sphere of Generalissimo Chiang Kai-shek'.[58] Furthermore, the US president's General Order No. 1, which laid down the principle for accepting the Japanese surrender, required all Japanese forces 'within China (excluding Manchuria), Formosa and French Indo-China north of 16 degrees north latitude' to 'surrender to Generalissimo Chiang'.[59] In line with the above, the Japanese should surrender Hong Kong to Chiang — an arrangement seen in London as harmful to British interests.

In China, Chiang designated the Thirteenth Corps under Shi Jue, which had been issued with US equipment and materials earlier in the summer, to take over Hong Kong.[60] Shi's corps was in the vicinity of Wuzhou, less than 300 miles from Hong

Kong, when the news broke.[61] Sun Liren's New First Corps, which was also in the same area, was ordered to liberate Canton. The two forces, which together numbered more than 60,000, could march to Hong Kong quickly. Chiang did not order either or both of them to proceed at all speed, for he had not expected a dispute over Hong Kong.

As soon as the news broke, the British government in London acted immediately to recover Hong Kong. On the day the Japanese surrender was announced, the British proceeded to detach and form a special naval task group from the British Pacific Fleet to sail towards Hong Kong.[62] Without delay, they sought the US naval authority's cooperation for this redeployment. On 16 August, the British government informed the Chinese of its plan, lest Chiang first hear the news from Wedemeyer (via US services' channels) and take offence.[63] The British ignored the fact that Hong Kong was in Chiang's theatre and that they should have obtained his consent beforehand. London now took the position that 'irrespective of operational theatres, wherever the sovereign power has sufficient forces available it should resume its authority and accept Japanese surrender in its own territory'.[64] There was no question of consulting Chiang about the British plan. The British did not wish to provoke Chiang into a hostile response, but fully intended to reach Hong Kong and liberate it from the Japanese before the Chinese army got there. Britain started what could have become a scramble for the liberation of Hong Kong.

The Chinese government was understandably offended when it was informed of the British action, which it deemed 'rather high-handed'.[65] It rightly suspected the British were concerned about Hong Kong's future. In the absence of Minister T. V. Soong, Vice-Minister K. C. Wu was in charge of the Foreign Ministry and the negotiations with the British. He tried to assure the British that China had no territorial ambitions in Hong Kong, that it would not take advantage of accepting the surrender to establish possession and that it regarded Hong Kong as a matter that would require eventual settlement through diplomatic channels.[66] The Chinese government also formally asked Britain to adhere to General Order No. 1, to act in concert with China as an ally to ensure peace and order in Asia in taking surrender from the Japanese, and to refrain from landing any forces in the China theatre without prior consent.[67] For its part, China pledged to respect all legitimate British interests and accord them every necessary protection. China tried to protect its interests by insisting on following the correct procedures. Its handling of the matter was reasonable and responsible.

Chiang did not order his army to race against the British fleet steaming towards Hong Kong. He stood by this decision even after his insistence that the usually legal-minded British should follow the agreed procedures proved fruitless, and the British turned down his offer of compromise, which from his point of view would have protected the honour of both sides. This seems remarkable, particularly since he had at his disposal some of his best trained and equipped forces, which could probably have beaten the Royal Navy in the race.

Chiang's decision can only be understood in a wider context. His primary concern was China proper. To begin with, the Chinese communist forces, which were in principle under his command, had openly disobeyed his orders about arrangements for the Japanese surrender.[68] Under Mao Zedong's leadership, they were preparing to 'struggle' against Chiang's hold over the country.[69] They were rushing to take over as much land in China proper from the Japanese as possible.[70] To Chiang, this was a race he could ill afford to lose. By comparison, the race against the British was of little consequence. Losing the former could pose a major problem for his postwar plans for the entire country. By contrast, he had little worry about Hong Kong, particularly since he already had an agreement with the British over the question of the future of the New Territories. He could raise the issue at any time. He also had to take into account the activities of the communist East River column, which had an independent Hong Kong–

Kowloon group operating in the New Territories.[71] By 20
August, the East River column's main force had seized
Shenzhen and was at the border of Hong Kong.[72] If Chiang had
ordered his US-trained units to race against the British, he
would have generated a nationalist fervour and provoked the
communists into competing. In such an eventuality, both he
and the British would probably have lost the race to the East
River column. Indeed, the Chinese government felt that if its
own forces could not liberate Hong Kong, it would rather this
were done by the British than the communists.

Also, Chiang could not afford to tie down his best units for
garrison duties in Hong Kong. This would be unavoidable
should he choose to confront the British. US Ambassador
Hurley had informed Chiang of his conversations with
Churchill the previous April. He believed the British would not
give up Hong Kong without a fight.[73] The Chinese ambassador
to London, Wellington Koo, confirmed his suspicion that the
British would take a strong stand. Koo had ascertained from Sir
Stafford Cripps that the new Labour government held the same
view of Hong Kong as Churchill's government.[74] At that time,
Chiang could not afford to use force against the British over
Hong Kong. With only 16 truly combat effective divisions in
the whole country — his remaining 250 plus divisions were of
'negligible' fighting value — he could not spare the New First
Corps' three divisions.[75] These crack divisions were needed
elsewhere — particularly for the reoccupation of Manchuria
and north China, where the communists were infiltrating.
Thus, though in principle Chiang had some of his most
powerful military units suitably located to back up a tough
stand over Hong Kong, they were largely irrelevant to his
diplomatic manœuvres. He could not afford to commit them in
a showdown with the British. In any event, because China had
just emerged as one of the five founding members of the
United Nations, Chiang had no intention of confronting the
British. His hands were tied.

As soon as the Sino–British diplomatic exchanges began to

turn into a serious dispute, the British ambassador in Chongqing, Sir Horace Seymour, rightly assessed that Chiang did not want a confrontation, but was 'upset' because the British had ignored his prerogatives as the Allied commander of the China theatre.[76] He also correctly judged that Chiang would agree to a settlement for a British fleet to liberate Hong Kong if his authority as supreme commander were not compromised. In the ensuing dispute, the senior British officer in China, Lieutenant-General Sir Adrian Carton de Wiart, also felt Chiang had justifiable grounds for his position.[77] The astute assessments of the British representatives in Chongqing proved to be of only marginal value, however, for they were overruled by London.

Officials in the Colonial and Foreign Offices were highly suspicious of Chiang's intentions. Their concern was that allowing Chiang to exercise authority of any kind in or over Hong Kong would be the thin end of the wedge to achieve his well-known objective over Hong Kong.[78] Chiang's predicament was not fully understood. More importantly, at this moment of victory, jingoism affected the judgement of the British in London. Chiang's responses were deemed 'unreasonable' because he 'could hardly have expected us not to wipe out the memory of the Japanese capture of Hong Kong'.[79] The obvious point that Chiang was being publicly humiliated by an ally did not catch anyone's imagination. Officials handling the matter in London felt a sense of righteousness in their hard-line approach.[80] Even Foreign Secretary Bevin felt Britain must first recover Hong Kong from the Japanese.[81] Indeed, within days of the dispute emerging, he publicly committed his government in a statement to the House of Commons.[82] London was psychologically prepared to face down Chiang over Hong Kong. Its capabilities to do so were enhanced day by day, for a powerful naval task group under Rear-Admiral (later Sir) Cecil Harcourt was steaming towards Hong Kong.

As the British and Chinese were unable to agree on the arrangements for the Japanese surrender, they both appealed to the USA for support. Chiang did so in general terms through the normal diplomatic channels as soon as the British made what was, to him, an unreasonable demand.[83] The British were a little slower off the mark, but were nevertheless more effective in securing US backing. On 18 August, Attlee, now prime minister, asked President Truman to instruct General Douglas MacArthur, supreme commander of the Allied powers, to order the Japanese in Hong Kong to surrender to the British.[84]

Unlike Roosevelt, Truman was not sentimentally attached to supporting Chiang over Hong Kong. In fact, he thought poorly of Chiang.[85] When he received Attlee's request he did not bother to check with Chongqing. While he failed to respond to Chiang's initial telegram, he responded to Attlee promptly. By the time Chiang appealed to him again on 21 August, Truman had already replied to Attlee three days earlier. Truman told Chiang he saw the dispute as 'primarily a military matter of an operational character' and had 'no objection to the surrender of Hong Kong being accepted by a British officer, providing military coordination is effected beforehand by the British with the Generalissimo'.[86] The death of Roosevelt and consequent change of US president earlier that year, ensured the British success in Washington. Isolated diplomatically as well, Chiang had to compromise with the British.

Chiang proposed to the British that, in his capacity as supreme commander, he would delegate authority to a British officer nominated by Britain to take the surrender in Hong Kong in the presence of a Chinese and an American officer designated by him.[87] He accepted the British wish to restore their military honour and reassured them that he respected legitimate British interests, including their return to Hong Kong.[88] To demonstrate his sincerity and to dampen jingoism from within his government, he even made an announcement at the Supreme Council for National Defence categorically stating that he did not intend to send troops to Hong Kong.[89] In the meantime, appropriate orders were duly issued to his forces.[90] He even personally told Ambassador Seymour that he desired to have good relations with Britain, though he also insisted that he must defend China's legitimate rights.[91]

In return, Chiang asked the British to undertake not to accept the Japanese surrender in Hong Kong before he had done so in the China theatre as a whole. This would include the handing over of Japanese ships and mechanized transport equipment in Hong Kong, and making the port and related facilities there available for the transshipment of Chinese troops to north and northeast China.[92] Chiang bowed to the political and diplomatic reality and, in the light of the rising communist challenge, to the military imperative as well. He was as accommodating to the British as anyone could reasonably have expected him to have been.

Deeply affected by their prejudice against Chiang, British officials in London rejected his face-saving formula. They suspected that if Chiang were allowed to delegate authority to the British commander, Rear-Admiral Harcourt, he could continue to exercise military authority through Harcourt after taking the surrender.[93] Chiang would be asked to waive his authority in the case of Hong Kong. When Seymour approached Vice-Foreign Minister Wu about the situation, the latter strongly advised him against putting the matter to Chiang. Seymour believed that Wu was sincere when he advised, on a private and completely confidential basis, that if Britain could not accept a delegation of authority, it should simply 'leave the matter alone and go ahead with surrender arrangements as planned'.[94] As Wu rightly assessed, Chiang felt very strongly about the issue and stood his ground.[95] He could not be moved. The final compromise was a British decision for Harcourt to represent both Britain and Chiang, as supreme commander of the China theatre, when receiving the surrender from the Japanese, an arrangement to which Chiang acquiesced.[96]

As the diplomatic saga unfolded, news of the Japanese emperor's announcement spread in the Stanley camp, where the senior British officer in Hong Kong, Franklin Gimson, was interned. Gimson was a courageous and far-sighted official who represented the best in the British Empire. He arrived in Hong Kong and took office as colonial secretary only days before the Japanese invaded. As the senior officer in the internment camp, he planned for Hong Kong's postwar reconstruction, including the introduction of a 'popularly elected' element to the local legislature.[97] Once he was certain that the Japanese were surrendering, he went to see the commandant. He informed the Japanese that, from then on, he would take charge of the administration. He asked for accommodation for himself and his officers and, pending the arrival of British forces, demanded that the Japanese troops continue to maintain order.[98] Shortly afterwards, on 23 August, an ethnic Chinese BAAG agent delivered the instructions London had ordered the BAAG to transmit to him. Once he knew London's intentions, Gimson promptly asked the Chief Justice in the camp, Sir Athol MacGregor, to administer the necessary oath for him to take over as officer administering the government. Frail and undernourished, Gimson and some of his fitter colleagues reclaimed British sovereignty over Hong Kong by sheer courage, stamina and dedication.[99]

On 29 August, a powerful Royal Navy Pacific Fleet task force under Harcourt's command, consisting of two aircraft carriers, a battleship, three cruisers and a number of destroyers and minesweepers, arrived off Hong Kong.[100] On the following day, having transferred his flag from the aircraft carrier HMS *Indomitable* to the cruiser HMS *Swiftsure*, Harcourt steamed into Victoria Harbour to take over from the Japanese forces. He was greeted by Gimson and his slender nucleus of a civil administration. On 1 September, Harcourt formally proclaimed the establishment of a British military administration and, on his own initiative, appointed Gimson lieutenant-governor. London later disallowed this last act, for a military administration with full powers coexisting alongside a civilian government created a constitutional anomaly. MacDougall and his civil affairs unit (formerly the Hong Kong Planning Unit) took over the administration when they arrived on 7 September. Gimson was repatriated for recuperation. Hong Kong's British administration was being restored to a level of efficiency that soon made it the most shining example of all the territories liberated from the Japanese.

On 16 September 1945, in Government House in the presence of Major-General Pan Huaguo and a US colonel, Harcourt formally accepted the Japanese surrender on behalf of both his own country and Chiang (as theatre commander). Hong Kong had finally returned to the British Empire's fold. Contrary to Foreign Office concerns, Chiang never made use of Harcourt having accepted the surrender on his behalf to attempt to exercise authority over him. Chiang handled the liberation of Hong Kong in good faith: it was the British who were high handed. Whether or not the British behaviour was justifiable, it soon proved to be of significant long-term value to them in deciding Hong Kong's fate.

4. Crown Colony For Ever? 1946–79

Hong Kong was restored as a Crown colony on 1 May 1946. The military administration under Harcourt and MacDougall had already made great progress in rehabilitating the territory. Being far-sighted and progressive minded people, both Harcourt and MacDougall recognized that there was a strong local public expectation of a new deal of some kind when civil government was reintroduced.[1] They also reported that their policies in Hong Kong were 'carefully scrutinized in China' and that anything that savoured of a return to the *status quo ante* would be 'seized upon to add to the clamour for the return to China of Hong Kong'.[2] British diplomats and senior non-official people visiting Hong Kong confirmed their reports to London. On 1 May 1946, Sir Mark Young, whom the Japanese had held as a prisoner during the war, returned to resume his interrupted governorship and to restore civil administration. The Crown colony system of government was reinstated and MacDougall was appointed colonial secretary. Although Young's return marked a restoration, he also brought with him a new deal.

Upon his return, Young declared that the British government had 'under consideration the means by which in Hong Kong, as elsewhere in the Colonial empire, the inhabitants of the Territory can be given a fuller and more responsible share in the management of their own affairs'.[3] This new deal was devised partly in accordance with the policy drawn up under Gent in the Colonial Office, and partly in response to Harcourt and MacDougall's recommendations. Young pursued political reform energetically because he believed that, 'given the Chinese Government's determination to recover Hong Kong, ... the only way to keep the colony British was to make the local inhabitants want to do so'.[4] In his view, this could be achieved by turning the local inhabitants from Chinese sojourners into citizens of British Hong Kong through popular political participation. Young's bold attempt to introduce representation into the local administration was linked to his wish to pre-empt the need to return Hong Kong to China.

The British government's recognition that postwar Hong Kong needed some kind of new deal meant that Young was given only one year before a new and younger man was to take his place.[5] In July 1947, Sir Alexander Grantham took over the governorship. A first-class administrator who started colonial service as a cadet in Hong Kong before moving on elsewhere, Grantham felt he understood the Chinese people in ways that Young never did. He thought that Young was misguided, for 'it was virtually impossible to evoke either a local loyalty or a greater sense of belonging to the British Commonwealth'.[6] Grantham partly based his argument on the fact that, until 1950, the majority of people in Hong Kong did not consider themselves settled there. This was hardly surprising given that there was free and considerable movement of people across the Sino–British border. Its population had increased from a little over 1 million before war broke out between China and Japan in 1937 to a peak of 1.6 million in 1941. It fell to about 600,000 in 1945 and then swelled to about 2.3 million in 1950.[7] Grantham believed that 'Hong Kong would continue as a British Colony' until 1997, when the New Territories lease would expire.[8] In his view, the entire colony, including the New Territories, would then be returned to China. He thus saw no point in Young's attempt at constitutional reform and skilfully abandoned this commitment over a period of five years.[9] While Young tried to pre-empt the fateful date of 1997, Grantham accepted it as an unavoidable appointment in history and tried to ignore it, for it was half a century away.

Preparations for Negotiations

The question of Hong Kong's future continued to receive attention in Britain and China after its liberation from the Japanese. Neither side needed to be reminded of their January 1943 agreement by which China reserved the right to raise the question of the New Territories' future after Japan's defeat. Both parties were equally aware that, in practice, this involved dealing with the future of Hong Kong as a whole. Once urgent matters associated with the end of hostilities were settled, officials in London quietly examined the Hong Kong question. The British success in recovering Hong Kong in August 1945 was generally understood to have strengthened Britain's hand, but not to have eliminated the need to negotiate with China.

At the Colonial Office, Gent continued to play a pivotal role in energetically making preparations for Hong Kong to face the brave new world. This continued until he left to become high commissioner of Malaya in 1946. The Colonial Office sought opinions and advice from various informed outsiders, including leading businessmen with extensive experience in Hong Kong. Retired Colonial Secretary Norman Smith floated an idea never examined before. It was to return most of the New Territories to China, if this should become necessary before 1997, but retain and incorporate into the colony proper the built up part of the mainland south of the Kowloon hills known as New Kowloon.[10] Smith's idea did not win any serious support, but it demonstrated the Colonial Office's concern to explore all possibilities. Under Gent's lead, the Colonial Office focused its attention mainly in two directions.

First, Gent advocated the need to restore Hong Kong's economic fortunes as quickly as possible so that it would become highly valuable to the Chinese again.[11] This involved preparing a new deal, including the introduction of genuine political reforms that would give the local people 'real power including real control over ... [their] own finances'.[12] The objective was to pre-empt the need, or at least reduce the pressure, to return Hong Kong or the New Territories. This line of thinking coincided with that of Harcourt, MacDougall and particularly Young, who implemented this policy with zeal.

The second was to submit a paper on Hong Kong's future for incorporation into a general document setting out Britain's postwar foreign policy, which the Cabinet Office's Far Eastern Planning Unit was preparing.[13] By seizing the initiative, the Colonial Office gained the advantage of providing the basis it itself had approved of for interdepartmental consultation. It also pre-empted the Foreign Office, which was likely to produce a paper that was unsympathetic to the Colonial Office view. The draft the Far Eastern Planning Unit presented in October 1945 was mainly based on the Colonial Office one. Its starting point was the need to prepare for the Chinese raising the question of the future of the New Territories. It listed four options for further consideration, namely:[14]

- Britain rejects any Chinese demand for the return of Hong Kong or the New Territories;
- Britain returns the New Territories with certain conditions;
- Britain enters into a lease-back arrangement whereby it cedes the sovereignty of Hong Kong proper to China, but leases the entire territory back for a specific number of years; or
- Britain retrocedes the entire colony.

Although the paper set out the arguments for each of these options, there was a preference that the last two should not be pursued if avoidable.

George Kitson, head of the Foreign Office's China Department and an old China hand, felt the need to respond to reports from the east that Hong Kong would need a new deal in the postwar era. In his mind, Britain could not 'go on treating Hong Kong as a Crown Colony on an island off the coast of China'. He felt that political reform there would not stop the Chinese demanding its retrocession.[15] He himself intended to produce a policy paper on the subject in late 1945, but was otherwise preoccupied. Sterndale-Bennett encouraged him to proceed in early 1946. The latter was concerned that the government had led British businessmen to believe that it would hold on to Hong Kong. He felt it would be 'wrong to let them continue in a fool's paradise' only to let them down later.[16] Before the end of February, Kitson duly produced a 14-page memorandum, which, if approved, would form the basis of a Cabinet paper.

Kitson's starting point was a strong sense of sympathy for the Chinese case. To explain the Chinese feeling he made an analogy with the Isle of Wight. He argued:

> Supposing the Chinese had taken the island against our will 100 years ago and covered it with pagodas, etc., and developed it by means which they had invented and we had not learned to use, doing all this for their own purposes, although talking a great deal about the material advantages to the United Kingdom, and all the time emphasizing the value of this haven of good government, a protection against insecurity, in the Isle of Wight. Even if they had created a heaven on earth in that small island we should have only one feeling about it. We should want it back.[17]

While Kitson restated the case for retaining Hong Kong, which the Colonial Office advocated, he felt it was essential not to reject outright any Chinese approach on the subject. He believed the Chinese not only had a strong case but also 'formidable means at their disposal'. These included the ability to paralyse Hong Kong by repeating the strike-cum-boycott of 1925/6, and refusing to cooperate with the British generally. Kitson believed Chinese cooperation was crucial for the restoration of British economic interests in China, for international peace and security, and for avoiding problems on the China–Burma border, in Tibet and even among the Chinese community in Malaya. He was convinced that, given the strong

Chinese feeling, Sino–British relations could 'not rest on a fully satisfactory basis until the Hong Kong issue is faced and fairly dealt with'.

He argued China's case more powerfully than any Chinese diplomat or leader had done. He advocated that Britain take the initiative to raise the matter with the Chinese. The reason was that the 'right sort of gesture would ... provide the Chinese government with an invaluable aid in overruling an opposition and keeping in check a public opinion which, in the absence of any encouraging sign from our side, might drive the government to extreme and inconvenient demands'. As to the possible solutions, he recounted the options listed in the Far Eastern Planning Unit paper.

He also added another proposal made by John Keswick, a leading Jardine Matheson & Company businessman who served as a political adviser to the supreme commander of the Southeast Asian Command during the war. This was to convert the Crown colony of Hong Kong into the 'Free Port and Municipality of Hong Kong'.[18] In Keswick's conception, this new Hong Kong would have no discrimination based on race, colour or creed, and an elected council would advise its chief executive officer. Kitson urged the British government to declare publicly that it was prepared 'as a gesture of goodwill and in a spirit of friendship for the Chinese nation to enter into negotiations' for the return of the New Territories 'on suitable conditions'.[19]

In preparing his paper, Kitson demonstrated a good understanding of Chinese feelings, but showed remarkable naïveté. However apt his analogy with the Isle of Wight might have been, it was utterly unacceptable to the mainstream British view. As Sterndale-Bennett pointed out, it had wider implications. For example, there was no question of Britain returning Gibraltar to Spain.[20] Kitson's wish to win Chinese gratitude and thus secure their friendship and cooperation by making a grand gesture over the New Territories was unrealistic. Given their feelings about Hong Kong, the Chinese would at best see the 'grand gesture' he proposed as correcting a wrong done to them. Furthermore, since the Chinese wanted to recover Hong Kong in its entirety, a gesture over the New Territories could hardly achieve Kitson's hope for Chinese gratitude, even in the short term.

The permanent secretary within the Foreign Office, Orme Sargent, rightly saw Kitson's assumption as 'a complete delusion and a very dangerous one', for its effect on China's policy towards Britain would 'either be nil or of very short duration'.[21] Sargent and Foreign Secretary Bevin felt Britain had only two reasons to give up Hong Kong or the New Territories — 'either because we have no longer the physical means (military and financial) to maintain our position or because we anticipate that sooner or later the Chinese Government will be able to hold us to ransom by paralysing our trade and administration in Hong Kong'.[22]

Following the usual procedure by which various interested parties in the foreign service were consulted, Kitson substantially revised the paper and presented it as a Foreign Office memorandum in July.[23] Although the reservations expressed by others were noted, this paper still recommended taking an initiative to open negotiations with China. It listed four options, not all of which were included in the Far Eastern Planning Unit paper. These were:

- the return of the New Territories in exchange for Anglo–Chinese control over the airport, reservoirs and other infrastructures in the New Territories;
- to turn Hong Kong in its entirety into an Anglo–Chinese condominium;
- to place Hong Kong under international control with China and Britain having a predominant share in its administration; and
- to retrocede Hong Kong in its entirety, but for a new treaty to be signed by which Britain would lease Hong Kong (with or without the New Territories) for a period of 30 years.

The paper recommended the last option. It was meant to be a compromise between the need to satisfy Chinese nationalist aspirations and Britain's reluctance to give up Hong Kong. However, it was a shortsighted one, which took no account of its implications for the local people or their views. The first option listed in the Far Eastern Planning Unit paper, which was to reject a Chinese demand for a return, was deleted from this new paper.

The Colonial Office and Governor Young reacted strongly against the Foreign Office paper. Thomas Lloyd had by then taken over from Gent as the supervising under-secretary. He shared Governor Young's view against taking any initiative or accepting the lease-back proposal.[24] Lloyd attempted to counter the Foreign Office's greater weight in Whitehall by proposing to enlist the support in interdepartmental consultations of other ministries likely to be sympathetic. These included the armed forces, the Board of Trade, the Ministry of Civil Aviation and, above all, the Treasury. The last was a particularly useful ally, for it was one of the most powerful ministries in Whitehall. Lloyd was certain he could get the Treasury on his side, for he knew how strongly it would oppose any proposal that required the British Exchequer to support a colony. In the stringent days of postwar Britain it was a particularly astute move. He argued that the opening of negotiations with China would 'materially affect the readiness of British and other firms to sink any further money into the colony for rehabilitation', and would 'preclude the colony itself from raising a loan for rehabilitation', which was at that time under consideration. All Lloyd would concede was for the Colonial Office to provide an alternative draft paper, which would incorporate the views of the Foreign Office. The Foreign Office paper was unacceptable to the Colonial Office, even as a basis for further consultation.

Lloyd's opposite number in the Foreign Office, Esler Dening, was, unlike Kitson, not personally committed to the paper. He accepted Lloyd's proposal.[25] A joint paper, which listed the options and arguments for and against each one of them, was finally produced in the following year, but it was never submitted to the Cabinet. By then, in 1947, China had descended into a full-scale civil war and the government's position was rapidly deteriorating.[26] There was no longer an immediate prospect of the Chinese government raising the New Territories' issue, and Foreign Secretary Bevin preferred to keep quiet about Hong Kong.[27]

Between the Japanese surrender in 1945 and 1949, there was a considerable amount of Chinese nationalist agitation for the recovery of Hong Kong. The head of the Chinese military mission in Hong Kong, Major-General Pan Huaguo, advocated opening negotiations with the British immediately after the end of the war.[28] The Foreign Ministry considered the issues involved and 'looked for the right moment' to open negotiations with the British.[29] By 1946, it took the position that whether China should raise the question of the New Territories or of Hong Kong as a whole must depend on what circumstances prevailed when negotiations could be started.[30] Later that year, when the British were examining the possibility of building a new airport in Pingshan in the northwest of the New Territories, the Ministry of Defence recommended considering this issue together with that of the future of the New Territories.[31] Whenever there were disputes in Hong Kong, such as over the old fort of Kowloon, numerous petitions from county or provincial assemblies in different parts of the country demanding the return of Hong Kong were submitted to the central government.[32]

Despite the public agitation, the Chinese government did not formally raise the question of either the New Territories or Hong Kong. As was the case during the war, Chiang defined the basis of China's policy. He did so when he spoke at the Supreme Council for National Defence during negotiations for the liberation of Hong Kong in the following terms:

China will not use the occasion of Japan's unconditional

surrender as a pretext for disregarding international agreements and infringing upon the rights of our allies. We will not take advantage of this opportunity to dispatch troops to take over Hong Kong, nor will we provoke misunderstanding among our allies. I wish to state here that the present status of Hong Kong is regulated by a treaty signed by China and Great Britain. Changes in future will be introduced only through friendly negotiations between the two countries. Our foreign policy is to honour treaties, rely upon law and seek rational readjustments when the requirements of time and actual conditions demand such readjustments. Now that all the leased territories and settlements in China have been one after another returned to China, the leased territory of Kowloon should not remain an exception. But China will settle the last issue through diplomatic talks between the two countries.[33]

The ties on Chiang's hands, which produced the restraint behind the above statement, got even tighter afterwards. In an important sense, the Japanese surrender came too soon for Chiang's government. Even as the country was enjoying the euphoria of victory, Chiang had to face the grim reality that his government and resources were largely confined to the south-western part of the country. The mountainous terrain and appalling communications that had helped his poorly equipped army hold off the Japanese invaders, now hindered his efforts to restore central authority. To reoccupy and rehabilitate a country the size of a continent he had a battered bureaucracy and, with the exception of the US trained divisions, an ineffective army supported by a war-torn economy suffering from hyperinflation.

The biggest problem Chiang faced was the communist challenge in north China, which was spreading fast into Soviet occupied Manchuria. However, most of his combat effective troops were in south and southwest China. They could easily march towards Hong Kong, but could not reach the north quickly. Eventually, Chiang had to swallow his nationalist pride and ask the USA to land 50,000 marines. This was to prevent vital port and communication facilities in north China from falling under communist control.[34] For the eventual dispatch of his crack divisions to the north — a high priority issue — he had to rely on British cooperation as well. He needed Hong Kong's port facilities to ship three corps of about 100,000 crack troops to north China and Manchuria. Until they had all passed through Hong Kong in the spring of 1946, Chiang could hardly afford to create tension over Hong Kong that might result in its transshipment facilities being denied to the Chinese army.

Chiang was also somewhat restrained by Britain's handling of Hong Kong's liberation. Britain's determination to recover Hong Kong, its ability to deploy a powerful fleet at short notice and the US endorsement of its position all left their marks on Chiang. British intransigence taught him a lesson: unless he had the resources to support a tough stand over Hong Kong, the British would humiliate him. The intelligence available to him also confirmed — in this case wrongly — that the British government would 'under no circumstances return Hong Kong'.[35] Given the enormity of his domestic task and given that he had no means to back up a hard negotiating position, Chiang understandably refrained from raising the question of the New Territories. With the communist challenge also rapidly turning into a full-scale civil war, the last thing Chiang needed was a slap in the face by the British, which is how his enemies would have portrayed a diplomatic impasse over Hong Kong's future.

This exercise in restraint did not mean that efforts were spared to test the British attitude. In June 1946, at a meeting prior to Ambassador Sir Horace Seymour's departure, Chiang took the opportunity to say that, until the Hong Kong issue was resolved, satisfactory relations between the two countries would be impossible.[36] He added that it would be fairly simple to arrange matters in such a way that the material interests of both sides could be furthered. Two weeks later, when it was Ambassador Wellington Koo's turn to bid farewell to London, Koo raised the issue with Minister of State Noel-Baker, in the absence of Secretary Bevin. Koo tried to find out whether there was any indication that the British government would meet the Chinese wishes.[37] He tried to ascertain whether the issue had been discussed at the top level. He had to be satisfied with the reply that it was not the right time for negotiations to commence and that the matter was not under Cabinet consideration. While Kitson cited the two meetings to support his advocacy to start negotiations, they confirmed in the Chinese mind that such a time had not come.

From that point onwards, the Chinese government accepted that the issue would have to be tackled at a later date, perhaps when it had re-established control in China. The preferred solution was still essentially based on Chiang's wartime idea that China would voluntarily turn Hong Kong into a free port after its return. Options that compromised Chinese sovereignty, such as turning Hong Kong into the Far Eastern headquarters of the United Nations, were deemed unacceptable.[38] In 1947, senior Chinese leaders close to Chiang announced China's decision to defer tackling the Hong Kong question. Both General Lo Chuoying, as governor of Guangdong, and Sun Ke, as vice-president of the Republic of China, announced the decision publicly in order to pacify public agitation.[39]

They held to this policy even when a major dispute developed over the old fort of Kowloon towards the end of the year. Although the immediate cause of the dispute was the Hong Kong government's attempt to clear the area for redevelopment, jurisdiction over the old fort was intricately related to the New Territories' lease. Despite this connection and even after public agitation turned violent in Canton in January 1948, the Chinese government continued to exercise great restraint and avoided relating the dispute to the future of the New Territories.[40] As long as a settlement would not prejudice China's sovereign rights, Nanjing's primary concern was to reach an amicable settlement as the country was then in the midst of a national crisis.[41]

A New Government in China

By the last quarter of 1948, the situation in China had become so desperate for the Chinese government that it was fighting for its very survival. The tide of the civil war had turned in favour of the communists. Three major battles, involving the deployment of almost 1.5 million troops on each side, were at that time raging in Manchuria and north China. By January 1949, the communists had won all three battles decisively and, in the process, had destroyed Chiang's original US trained and equipped crack divisions in Manchuria.[42] The back of the Kuomintang's military power had been broken.

The rest of 1949 was a nightmare for the Chinese government. Communist forces under Mao Zedong crossed the Yangtze River and captured the capital Nanjing and the financial centre Shanghai in April. By October, they had swept south, taken over Canton and reached the Sino–British border. The Kuomintang government had fled first to Canton, then to Chongqing and eventually, before the year ended, to Taipei. Though Chiang formally 'withdrew' from the presidency in January, he was still directing the Kuomintang behind the scenes. He resumed the office of president of the Republic of China (ROC) the following year and, until his death in 1975, continued his struggle against the communists from his island redoubt of Taiwan.

In the meantime, on 1 October 1949, Mao proclaimed the establishment of the People's Republic of China (PRC) in Beijing. For better or for worse, China had a new government of a communist persuasion and this now handled the Hong Kong question.

Foreign policy seriously came on to the Chinese communists' political agenda when a US army observer group, known as the Dixie Mission, arrived in Yenan (their capital at the time) during the Pacific war. The Americans had gone there to assess whether the USA should give them military aid for their common struggle against Japan. In its early days, the Chinese communists' foreign policy was based more on pragmatism and opportunism than on ideology.[43] Their treatment of Taiwan was a good example of such pragmatism. Prior to 1943, the communists excluded Taiwan from their list of China's lost territories. Instead, they put it in the same category as Korea, namely as a victim of Japanese imperialism that should be given independence. Mao himself had told this to a US journalist, Edgar Snow.[44] However, when Chiang persuaded Roosevelt and Churchill at the 1943 Cairo Conference to include Taiwan as a territory to be returned to China after Japan's defeat, Mao and his comrades changed their position. Henceforth, they 'treated Taiwan a priori as an integral part of Chinese territory and thus denied any potential political sovereignty to the Taiwanese people'.[45]

In the immediate postwar period, the Chinese communist view of the world order was based on the existence of the Cold War between the Soviet and US blocs.[46] Within China itself, the communists focused their foreign policy on strengthening their power as much as possible. This was while US statesman George Marshall was trying to mediate between them and the Kuomintang in the Chinese civil war. When this failed in January 1947, the communist leadership put foreign policy on the back seat while they concentrated on the military campaigns. Towards the end of 1948, the picture began to change again. Mao recalculated how much time would be needed to defeat the Kuomintang. He estimated that it would probably take about another year, rather than three more years as previously calculated.[47] Their victories in Manchuria and north China gave the communists control over major cities such as Beijing and the coastal regions in north China in early 1949. It had become necessary to work out a detailed policy towards the Western presence there.[48]

Mao was the most important party leader in terms of making foreign policy.[49] Though, by most Western accounts, Premier Zhou Enlai might have personified the PRC's diplomacy, he was more responsible for implementing rather than making foreign policy.[50] Mao's thinking was deeply affected by his own experiences as a revolutionary and in the civil war. As a master strategist, he consistently emphasized the importance of holding the initiative.[51] This requirement, which was based on his military thinking, was adopted as one of the PRC's basic foreign policy principles.[52] From his view of the world, Mao considered China in an 'intermediate zone' between the USA and the Soviet Union, and stressed the need to lean to the latter.[53] Mao also showed a strong Sino-centric view of the world. The mixing of these factors produced an unusual approach to foreign policy. While Mao was keen to restore China to its 'rightful place' in the world, he did not intend simply to abide by the rules and conventions of international relations. Under Mao, China tried to define its own terms for participating in the world community.

In handling its relations with Britain, the PRC took London and the rest of the world by surprise. At that time, Britain was unquestionably the second most powerful country in the non-Soviet camp. When it extended recognition to the PRC in January 1950, instead of simply reciprocating, as was the convention, Beijing responded by imposing conditions for establishing relations.[54] Acting on Mao's instructions, the PRC merely permitted the British to send a representative to Beijing to negotiate the establishment of diplomatic relations.[55] Although the British maintained a mission in Beijing, diplomatic relations were not established until June 1954.[56] Normal relations with ambassadorial representation had to wait until 1972.[57] This was extraordinary because it would have been to the PRC's advantage to secure British recognition at an early date. However, in Mao's calculation, this was of minor importance compared with keeping the initiative in Beijing's hands.

Hong Kong occupied an unusual place in Chinese communist calculations. Unlike Chiang's government, which essentially considered it a foreign policy matter to be resolved by diplomacy, the PRC placed Hong Kong somewhere between foreign policy and domestic policy. In Beijing's view, the treaties that governed the status of Hong Kong and the New Territories were 'unequal treaties' and therefore invalid.[58] It saw Hong Kong as a matter 'left behind by history', which 'could be resolved through negotiations when the conditions were ripe'.[59] However, unlike most international disputes, it was an issue that Beijing maintained 'the United Nations had no right to discuss' as soon as it became a member of this international organization.[60]

When the communists and the Kuomintang were about to resume their civil war in full force at the end of 1946, Mao told a handful of Western journalists that he did not at that stage seek the early return of tiny Hong Kong.[61] In a fuller account by Gordon Harmon, a British journalist in the group, Mao reportedly said:

China has enough trouble in her hands to try and clean up the mess in her own country, leave alone trying to rule Formosa, for us to clamour for the return of Hong Kong. I am not interested in Hong Kong; the Communist Party is not interested in Hong Kong; it has never been the subject of any discussion amongst us. Perhaps ten, twenty or thirty years hence we may ask for a discussion regarding its return, but my attitude is that so long as your officials do not maltreat Chinese subjects in Hong Kong, and so long as Chinese are not treated as inferior to others in the matter of taxation and a voice in the Government, I am not interested in Hong Kong, and will certainly not allow it to be a bone of contention between your country and mine.[62]

Still headquartered in the remote northwest with his chosen

sites for decisive battles in north and northeast China, Hong Kong was too far away to command Mao's immediate attention. In any case, it had an important value to the communists under British rule. The Hong Kong government had a long tradition of providing 'a home of refuge for any party in China out of power' on condition they 'obey the law and do not behave so as to damage relations between His Majesty's Government and the Government of China'.[63] Working within such a framework, for a short time after the war when it was unsafe for it to operate in south China, the Communist Party surreptitiously located its South China Bureau inside Hong Kong.[64] Even after the bureau could be re-established in China proper, it continued to keep a sub-bureau in Hong Kong.[65] The British ignored its existence because its cadres did not openly break Hong Kong laws, made no attempt to challenge or even criticize British imperial rule there, and there was no evidence of any subversive activity against the government of China.[66] To the communists, Hong Kong was 'more a regional than a purely local centre' from which to coordinate and aid the struggle for power on the mainland, and 'for transmitting directives to neighbouring countries'.[67]

As victory over all China loomed, the Communist Party sought to reassure the British of its policy towards Hong Kong. In late 1948, the local head of the Xinhua News Agency, Qiao Guanghua, an alternate member of the Communist Party's Central Committee and its *de facto* representative in Hong Kong, reaffirmed his party's position. Through the Reuters' correspondent in Hong Kong, he told the British that 'it was not the Communist Party's policy to take the British colony by force when they come into power in China'.[68] He further 'inferred that his Party would not agitate for the return of Hong Kong'.[69] A few months later, when Anastas Mikoyan (then a personal representative of the Soviet leader Joseph Stalin) tried to ascertain Mao's views on foreign policy and imperialism, Mao explained his policy towards Hong Kong. He said that he had decided 'to defer the seizure of the colonial bastions of

Hong Kong and Macao because of their economic value to China'.[70] As the communists became the ruling party responsible for rehabilitating China, Hong Kong became more important as a base for revolution than for its economic value.

The establishment of the PRC did not fundamentally change the Communist Party's Hong Kong policy. When communist forces were about to reach the Hong Kong border, the local commander was specifically instructed not to let any incident happen.[71] A new dimension, however, was added in the early 1950s as a result of the Korean war. Huang Zuomei, the party secretary and head of the Xinhua News Agency in Hong Kong, was instructed to follow the leadership's decision. This was that, in the light of the Cold War, the PRC would not attempt to take Hong Kong from the British, for it was a valuable instrument with which to divide the British from the Americans.[72] When he issued this instruction, Premier Zhou Enlai also stressed Hong Kong's value in helping the PRC break the embargoes the USA and UN had imposed on it after the outbreak of the Korean war. As Politburo member Peng Zhen explained to cadres within the party, it would be 'unwise for us to deal with the problem of Hong Kong rashly and without preparation'. This would 'not only bring unnecessary technical difficulty in the enforcement of our international policy but would also increase our burden'.[73] In 1954, Zhou admitted privately that, up to then, the PRC government had not deliberated on Hong Kong's future.[74] In 1959, Mao reaffirmed the policy to keep the status quo there because of its value to China.[75] The party's Central Committee subsequently issued a directive to the effect that Hong Kong, together with the Portuguese colony of Macao, should be fully utilized to further the country's long-term interests. This emerged as (and has remained) the guiding principle for the PRC's Hong Kong policy. It survived the upheavals of the Cultural Revolution and came to be reaffirmed after reviews in the 1970s and 1980s.[76]

Since late 1948, the PRC has continuously maintained that

the Hong Kong question would be settled through negotiations at a time of its choosing. Unlike China under the Kuomintang, the PRC rejected the relevance of a technical distinction in legal status between the New Territories and Hong Kong proper. It expected to recover Hong Kong in due course. When Sino–British relations were normalized in 1972, Premier Zhou spoke to a British journalist about the PRC's intentions over Hong Kong. He expected to settle the question through negotiations and had 1997 in mind as the appropriate time for a solution.[77] Beijing could afford to take a relaxed attitude because, as I explain below, the British did not publicly challenge its position and thus allowed it to feel it had retained the initiative over Hong Kong.

Basis for a Future

While the three decisive battles of the Chinese civil war were raging in December 1948, the British government had already rightly concluded that 'Communist domination of China' would 'only be a matter of time'.[78] It had started to work out a new China policy. It had no illusions about Chinese communists being 'agrarian reformers'; it recognized they were orthodox Marxist–Leninists.[79] A small cache of communist documents the Hong Kong police accidentally captured in a routine operation confirmed their assessment.[80] In the light of the communist nature of the new regime, the British accepted that their relations with China would undergo basic changes. Nevertheless, they decided against abandoning their position in China and tried to keep 'a foot in the door'.[81]

As 1949 unfolded, British concerns about Hong Kong's future underwent a basic change. The prospect of Chiang's government raising the question of the New Territories had diminished so much that it now ceased to be relevant. This removed an underlying worry about Hong Kong that had divided the Foreign and Colonial Offices for much of the 1940s. The new consideration was whether the Chinese communists would allow a 'well-organized, well-run British port convenient for their trade with the outside world' to exist, or whether they would seek to get it back by using 'every method short of war'.[82] The British did not doubt that the communists intended to recover Hong Kong, but thought that it was not imminent. They did not expect a communist attack.[83] The British saw the most serious threat as internal unrest 'inspired by the Communist-dominated' trade unions.[84]

Before the end of the year, the British government nevertheless massively reinforced Hong Kong's garrison from one infantry brigade to about 30,000 troops. These were supported by tanks, heavy guns, a powerful fleet, including an aircraft carrier, and a sizeable air force.[85] This was not so much because of a changed assessment of threat as because of an unexpected incident that occurred more than 700 miles away from Hong Kong.

On 20 April, a British frigate HMS *Amethyst* was shelled and badly damaged on a routine mission sailing up the Yangtze River to Nanjing. It was held captive by communist artilleries massed on the northern bank of the river who were preparing to attack Kuomintang forces on the south of the river. In the absence of the China Squadron's commander in chief, the second in command, Vice-Admiral Alexander Madden, immediately organized a rescue mission. This consisted of three ships headed by his flagship, the cruiser HMS *London*. They were all beaten back by heavy communist fire after sustaining major damages and casualties.[86] Under cover of darkness, on 30 July HMS *Amethyst*, whose original captain had been killed in action, eventually made a daring escape under the command of Lieutenant-Commander J. S. Kerans, a deputy naval attaché. They reached safety the following morning after an ordeal lasting 101 days.

The failure of Madden's rescue mission was seen in Hong Kong as the Royal Navy's greatest humiliation in the East since the sinking of HMS *Prince of Wales* and *Repulse* at the beginning of the Pacific war.[87] It also had a major impact on public opinion in Britain. The government tried to calm its critics and demonstrate its determination to protect British interests in the Far East by immediately dispatching a brigade to strengthen the Hong Kong garrison.[88] It also sent the minister of defence, A. V. Alexander, on a high profile visit to the colony to enhance its security.

In this period, the communists had posed no greater threat to Hong Kong. Despite his public rhetoric, Mao was convinced that the *Amethyst* incident had been an accident.[89] He failed to understand its relationship with the reinforcement and wondered for a while whether the British move in Hong Kong was intended as a prelude to intervention in the Chinese civil war.[90] He urged his generals to watch the British deployment, but took no other action. Irrespective of the communist threat, once the Hong Kong garrison had been doubled and the British had committed their prestige to its defence, it became vitally important not to risk losing Hong Kong and its defence force. In the view of the chiefs of staff, 'failure to do so would have a disastrous effect on morale in Southeast Asia'.[91] For a short time, Hong Kong came to be seen as the most exposed of a line of dominoes vulnerable to pressure from the communist camp.[92] The British government felt it had to reinforce Hong Kong massively to deter a communist attack.[93]

The reinforcement of Hong Kong pushed the question of its future higher up the political agenda. After a period of inter-departmental consultations and several discussions in the Cabinet, a new policy was produced in August. The Foreign and Colonial Offices jointly submitted the Cabinet's policy paper. By then, Hong Kong's future had come to be seen more from the perspective of the Cold War than from that of fending off a Chinese claim for retrocession. The British concluded that the situation they faced in Hong Kong was like that in Berlin. Just as Britain could 'not foresee with certainty how the future of Berlin' would develop, but were 'convinced of the necessity of remaining there', it felt 'impelled to remain in Hong Kong without any clear indication of the extent or duration of the military commitment involved'.[94] Such a policy was partly based on the armed forces' assessment of the situation. They took the view that the reinforced garrison had 'a good chance of holding Hong Kong against a full-scale attack by Chinese communists unless the latter were receiving appreciable military assistance from Russia'.[95]

The Cabinet paper outlining the new policy laid down that Britain 'should not be prepared to discuss the future of Hong Kong with the new Government unless it were friendly, democratic, stable and in control of a united China'.[96] It further explained:

> We cannot agree to negotiate about Hong Kong with a Government which is unfriendly, since we should be negotiating under duress. We should equally refuse to discuss the future of Hong Kong with a Government which is undemocratic, since we should not be prepared to hand the people of Hong Kong over to a Communist regime. Finally, we should be unwilling to discuss Hong Kong with a China which is not united, because its future would be likely to become a pawn in the contest between conflicting factions. Unless there were a stable Government we could not rely on it to preserve Hong Kong as a secure free port and place of exchange between China and the rest of the world.

Since it was obvious that the new communist government to be set up in China could not meet any of the above conditions, the issue of discussing Hong Kong's future was treated as academic. The New Territories' lease, which was due to expire in 1997, posed a different problem. The Cabinet paper suggested:

> It does not seem likely that when that time comes any Chinese Government will be prepared to renew the lease. Without these territories Hong Kong would be untenable, and it is therefore probable that before 1997 the United Kingdom Government of the day will have to consider the

status of Hong Kong. But we are surely not justified some two generations in advance of the event in attempting to lay down the principles which should govern any arrangement which it may be possible to reach with China at that time.

When the issues involved were discussed in the Cabinet, there was a strongly expressed view that Hong Kong could only be held in the long term with US support.[97] Furthermore, the Cabinet agreed to remove 'democratic' from the conditions to be met, for it precluded discussions with a communist government of China. The British government expected the communists to stay in power on a long-term basis and had resigned itself to dealing with the Hong Kong question prior to 1997.

Britain's attempt to secure US support for Hong Kong's defence proved problematic. To begin with, the two countries responded very differently to the communist victory in China.[98] Furthermore, the US government had an ambivalent attitude towards Hong Kong. This was partly because of its colonial status, but there were also wider strategic considerations. On the one hand Washington saw that, with its 'strongest ally ... threatened with a state of war or a serious loss of prestige' over Hong Kong, its 'interests in the Far East would be involved'.[99] On the other hand, it recognized the disparity between its capabilities and worldwide obligations.[100] In the US assessment, defending Hong Kong 'would require the establishment of a military position well inland' and would involve 'a movement of large-scale forces into China', which would risk global war.[101] The USA decided against helping to defend Hong Kong. It did not 'expect to retain by force any foothold in continental China' in the event of a world war.[102]

By 1960, the military build-up during President Dwight Eisenhower's administration had considerably strengthened his confidence in US power. He now had the resources to contemplate military intervention to support a determined British attempt to defend Hong Kong.[103] Nevertheless, he refrained from making a firm commitment. US policy subsequently remained noncommittal, even in 1967 at the height of the Vietnam war and Cultural Revolution when local communists challenged the Hong Kong government's authority.[104] Thus, though the British had at times expressed confidence that the USA would come to Hong Kong's aid should it come under attack and that US nuclear retaliatory power served as a deterrent to the PRC, they were always aware that there was no US undertaking to defend Hong Kong.[105]

Masterly Inactivity

Essentially left on their own in Hong Kong, the British were mindful of their vulnerability and of the day the Chinese would demand retrocession.[106] After 1949, Britain's basic task was 'to postpone this evil day as long as' it could.[107] The disparity between Britain's worldwide obligations and the resources available to it made Hong Kong even more vulnerable. Within a year of the local garrison being dramatically strengthened, it was run down. Two battalions left for Korea when war broke out there, and Britain could not spare more troops for the Far East.[108] The size and fire power of the British forces in Hong Kong were subsequently reduced further. Before the 1950s ended, the army had redeployed most of its heavy equipment and much of the garrison elsewhere. The Royal Air Force had done the same with its combat aircraft. The Royal Navy had reduced its once mighty presence to a frigate and six minesweepers. By then, the British garrison was so small that the Foreign Office admitted privately that, in the event of a full-scale Chinese attack, 'all would be over before we could reinforce'.[109] The British military weakness made it vital for them not to provoke the Chinese over Hong Kong.

Responsible British government officials periodically continued to review their policy on Hong Kong's future. In 1957, a working party was formed to take stock interdepartmentally of Britain's position in Hong Kong.[110] However, such exercises could do woefully little about devising a new policy. The communist regime's consolidation in China, the stalemate across the Taiwan Straits, and the continuing decline in British military might and economic power imposed severe constraints, which got tighter over time. Masterly inactivity was Britain's only realistic policy; and this meant avoiding raising the issue of Hong Kong's future for the next two decades. By the 1970s, it also required the British not to challenge the PRC when, on joining the United Nations, it stated that it regarded Hong Kong as a legacy of history to be dealt with at a time of its choosing.[111]

A more positive policy complemented the passive one of doing nothing. It consisted of striving to prevent Hong Kong being turned into a flash point in the Cold War, or being sucked into the unfinished civil war between the communists and Kuomintang in Taiwan. In practice, this meant that, as far as possible, the Hong Kong government had to adhere to a policy of strict neutrality in Chinese politics, supported by an attitude of non-provocative firmness towards the two Chinese regimes.[112] Governor Grantham explained the rationale behind this policy:

> The strength of our position in Hong Kong depends largely upon non-involvement in political issues. This can be achieved only by maintaining strict legality and impartiality in any issues with a political tinge. We have followed this attitude in relation to Chinese political activities in the colony, e.g. treating both [the Kuomintang] and Communists exactly similar and absolutely according to law. Any departure from this . . . would weaken our position, both externally and internally.[113]

In addition, the Hong Kong government also tried 'to administer the territory in the interests of the inhabitants, including those numbering nearly a million who have come from China in recent years' and to prevent it being used 'as a base for hostile activities against China'.[114] Increasingly, the

Hong Kong government fulfilled the expectations Mao set out for Gordon Harmon as requirements for the communists not to raise the Hong Kong question at the end of 1946. By the end of the 1970s, it had also turned itself into as good a government as possible in the Chinese political tradition. In political terms, Hong Kong did not become a thorn in the PRC's side.

Economically, Hong Kong became increasingly valuable to the PRC. In the 1950s, its existence helped procure certain strategic materials, which were smuggled into the PRC despite the US and UN embargoes imposed because of the Korean war.[115] In the early days, local residents' remittances to relatives on the mainland provided valuable foreign exchange. During the famine caused by the failure of the Great Leap Forward in the late 1950s and early 1960s, food parcels and other support from the people of Hong Kong was a vital lifeline for many in the PRC. Hong Kong's economic takeoff in the late 1960s and early 1970s greatly enhanced its value, particularly since Hong Kong resumed its pre-1950 role as the PRC's main entrepôt.[116] Once the PRC embarked on its programme of 'four modernizations' in the 1970s, Hong Kong became the principal channel through which the PRC acquired modern technology, management skills and capital.[117] Hong Kong contributed almost one-third of the PRC's foreign exchange earnings.[118] It also provided crucial financial services that were unavailable in the PRC.[119] After 1949, Hong Kong became the PRC's goose that laid the golden egg.

Because the policy of masterly inactivity over Hong Kong's future was complemented by good government and the conditions for an economic miracle, Britain gave the PRC no reason to feel concerned about Hong Kong. Until the end of the 1970s, the policy of masterly inactivity gave Beijing the impression that it held the initiative over Hong Kong. It had no reason to disturb the goose that so obligingly laid bigger and bigger golden eggs. The people of Hong Kong also chose to ignore the fact that the New Territories' lease would expire in 1997 and that something would have to be done about it, at least about the expiry of British jurisdiction there. Because the PRC regarded the 'unequal treaties' as invalid, many people thought that the PRC might choose to ignore this particular appointment in history. Some even indulged in the comforting thought that the PRC might allow the status quo to continue in Hong Kong for as long as it proved advantageous to it. In the 1970s, Hong Kong gave the false impression that it would continue as a Crown colony for as long as anyone cared to look ahead. Most people, however, preferred not to look beyond the short term.

5. Towards the Joint Declaration: Negotiations, 1979–84

Hong Kong's future and Sino–British relations were tossed like a cork upon an angry sea of Chinese turbulence for almost three decades from 1949. Periods of reasonable cooperation were interspersed with times of difficulty and even hostility.

Upon taking power, the PRC government tried to drive out foreigners by turning their investments into liabilities. It put so much pressure on British investors on mainland China that those who managed to leave by handing over their assets to the Chinese authorities by 1952 were the lucky ones.[1] The less fortunate had to continue to transfer funds into the PRC for a few more years. These were to pay for the various demands of the authorities and of the Chinese labourers, who had no work to do but could not be made redundant. Payments were also made to protect British personnel who were practically held as hostages.

By 1952 such transfers amounted to £6.5 million[2] — a small sum compared with the losses British investors sustained in China. By then, £80 million in outstanding loans to China and a staggering £200–300 million in investments and commercial property had effectively been written off or lost.[3] It puts the scale of the losses in perspective if one compares them with the estimated total value of British investments in Hong Kong, which amounted to only £156 million in 1949.[4]

A spell of reasonable cooperation followed the 1954 Geneva

Conference when Chinese Premier Zhou Enlai and British Foreign Secretary Anthony Eden agreed to exchange chargés d'affaires. Sino–British relations reached their lowest ebb during the Cultural Revolution when Red Guards burned down the British mission in Beijing. The only real bilateral breakthrough occurred after US President Richard Nixon visited the PRC in 1972. Later that year Britain and the PRC finally normalized their relations when they exchanged ambassadors — 22 years after Britain first extended recognition — and a more cooperative mood returned.

As the extremist policies of the Cultural Revolution finally ended with the death of Mao and the fall of the so-called 'Gang of Four' in 1976, China began to project a new image.[5] It was one of pragmatism and relative moderation with a clear emphasis being put on revitalizing its economy. Better relations with Britain developed. By the late 1970s, Hong Kong's relations with the PRC had also significantly improved from the nadir of 1967. In that year the Cultural Revolution spilled over into Hong Kong and the local Maoists organized riots and an indiscriminate bombing campaign. The Hong Kong government, which enjoyed broad public support, suppressed what the locals referred to as 'the confrontation'.[6]

Domestic political changes in the PRC partly explain the improvements in Sino–Hong Kong relations in the 1970s. To pursue its new focus on 'the four modernizations', the PRC needed Hong Kong's cooperation, facilities and assistance. The Hong Kong government's outlook had also changed, not least because of the arrival in late 1971 of a career diplomat, Sir Murray (now Lord) MacLehose, as governor. Under his administration, the Hong Kong government improved relations with the director of the Xinhua News Agency, the PRC's *de facto* representative in Hong Kong since 1949.[7] Departing from his predecessors' practice, for the first time MacLehose gave public blessings to the Xinhua News Agency's presence. In October 1978, he attended the PRC's national day celebration.[8] This marked a new era of cooperation, even friendliness.

A British Initiative

The year 1979 proved to be crucial in Hong Kong's history. With an official visit by Governor MacLehose to Beijing, it marked the beginning of the process that led to the opening of formal negotiations between Britain and the PRC in September 1982. At that time, MacLehose's intention was more to test the water than to start negotiations. However, although the visit received wide coverage in the media, very few people recognized its real significance.

The visit originated from an invitation by the Chinese minister for foreign trade, Li Qiang. The Chinese intended to use it to improve Sino–Hong Kong relations generally and, in particular, to enhance Hong Kong's contribution to the PRC's programme of 'four modernizations'. MacLehose had an additional idea: he wanted to use the occasion to find out the PRC's real design for Hong Kong's future. This was a major step forward. The PRC's position on Hong Kong had not been examined since Anthony Royle, a junior minister in the Foreign Office, had headed a committee in London almost two years earlier.[9] Also, the Royle Committee had only explored the question in general within the foreign service.

Aware of the delicacy of such an operation, MacLehose opted to keep his intention secret. It was to be a trial balloon. In Hong Kong he consulted Sir Yuet-keung Kan, a particularly trusted senior non-official member of the Executive Council, but kept Kan's colleagues in the dark. Among the civil servants, only Dr David (now Lord) Wilson, his political adviser on secondment from the foreign service, was closely involved. MacLehose also informed the chief secretary, Sir Jack Cater, but did not seem to have consulted him much. In the wider context of British policy making, the key figures engaged in the planning were Sir Edward Youde, former ambassador to Beijing and at that time deputy under-secretary supervising Far Eastern affairs at the Foreign Office, and Sir Percy Cradock, then ambassador in Beijing. The operation received the blessings of Foreign Secretary David (now Lord) Owen.[10]

MacLehose cleverly devised his bold initiative. He had a general idea of what the Chinese intended to derive from his visit and reasonable grounds to believe that they would discuss the subject of Hong Kong's prosperity and value to the PRC. He planned to use such a discussion to raise the question of individual land leases in the New Territories. These were all due to expire three days before the New Territories lease itself. He hoped to persuade the Chinese that if they could do something to blur the 1997 deadline, this would sustain confidence in Hong Kong, which would then be able to continue to assist the PRC's modernization.[11]

A positive Chinese response would imply their consent to a non-offensive British effort to amend the Royal Order in Council of 1898 on which the extension of British jurisdiction in the New Territories depended. If successful, this scheme would remove the terminal date on the future of the New Territories and therefore of Hong Kong without provoking the PRC to take a nationalistic stand. The latter would be unavoidable if either side raised the question of the New Territories' lease itself. The success or failure of the MacLehose initiative depended on four factors:

- whether the Chinese leaders understood the subtle differences between the Crown and New Territories leases;
- whether they would treat the two as being distinct and separate even if they understood;
- whether it would be possible to produce the perfect interpretation required to ensure that the subtle but vital differences were not lost in translation; and, most important,
- whether the Chinese were so committed to achieving their economic objectives that they would formally agree to put aside a matter involving what they saw as national dignity and integrity until an undefined date in the future.

It is interesting and important that Youde, Cradock and Wilson, who were among the best China hands in the Foreign

Office, all went along with MacLehose's idea. Even then, according to his memoirs, Cradock doubted the Chinese would put nationalist considerations behind economic reform.[12] Nonetheless, whatever his personal reservations, Cradock backed MacLehose's proposed course. The British did not fully understand Chinese feelings about Hong Kong — which remained essentially the same as those captured in Kitson's Isle of Wight analogy of 1946.

To understand MacLehose's boldness one must look at his record and achievements as governor. Though he mainly built on the Hong Kong government's achievements in the postwar era, by a series of audacious initiatives he managed to change the colonial government's public image. He established an Independent Commission Against Corruption, which broke the back of high-profile organized corruption. He broke with tradition by calling in an outside consultant to help reform the colonial administration and make it more responsive to public opinion. He publicly committed his government to a ten-year housing scheme that gave the colonial administration a caring image. He also presided over a period of spectacular growth and prosperity following the economic takeoff of the 1960s.

These changes and other policies transformed the old colonial style good government into one that fulfilled the expectations of as good a government as possible in the Chinese political tradition.[13] It was a stunning achievement of which MacLehose could justifiably be proud. He probably felt he was personally responsible for much of this feat, for he was intellectually superior to most of his lieutenants and, as governor, had a habit of leading from the front. By the end of the 1970s, MacLehose had been in his position for longer than most, if not all, of his top aides.

He had reason to think that he knew what was best for Hong Kong better than almost anyone else — in the government or in the territory. He no longer felt he always needed their advice and was becoming increasingly autocratic. In short, he had by then established himself as a genuine giant who dominated

Hong Kong's politics and rivalled Sir Alexander Grantham as the greatest of Hong Kong's governors. He seemed to suffer from what Grantham had called the long-serving colonial governor syndrome — excessive self-confidence produced by being 'next to the Almighty' for too long. It gave people whose subordinates had reassured them of their infinite wisdom every day for many years a sense of infallibility.[14] MacLehose also felt a sense of responsibility to the people under his charge and sought to secure their future. He was aware of the delicacy of the subject matter, but his great self-confidence and desire to crown his governorship with an historic achievement clouded his judgement.

MacLehose's personal role and the sense of responsibility shared by those involved were not the only factors, but they were the most important. In 1979, some people in business circles began to express concerns about Hong Kong's future.[15] Because only 18 years remained before 1997, the time was approaching for banks to consider altering their usual 15-year mortgage term. However, it was at least a good two years before the banks actually had to decide, and Hong Kong operated on the basis of five-year money back investments. On the whole, Hong Kong was unconcerned about its future and the economy showed no sign of being affected by the '1997 factor'. The local stock market indicator, the Heng Seng Index increased from 495 at the end of 1978 to 879 in 1979. Even more telling, from a base index of 100, domestic property prices continued to rise to 121 in 1979 and further to 148 in the following year, before dropping in 1982.[16] It was only then, three years later when formal negotiations began, that the '1997 factor' had a significant impact on economic confidence and performance.[17]

MacLehose and his colleagues planned a pre-emptive strike. They took the initiative because they shared a sense of 'moral responsibility' towards the local inhabitants. To sit on their hands and do nothing about the future of more than five million people under their charge was simply unacceptable.

They felt that the responsible thing to do was to seek a solution before a crisis developed: a crisis would limit the options available to them and, by implication, to the people of Hong Kong. It never occurred to them that they should have sought the views of the more than five million people with whose future they were dealing.

This might seem to be incredibly arrogant and presumptuous: but they acted as paternal figures and thought they were doing so in the best interests of the people of Hong Kong. Although most of these people were British subjects by birth, British officials did not at heart regard them in the same light as they did the citizens of the British Isles. Indeed, the officials' shared sense of 'moral obligation' to the people of Hong Kong is indicative of this mentality. If the British officials had thought of Hong Kong's British subjects as British rather than Chinese, they would have spoken of their obligations rather than their 'moral obligations' to them.

At that time the policy makers further believed that with the pragmatic Deng Xiaoping in charge of the PRC, Hong Kong, the metaphorical goose, had the best chance of getting what it wanted. This was a stay of execution in return for producing more and bigger golden eggs for the PRC.[18] Except for the conviction of MacLehose, who enjoyed the support of his senior diplomatic colleagues, as yet Britain had no compelling reason to take the bold initiative.

While MacLehose's visit was presented to the public as very successful, his attempt to find a solution for Hong Kong's future was a disaster. When the Chinese Foreign Ministry learned of his intention, it was taken by surprise. According to a Chinese insider, the Foreign Ministry specifically asked the British not to raise the issue when they met Deng Xiaoping.[19] At that time, Deng had not yet firmly established himself as the paramount leader, but he was assiduously consolidating his power and took the official position of vice-premier.[20] In any event, nobody had briefed him of MacLehose's intention. In the meeting Deng said:

It has been our consistent view that the People's Republic of China has sovereignty over Hong Kong while Hong Kong also has its own special position. A negotiated settlement of the Hong Kong question in the future should be based on the premise that the territory is part of China. However, we will treat Hong Kong as a special region. For a considerable length of time, Hong Kong may continue to practise its capitalist system while we practise our socialist system.[21]

MacLehose used this opening to raise the question of the Crown leases, which seemed to have been confused in interpretation with the New Territories lease. Wilson interfered to correct the mistake and this annoyed Deng. Deng responded by asking the governor to tell investors in Hong Kong to put their hearts at ease, but reiterated that the PRC would recover Hong Kong.[22] In line with PRC practice, once the most senior leader responsible has spoken on a subject, no one contradicts him. MacLehose and his colleagues' subsequent discussions with other Chinese leaders produced no softening of Deng's stand.

On his return to Hong Kong MacLehose put the best gloss over this secret fiasco and skilfully encouraged the media to produce an optimistic illusion. Retrospective popular belief in Hong Kong and most accounts, including scholarly works on the subject, do not do justice to MacLehose. They generally charge him with either lying or being economical with the truth about his meeting with Deng.[23] They accuse MacLehose of omitting half of Deng's message — namely that the PRC would recover Hong Kong — and of merely reporting that investors had nothing to fear. The truth is more complicated. The day after his return, MacLehose made a public statement, in part of which he said:

You know the long-standing Chinese position on Hong Kong, that it is part of China and a problem that will be solved when the time is ripe. But the point that was repeatedly stressed to us at all levels was the importance which the Chinese leaders attach to the value of Hong Kong, to the contribution that it could make to the modernization programmes, to the importance of maintaining investment and confidence in Hong Kong, and of increased Hong Kong investment in China. Indeed Vice-Premier Deng Xiaoping formally requested me to 'ask investors in Hong Kong to put their hearts at ease'; he also asked for encouragement of investment in Guangzhou [sic] Province and the rest of China.[24]

In the rest of his press statement, by emphasizing the good news, MacLehose effectively encouraged the journalists and local people to focus on the more positive side of his visit. He did not omit the bad news: the media and the people of Hong Kong merely chose to ignore it. Their response to Deng's message of assurance almost amounted to euphoria.[25] They did not want to worry about the future. They simply chose to celebrate the good news and avoid studying the governor's full statement carefully. This reflected the mentality of the people at that time.

Cruel as it was to let the local people continue to live in a fool's paradise, the governor must have deemed it irresponsible to set off a panic by being candid. A panic before working out a plan to pre-empt such an eventuality might have gravely undermined public confidence and thus damaged the economy. It is unclear whether or not MacLehose also felt concerned about the impact on his personal reputation.

The MacLehose initiative was a well-intentioned piece of secret diplomacy that backfired. It brought no tangible advantage to either the British or the people of Hong Kong. However, contrary to retrospective popular belief in Hong Kong, it was not part of a sinister plot to minimize British responsibilities to the people of Hong Kong. Despite a rising sentiment in the UK against the immigration of coloured people from the Commonwealth in the late 1970s, the MacLehose initiative bore no relationship to the subsequent passing of a British Nationality Bill. The bill created a new category of citizenship for Hong Kong's British subjects and completely removed their right of abode in the UK. But this right had already been substantially eroded by the Commonwealth Immigrants Act of 1962. Had the future of Hong Kong been a major factor for the new nationality bill, the British government would have waited until it was passed before allowing MacLehose to test his idea. A delay was possible because, as explained earlier, in 1979 there was no compelling reason to take the initiative.

Understandably, this disappointed the British. In the following two years they took every opportunity they could find to probe the Chinese attitude further. The British government quizzed the PRC's Premier Hua Guofeng and Foreign Minister Huang Hua during their separate visits to Britain towards the end of the year, but they said nothing new. When former Prime Minister James Callaghan visited the PRC in May 1980 and Foreign Secretary Lord Carrington went in April 1981, both returned empty handed. The Chinese did not wish to give away anything while they were working out their Hong Kong policy. They kept the initiative in their hands.

Beijing's Reactions

MacLehose's visit had put Hong Kong on the Chinese leadership's political agenda.[26] Deng Xiaoping had thought about Hong Kong and about the reunification of China, but until then he had not put the two together. Hitherto, his thinking on Hong Kong had mainly been about how to utilize it to the full to support the PRC's modernization. With respect to unification, Deng mainly had Taiwan in mind, the island redoubt to which Chiang Kai-shek and his supporters had withdrawn in late 1949. Its existence marked the Communist Party's failure to conclude the Chinese civil war, which was a long-standing Communist Party objective.

When MacLehose visited, Deng had just made a major foreign policy breakthrough that promised to provide an opportunity to resolve the Taiwan issue. This was the reaching of an agreement in December 1978 to normalize relations with the USA.[27] It involved terminating the USA's defence treaty with the Republic of China (or Taiwan) in a year's time.[28] This meant that the USA would remove its Seventh Fleet, which since June 1950 had been a major obstacle in the way of the PRC gaining control of Taiwan. From Beijing's point of view, this heightened threat might persuade Taipei to respond to China's wooing.

These endeavours culminated in one of Deng's close political allies, Yeh Jianying, issuing a nine-point statement in September 1981. An intensive campaign to elicit a positive response from Taipei followed his statement, which set out the basis for reunification. The Kuomintang government in Taiwan stone-walled. Before the end of the year Deng decided to alter the PRC's priority in the unification plan. He now wanted to take advantage of the British initiative over Hong Kong, which implied a willingness to compromise. He resolved to seek the return of Hong Kong and use it as an example to persuade Taiwan to rejoin mother China.

Though it was originally devised with Taiwan in mind, he thus applied the idea of 'one country, two systems' to Hong Kong. It is possible to trace its genesis to Yeh's nine-point statement. This pronounced that, 'after reunification of the country, Taiwan could become a Special Administrative Region, enjoy a high degree of autonomy and keep its armed forces'.[29] It adds that 'the central government would not interfere in the local affairs of Taiwan'.

The PRC had started to build up a new bureaucratic infra-structure to deal with Hong Kong in late 1978 when Deng planned to make the most of Hong Kong for the modernization of the country. He entrusted this matter to a close colleague and veteran 'Hong Kong hand', Liao Chengzhi. Liao had headed the communist organization in Hong Kong before the war and had for a long time handled overseas Chinese affairs.[30] In 1978 he was a Central Committee member and held ministerial rank. Consequently, his new office, the Hong Kong and Macao Affairs Office (HKMAO) under the State Council, was given ministerial status. Under Deng's supervision, he was largely responsible for Hong Kong affairs until his death in 1983.[31]

Liao's two principal assistants were Li Hou and Lu Ping, who later became closely involved in the formal negotiations between the PRC and Britain, and in the drafting of a Basic Law for Hong Kong. Until 1981, the focus of HKMAO's work seems to have been on building up a broad united front with the people of Hong Kong rather than on working out a scheme for its return. It is impossible to say with certainty whether the PRC on its own would have raised the Hong Kong question later in the 1980s. However, it is beyond doubt that the PRC's decision to tackle the Hong Kong question was a reaction to the British initiative.

The Communist Party Politburo made the first major decisions on Hong Kong during a meeting in March 1981. It decided to recover sovereignty in 1997, ensure Hong Kong would continue to serve the PRC's economic and political interests, and devise an appropriate arrangement to fulfil the first two requirements.[32] Over the rest of the year Liao Chengzhi and his colleagues tried to work out the details on the basis of this Politburo decision. However, there was resistance from within the top leadership to the suggestion that the idea of 'one country, two systems' should apply to Hong Kong.

Li Xiannian, a senior leader who headed the party's Foreign Affairs Leading Small Group, was the most ardent opponent. He felt that permitting a capitalist enclave to continue within the PRC would leave the communist revolution incomplete. He also worried that it might become the first step towards the restoration of capitalism in the PRC. Others suggested exploring the option of turning Hong Kong into a socialist society.[33] In the end Deng, who had by then fully established himself as paramount leader, prevailed over his colleagues. To him, the starting point was the reality in the PRC. To his mind, since the PRC had both 'a Hong Kong problem and a Taiwan problem', the only way out was 'to seek a peaceful resolution' by implementing the idea of 'one country, two systems'.[34] He assured his colleagues that tolerating capitalism in Hong Kong would not affect the upholding of socialism in the PRC. Deng had intended the 'one country, two systems' policy to benefit, not undermine, Communist Party rule in the PRC.

By January 1982 Deng had carried his colleagues with him, and the Chinese government was therefore ready to respond to the gentle prodding of the British over Hong Kong. It did so during a visit by the Lord Privy Seal Humphrey Atkins, who was responsible for Hong Kong in the Foreign Office. Premier Zhao Ziyang told Atkins that the PRC had evolved general plans for Hong Kong, which would maintain its prosperity and safeguard the PRC's sovereignty over it.[35] The British were also advised to consult Yeh's nine-point statement for Taiwan. Since Atkins had instructions to enquire into Chinese intentions for Hong Kong and to prepare for a visit the following autumn by Prime Minister Thatcher, he responded positively. The ground was now clear to open formal negotiations.

At that stage, however, the Chinese had not worked out more than the basic framework for their Hong Kong policy. For the following nine months, Liao Chengzhi headed an inter-departmental task group to turn the general principle laid down by Deng into a clear policy. For this purpose, the Chinese tried to improve their understanding of Hong Kong by inviting a stream of prominent Hong Kong citizens to visit Beijing. They did not, however, really achieve their objective. Most Hong Kong visitors lost their resolution to speak frankly in the presence of Chinese leaders who did not welcome negative comments about the prospect of a Chinese take-over.[36]

When three eminent members of Hong Kong's Executive Council led by Sir Sze-yuen Chung spoke their minds at a later stage, Deng humiliated them. He dismissed their positions in Hong Kong society, told them they represented no one but themselves and stressed that the Chinese leadership knew what

Hong Kong really wanted.[37] This exercise of inviting influential Hong Kong figures to visit Beijing was also standard practice in the Chinese communist united front. The PRC government sought to win them over and increase its influence in Hong Kong, which would strengthen its position in the forthcoming negotiations with the British.[38]

By August 1982, a month before Thatcher's planned visit, Liao's group produced a draft paper and submitted it to the Politburo. The paper contained 12 points, mostly on arrangements to maintain Hong Kong's stability and prosperity, but also included measures to uphold public confidence. It formed the basis for discussions among the top leaders, including Deng, Party General Secretary Hu Yaobang, Premier Zhao, members of the Politburo and other senior leaders. The paper's final draft after Thatcher's visit underlined the importance of protecting Chinese sovereignty over Hong Kong.[39] It also became the Chinese team's basic brief for formal negotiations with Britain.[40]

Beginning of Negotiations

In 1982 British diplomats and officials worked hard to prepare for Prime Minister Thatcher's visit to Beijing scheduled for September. Its original intention was to reciprocate Premier Hua Guofeng's 1979 visit to London. However, it took on new significance after Atkins's visit early in the year. As a result of the Falklands war, the British position over Hong Kong hardened. Thatcher felt that both her personal standing and Britain's position in the world had been greatly enhanced.[41]

She planned to make a stand in the first instance on the grounds that treaties protected British sovereignty over Hong Kong island and the tip of the Kowloon peninsula.[42] Dick Cliff and Alan Donald in London, Cradock in Beijing, and Youde, who had succeeded MacLehose as governor in Hong Kong in May, were the main senior officials responsible for working out Britain's position. The foreign secretary of the day, Francis Pym, did not play a significant role, for he did not enjoy the prime minister's confidence or respect.[43] Thatcher had felt let down by the Foreign Office's handling of the Falklands crisis before the war, so tackled her diplomats on any proposal that smacked of pre-emptive surrender of British sovereignty over Hong Kong.

The debates among the British policy makers were mainly between the senior officials and Thatcher. They focused on what Britain could hope to achieve and the best way to approach the Chinese. The British based their position on the understanding that Hong Kong was militarily indefensible and that the permanently ceded territories were not viable without the New Territories.[44] Thus, reverting the whole territory's sovereignty in 1997 in exchange for terms most acceptable to the British government and to the people of Hong Kong was a matter of a negotiated settlement. To Thatcher, it meant 'continued British administration of the entire Colony well into the future'.[45] The British did not fully understand the strength of Chinese feelings about Hong Kong.

Deng Xiaoping defined the Chinese government's position. To him there were three issues — the question of sovereignty, how China would administer Hong Kong after 1997 to maintain its prosperity, and how to ensure an undisturbed transition.[46] He insisted that the PRC should exercise no flexibility in the question of sovereignty. While he desired an agreement for cooperation with Britain and valued highly Hong Kong's prosperity and stability, he refused to achieve them by making any concession over sovereignty. The old anti-imperialist jingoism of the communist movement in its early days affected Deng. He was determined to use Hong Kong to wipe out China's humiliation by the West in the preceding century.

To his mind, making any concession over Hong Kong's sovereignty would put him in the same category as those whom he called traitors. This is how he regarded Li Hongzhang, the veteran mandarin diplomat who signed the New Territories lease in 1898. Deng felt very strongly that if the PRC's resumption of sovereignty over Hong Kong should bring about cataclysmic results, then the PRC 'would courageously face up to this catastrophe'.[47] At heart, he did not believe Hong Kong's prosperity could only continue under British administration, and was confident that the PRC could somehow successfully take it over even without British cooperation.[48] Thatcher's bottom line, which was a kind of lease-back arrangement, was unacceptable to Deng and to the Chinese government.

When Thatcher visited Beijing in September, she negotiated directly with both Premier Zhao and Deng. As was the general practice in the PRC, she met Zhao first before calling on the paramount leader. The discussions about Hong Kong in the two meetings essentially had the same thrust, for Zhao could not but stick entirely to the prepared script approved by Deng. The main difference between the two meetings was in the atmosphere. Thatcher's talk with Zhao was much more friendly and businesslike than the one she had with Deng, which involved some heated exchanges. In their meetings both sides stated their positions openly.

Thatcher affirmed that Hong Kong's prosperity depended on confidence, which in turn required continued British administration.[49] She tried to entice the Chinese to accept her proposal. She did this by stressing that she would consider the question of sovereignty if they agreed to an arrangement that was acceptable to the British Parliament and to the people of Hong Kong. The Chinese did not know enough about how Hong Kong worked to see the force of her argument, which they in any event did not accept. Deng stated the Chinese position, which was that the PRC would recover Hong Kong in 1997 and make suitable arrangements to assure its prosperity.[50] He rejected the British position, particularly the validity of the treaties. He said that he would allow a year or two to reach an agreement with Britain but would then announce a unilateral solution should the negotiations prove fruitless.[51]

The PRC government under Deng was by then determined

to have its way over Hong Kong. It was so confident of its ability to force the British to accept its position that it leaked the gist of the 12-point policy paper to the Hong Kong media. This was even before formal discussions with Thatcher began.[52] This public statement that sovereignty over Hong Kong belonged to China and was not negotiable demonstrated how rigidly the Chinese government held this position. The strong sense of conviction with which Thatcher put the British case had mixed results. On the one hand, it strengthened the hand of British diplomats in subsequent negotiations, for the Chinese knew how strongly the prime minister felt about the subject. On the other hand, it also toughened the Chinese stand over sovereignty, for they realized that this would be a point of attack from the British. The main achievements of Thatcher's visit were to open negotiations over Hong Kong's future and to make known to each other their respective views. Apart from the common wish to maintain stability and prosperity in Hong Kong, a great gap separated the two. If there had been any illusion that subsequent negotiations would be anything but tough, it was shattered.

In Hong Kong the mood changed in 1982. Once it was clear that the Chinese government was devising a policy on Hong Kong's future, an air of anxious anticipation prevailed. Sir Sze-yuen Chung, the Executive Council's unofficial leader, greeted Sir Edward Youde with a clear request when he arrived to take over the governorship in May. Chung voiced the public wish that the new governor should put the future of Hong Kong on the top of his agenda, and maintain public confidence while he resolved the issue. The local people had very mixed views on the subject.

On the one hand, Chinese nationalist writings and communist propaganda had made most local residents believe that the British acquired Hong Kong through the so-called 'opium wars' and that colonialism was inherently bad. They felt they should be proud of being Chinese and should desire the early departure of the British 'imperialists'. On the other hand, the idea of being handed over to a communist regime whose atrocious record some had experienced first hand and others knew of through relatives and friends terrified them. Most of them had seen the great differences between the Hong Kong and the Chinese governments at work.

The economic miracle of postwar Hong Kong had also given them vested interests to protect. They had a way of life different from that in the PRC. Only a handful dared to say it publicly but the overwhelming majority clearly did not want a PRC takeover of Hong Kong. However, most Hong Kong citizens were realistic enough to recognize that independence was not an option, for the PRC would never accept it. What they hoped for was similar to Thatcher's bottom line — a kind of lease-back arrangement. Instead of attempting to control their own destiny actively they responded as they had always done. They looked to the British and the Hong Kong governments to secure their future.

Most Hong Kong citizens naïvely thought that Deng's pragmatism would prevent the Chinese leaders' irrational reactions based on nationalism from destroying Hong Kong — the goose that was laying the golden eggs. They were themselves affected by Chinese nationalism, but could not believe that the Chinese leaders would put nationalism above Hong Kong's economic value. They therefore watched Thatcher's visit with intense interest. They became very jittery about their future when they saw Thatcher failing to deliver an upbeat report, as MacLehose had done in 1979. The stock market, the property market and the value of the local currency reflected their hidden fears.[53] Within ten days of Thatcher leaving China Hong Kong's stock market lost 25 per cent of its value and, within a month, the Hong Kong dollar depreciated by 12 per cent. Nevertheless, most people in Hong Kong continued to hope that a diplomatic miracle would somehow be possible and an acceptable agreement eventually reached. This latent sense of optimism or naïveté was an important element of Hong Kong's resilience as it entered a period of considerable uncertainty.

The so-called first phase of negotiations defined the basis on which to conduct the talks and set out the agenda.[54] It lasted from October 1982 to June 1983. To the Chinese, the object of the exercise was to secure British cooperation to maintain stability and prosperity in Hong Kong. Since the Chinese refused to accept the validity of all three treaties that governed Hong Kong, they declined to discuss its sovereignty. They simply ignored the convention in international law by which a territorial cession implemented by a treaty remained valid unless and until superseded by a new one.[55] Before getting down to serious negotiations, the Chinese demanded that the British acknowledge their sovereignty over Hong Kong. This was a precondition. The British resisted it. Ambassador Cradock debated repeatedly with Vice-Foreign Minister Zhang Wenjin, and later with his successor Yao Guang, but there was no real progress for eight months.[56]

In the meantime, the PRC's policy-making establishment and propaganda machine shifted to high gear. Under Liao Chengzhi, Chinese officials revised the 12 points and, as part of their united-front work, released increasingly more details to the media of their blueprint for a post-1997 Hong Kong. In December 1982, the Chinese National People's Congress (NPC) also passed a new constitution, which contained an Article intended for Hong Kong, Taiwan and Macao. Article 31 specifically provided for the establishment of 'special administrative regions when necessary'.[57] Thus, as diplomatic talks ground to a halt, the Chinese seized the initiative to shape Hong Kong's future. By spring 1983, Cradock had concluded that Britain was facing 'the danger that we could be locked out of meaningful discussion, while Hong Kong's fate was decided, and promulgated, in Peking'.[58]

The Breakthrough

A series of what Cradock called 'finesses' overcame or set aside the many areas of major disagreement in the Sino–British talks, which lasted until September 1984. The first was a letter from

Thatcher to Premier Zhao in which she slightly modified her previous position. She did not formally accept the PRC's precondition of Chinese sovereignty, but wrote that if the people of Hong Kong accepted the outcome of the negotiations, she 'would be prepared to recommend to Parliament that sovereignty over the whole of Hong Kong should revert to China'.[59]

From China's point of view, Thatcher's *démarche* — delicate policy and diplomacy — meant that the British had accepted the precondition in disguise.[60] Since the negotiations were only about practical arrangements, the Chinese interpreted the British prime minister's undertaking as implying that she no longer contested whether or not the precondition was acceptable.[61] Given their own experiences of the rubber-stamping NPC, the Chinese leaders believed that the British Parliament would accept an agreement. The gap that originally separated the two sides appeared to have been bridged when Deng decided to use Thatcher's letter to let the British climb down with a semblance of dignity. This was to secure their cooperation in transitional matters.[62] To the British it was a finesse, but to the Chinese it was a British capitulation. As a result, the Chinese allowed the negotiations to enter a second phase in July 1983. Only then did detailed discussions on matters of substance start.

The two governments thus assembled their negotiating teams. The Chinese one consisted of diplomats from the Foreign Ministry's Western European Department, a legal adviser, Lu Ping of HKMAO (who formally took part as a consultant to the Foreign Ministry) and Li Jusheng, a deputy director of the Xinhua News Agency in Hong Kong. Its leader was Vice-Foreign Minister Yao Guang, who was later replaced by Assistant Foreign Minister Zhou Nan.

On the British side, Cradock headed the team until his retirement at the end of 1983, at which point Ambassador Sir Richard Evans took over from him. Governor Youde, Hong Kong's political adviser Robin (now Sir Robin) MacLaren, four diplomats from the embassy and the Hong Kong government's main interpreter supported the British leader. There was an unspoken understanding in British and Hong Kong circles that Governor Youde would represent Hong Kong. However, when Youde confirmed this in a press interview, the Chinese government challenged his role. The Chinese Foreign Ministry then issued a repudiative statement saying that Youde did not represent Hong Kong and was acceptable to the PRC only as a member of the British delegation.[63] The PRC government considered the negotiations to be strictly between itself and the British government.

The people of Hong Kong took no part in the negotiations: they had no elected representative to speak for them. Nonetheless, their views and concerns were constantly conveyed to the British team. Under the leadership of the highly conscientious and utterly incorruptible Sir Sze-yuen Chung, the unofficial members of the Hong Kong Executive Council tried to fill the void. The governor appointed Chung and his colleagues as confidential advisers on government policy. Although these advisers were mostly from business or professional backgrounds, their fellow citizens basically shared their preferences for the outcome of the negotiations. Chung also felt a personal sense of responsibility to his fellow citizens and to his place in history. With Governor Youde's support, they were briefed and consulted regularly in the course of the negotiations. They actively involved themselves in internal debates and played a significant role in working out Britain's policy.[64]

Although the PRC government openly dismissed the idea of a 'three-legged stool' and thus denied Hong Kong a direct role in the negotiations, it nevertheless claimed to represent the local people. Just as the talks were entering the second phase in July 1983, the Chinese government appointed Xu Jiatun to become its *de facto* representative in Hong Kong. He was a member of the Communist Party Central Committee and a ministerial rank cadre. In public, he was director of the local Xinhua News Agency. In private, he was the secretary of the party's local branch. He was not only the most senior PRC cadre ever appointed to Hong Kong, but he was also an exceptional one.

Despite his own limited and sometimes faulty understanding of Hong Kong, Xu recognized that Beijing held a highly distorted picture of public opinion there. It was almost the exact opposite of the actual situation.[65] In trying to rectify the misconception, he encouraged Chung and two of his Executive Council colleagues to call on Deng and speak their minds.[66] Xu also thought the British were manipulating public opinion in Hong Kong, and took it upon himself to counter it. A great master in the art of the united front he tried to win over public opinion by mobilizing the media and by meeting and talking to a wide spectrum of Hong Kong society. His united-front work was very successful and considerably reduced local antipathy towards the PRC.[67] Though Xu improved the PRC's understanding of Hong Kong, there were limits to his positive influence. These became apparent when he arranged for Chung and two other Executive councillors to visit Beijing, only to be rebuked and publicly humiliated by Deng for very politely speaking the truth.[68] Deng insisted that he knew the Hong Kong people better than they themselves did and that he acted in their best interests.[69] The Chinese government remained convinced that it and it alone represented the people of Hong Kong — whatever the latter thought.

The rigidly structured formal negotiations were mainly conducted by the leaders of the two teams. In keeping with British tradition, a major input came from the person on the spot — the forceful and sharp minded Cradock. Evans carried less weight when he took over.[70] Although Cradock had reached retirement age, his services were considered too valuable to lose. So, contrary to the usually strict Foreign Office retirement rules, the prime minister installed him as a deputy under-secretary in the Foreign Office and made him a special adviser on foreign affairs. He in effect became the supremo of officialdom and took charge of the negotiations on a daily basis. Other major figures determining British policy were the prime minister herself, Sir Geoffrey Howe (after he became foreign secretary in July 1983) and Youde. Unofficial members of the Hong Kong Executive Council, the assistant under-secretary concerned and the head of the Foreign Office's Hong Kong Department also participated.

The leader of the Chinese team had much less flexibility or influence than his British counterpart. In line with Chinese communist negotiating practice, he spoke mainly from a prepared brief from which he rarely departed. The change from Yao Guang to Zhou Nan made no difference other than that Zhou argued the PRC's case more forcefully. Although the Foreign Ministry was formally responsible, the Communist Party's Central Foreign Affairs Leading Small Group headed by Li Xiannian, with Premier Zhao as his deputy, supervised the negotiations. Ultimate authority rested with Deng himself. In accordance with established practice, the Chinese also fully utilized the fact that they were hosting the negotiations.[71] They selectively leaked the contents of the negotiations to the media to strengthen their negotiating position.

From the beginning, the second phase of the negotiations ran into serious difficulties. The stumbling block was Britain's role in the administration of Hong Kong after 1997. The basic British position was not to retain sovereignty but to relinquish it in exchange for continuing to administer Hong Kong for as long as possible beyond 1997.[72] The Chinese rejected the idea that it was possible to separate sovereignty and administration. As Zhou Nan saw it, to do so meant replacing 'an old unequal treaty with a new one'.[73] His government was 'determined to recover complete sovereignty and administration of Hong Kong'.[74]

Hong Kong and its financial market reacted with mild panic to the impasse, which continued into the autumn of 1983. By late September, the Hong Kong dollar had fallen to a low of 9.5 to the US dollar, as compared with 5.9 in the previous year, before the negotiations had begun. Local residents started to stock up on essentials.

In October, with the help of the Bank of England, the British and Hong Kong governments finally came up with an arrangement to restore public confidence. They linked the local currency to the US dollar, and this did the trick.[75] Though a major economic crisis was averted because nobody wanted it to happen and the British made the right gesture, the Chinese saw the near crisis as a result of deliberate British manipulation.[76] They did not understand that Hong Kong's government could not control its entirely open economy. The PRC government announced that, unless they reached an agreement within a year, it would impose a unilateral solution.[77] It remained firm and unshakeable in its insistence on ending British administration in 1997.

In the face of Chinese intransigence, the British eventually accepted that they would be unable to administer Hong Kong after 1997. Since avoiding a breakdown in the negotiations then became their overriding objective,[78] they authorized Cradock to attempt what he called 'the second finesse'. In November 1983, the British formally conceded that they 'intended no link of authority between Britain and Hong Kong after 1997'.[79] While Cradock justifiably called the first British climb down a finesse, this was much more like a major retreat, for Britain actually abandoned its previous bottom line. However, it created a breakthrough in the negotiations because it finally cleared the way for serious discussions that could lead to an agreement.

After their orderly retreat, the British regrouped and worked out a new strategy. This was aimed at 'extracting concessions of substance from Peking and enshrining them in a binding agreement ... within the Chinese timetable'.[80] Cradock rightly believed that 'pressure of time would in the end work for us as well as for the opposition'. Otherwise, we, the British, would have 'little chance of inserting our substance and details into the outline [of] Chinese principles'.[81] Cradock was right because the 12 points devised under Liao Chengzhi merely laid down the general principles. There were few if any details in the Chinese plan for post-1997 Hong Kong: the Chinese government did not in fact wish to have a detailed agreement.

The eventual compromise was a short agreement with three annexes; the longest of these, Annexe I, sets out China's policy towards Hong Kong after 1997. The British made a significant input by providing ideas and explaining why the Hong Kong system worked. A special department in the Hong Kong government headed by L. M. Davies carried out much of the preparatory work. The British also made comments on the Chinese drafts of the annexes. The intention was to supply the Chinese with ideas in the hope that they would adopt as many of them as possible. As the deadline imposed by Deng approached in the summer of 1984, the Chinese negotiators acted as Cradock predicted. In order to meet the deadline, they became more willing to cooperate with the British in reaching agreements on what remained of the so-called matters of detail.[82]

Until the late summer of 1984 the negotiations continued to be very tough. The most difficult issue concerned the Chinese proposal to set up a joint commission in Hong Kong to oversee the transition.[83] Deng suspected that the British would strip Hong Kong of its assets and create an undesirable political *fait accompli* before 1997 and it was he who suggested the proposal.[84] Deng and most of his colleagues found the idea of British 'imperialists' seeing it as a matter of honour and moral responsibility to run Hong Kong as well as possible too alien to take seriously. He wanted to create a special agency or commission to supervise the 13 years of the transition.[85]

Although the Chinese did not intend the commission to become a shadow government, when news of it leaked out most people in Hong Kong feared that this was exactly what would happen.[86] Governor Youde himself found the creation of such an institution unacceptable: he thought it would make Hong Kong ungovernable.[87] Hong Kong's initial resistance softened as negotiations over the commission dragged on and the Chinese again proved adamant.

Hong Kong's governor and Executive Council turned their attentions towards devising compromises to make the commission less objectionable. In the end, Britain's counterproposals amounted to setting up a Sino–British Joint Liaison Group (JLG), which would be an institution for consultation and not an organ of power. The JLG would continue to exist beyond 1997 and, for the first few years of its existence, it would not be located in Hong Kong itself.[88]

In the meantime, the Chinese side had also had a number of internal discussions. The British suggestion that it should not be an organ of power was acceptable, for the Chinese had never planned to take over or supervise the administration of Hong Kong immediately. Xu Jiatun, who understood Hong Kong's situation better than most, recommended allowing the JLG to continue for a few years after 1997.[89] The final compromise was for it to come into existence when the Sino–British agreement came into force and to last until the year 2000.

Interestingly, despite Hong Kong's Executive Council specifically requesting it, the British government did not ask for reciprocity over the existence of the JLG.[90] That would have meant creating the JLG in 1985 and having it last until 2009, 12 years on either side of 1997. It is unknown whether such a British proposal would have secured Chinese consent. The final compromise came when Foreign Secretary Sir Geoffrey Howe visited Beijing at the end of July. With this major hurdle removed an agreement became possible.

Other details in the final agreement defined the scope of political developments in the period of transition and the basis for Hong Kong's future: they were in fact important provisions. The main emphasis was on securing the territory's prosperity and stability. The final agreement also settled any questions that touched on sovereignty, as defined by the Chinese in line with the PRC's demands. The most notable example here was Deng's decision to station a Chinese garrison in Hong Kong. He announced this plan in May, in front of a group of Hong Kong journalists, who immediately broadcast the news in

Hong Kong. Not surprisingly, it had a very negative impact on public confidence.[91]

Though the Chinese government was keen to protect public confidence in Hong Kong, its top leader had little real understanding of what engendered confidence. There was more give and take over practical arrangements that did not involve sovereignty. The British persuaded the Chinese to abandon their original idea of making parallel announcements of their agreements and to opt for a joint declaration. Many of the details of the arrangements were agreed in the final months of the negotiations. In a few cases, these were written in language that later laid them open to different interpretations. In any event, the negotiators met Deng's deadline and produced the final draft of an agreement towards the end of September.

Agreement

On 26 September 1984 Sir Richard Evans and Zhou Nan initialled the agreement known as the Sino–British Joint Declaration in Beijing. The relatively short Joint Declaration has three annexes, which are equally binding as the main document. All together they make up a formal international agreement registered at the UN. The Joint Declaration was formally signed in Beijing on 19 December by Prime Minister Thatcher and Premier Zhou. After ratification in May 1985, the agreement came into force and the transitional period began.

By the Joint Declaration both sides agreed that sovereignty over the whole of Hong Kong would be transferred from Britain to the PRC on 1 July 1997. It provided that, in the transitional period, Britain would be 'responsible for the administration of Hong Kong with the object of maintaining and preserving its economic prosperity and social stability' to which the PRC would 'give its cooperation'.[92]

The Chinese government also defined its basic policies towards Hong Kong, which were elaborated in Annexe I. The Chinese government commits itself in the Joint Declaration to establish 'a Hong Kong Special Administrative Region [SAR] upon resuming the exercise of sovereignty over Hong Kong'. This will come 'directly under the authority of' the Chinese government. The SAR will 'enjoy a high degree of autonomy, except in foreign and defence affairs'. It will be 'vested with executive, legislative and independent judicial power, including that of final adjudication', where the 'laws currently in force in Hong Kong will remain basically unchanged'. Its government 'will be composed of local inhabitants' and its chief executive will be appointed by the Chinese government 'on the basis of the results of elections or consultations to be held locally'.

The SAR's principal officials will be 'nominated by the chief executive ... for appointment by' the Chinese government. 'Foreign nationals previously working in the public and police services in the government departments of Hong Kong may remain in employment'. It will keep the current social and economic systems as well as the existing life-style, whereby 'rights and freedom, including those of the person, of speech, of the press, of assembly, of association, of travel, of movement, of correspondence, of strike, of choice of occupation, of academic research and of religious belief will be ensured by law'. Private property, ownership of enterprises, legitimate rights of inheritance and foreign investments will also be protected by law.

As an SAR, Hong Kong will remain 'a free port and a separate customs territory'. It will 'retain the status of an international financial centre, as well as its markets for foreign exchange, gold, securities and futures'. It will continue to enjoy the free flow of capital and a freely convertible currency. It will not be subject to taxation from China and will have independent finances. It will have the right to 'establish mutually beneficial economic relations with the United Kingdom and other countries', and 'conclude relevant agreements with states, regions and relevant international organizations' for economic and cultural purposes. Its government 'may on its own issue documents for entry into and exit from Hong Kong' and will have responsibility for maintaining public order there. Finally, the Chinese government pledged to implement its commitments in a Basic Law for the SAR to be promulgated by its NPC, which 'will remain unchanged for 50 years'.[93]

As elaborated in Annexe I, the Joint Declaration enshrines China's blueprint for a post-1997 Hong Kong. It provides the future basis on which Hong Kong and its people will depend. Although the Joint Declaration contains specific provisions or omissions that are open to criticism, as a whole it is acceptable to the people of Hong Kong. This is so long as it is enforced honestly and in full, which is a responsibility both signatories are to share equally. However, implementation of the Chinese promises ultimately depends on the promulgation and enforcement of a PRC law, which Beijing sees as a domestic affair and permits no foreign interference.

The intransigence the Chinese government demonstrated in the negotiations towards any issue remotely connected with sovereignty points to problems ahead. It implies a non-cooperative Chinese approach to any British attempt to enforce the Joint Declaration in the event of a major disagreement over interpretation. The British approach to the negotiations has also revealed a harsh fact of reality. While the British government can be expected to try to enforce the agreement and to use every available negotiating means to do so, it does not have the will or might to require the Chinese to abide by the agreement should the latter deviate from it.

Implementation of the Joint Declaration will ultimately depend on Chinese goodwill, sincerity and the ability to interpret its terms correctly. There is no need to doubt the first two factors. The Chinese government would not have gone into such lengthy and difficult negotiations only to reduce its final product to a worthless piece of paper. However, interpretation remains a major problem, not least because the Chinese did not understand what made Hong Kong tick when they signed the agreement. In an important sense, they did not really know what they had committed to maintain unchanged for 50 years.

The Joint Declaration was supposed to assure Hong Kong's future, but it has not — at least not entirely or securely.

When, after two years of inordinate tension and uncertainty, the contents of the agreement were announced in the autumn of 1984, Hong Kong responded with relief. Though some individuals expressed reservations, the majority of local people accepted the Joint Declaration — after all, their only choice was to accept it or not have an agreement at all.[94] One might have expected stronger expressions of doubt about the value of the Joint Declaration. After all, the nature of the communist regime in the PRC, on which the enforcement of the document depended, had not changed. However, the citizens of Hong Kong wanted to look forward to a bright tomorrow rather than a future with a dark cloud hanging over their heads. Serious doubts and the re-emergence of uncertainty and fear belonged to a later time. The end of September 1984 was a time when most people in Hong Kong bravely looked forward to building a future on the basis of the Joint Declaration.

6. Hong Kong in Transition: 1985–9

When the Joint Declaration came into effect in 1985, it opened a new chapter in Hong Kong's history. This was one of the most remarkable — perhaps unique — episodes in the long history of the British Empire and in the story of decolonization. Here was the last, and one of the most outstanding, bastions of the empire and of Britain's lingering imperial interests. It was a Crown colony that was rich, successful and deeply embedded in Western capitalism, but soon to be absorbed by the PRC. Perhaps, under Deng's pragmatic leadership the PRC was embracing capitalism and the market economy. However, it was still a totalitarian communist state and deeply aware of the history of past Western intervention in China (and of Hong Kong's role), and imbued with an irredentist nationalism. The British government, and the official and unofficial community in the colony, seemed to hope for the best and avert their gaze from the ultimate result of the PRC's *realpolitik*. The period of transition leading to the territory's retrocession in 1997 had begun.

As required by the Joint Declaration, Britain continued to administer Hong Kong for the meanwhile, and the PRC officially committed itself to give its full cooperation. Annexe I of the Joint Declaration stipulates that the future SAR legislature should 'be constituted by elections'. However, since Hong Kong's legislative council consisted entirely of appointed members, the British had to introduce certain reforms during the transition.[1] Democratic Britain needed to reform Hong

Kong's legislature to meet socialist China's 'democratic' standards. Further complicating the situation was the fact that introducing elections for the legislature involved handing over certain political powers to the local population, which would contradict the Chinese intention or expectation. The Joint Declaration makes no provision on how to resolve this inherent contradiction.

British Policy in Perspective

Britain sees its role in the transitional period as that of a custodian of its own and Hong Kong's best interests. It also recognizes the need to secure the blessings of the PRC for its policies there. Once the lease-back option had become untenable in the negotiations, the rationale behind Britain's Hong Kong policy was to withdraw with honour. For this purpose, it was necessary to secure the territory's stability and prosperity. Public statements by Prime Minister Thatcher and other senior political figures that Britain intended to discharge its 'moral responsibility' to the people of Hong Kong were more than rhetoric. They represented the general feeling in the British establishment.

The limit to this commitment is Britain's own national interest. However, Britain and Hong Kong's requirements generally coincide. If Britain mismanaged the transition and public confidence snapped, Hong Kong's economy would collapse. The British Treasury would then have to bail Hong Kong out until arrangements could be made for the PRC to take over ahead of the appointed date. An exodus from Hong Kong in a crisis would likewise create a huge problem of refugee relief for which Britain could not but play the leading role. In other words, British interests also demand a successful transition in Hong Kong.

A sense of honour and national interest aside, the British approach to the transition has also been affected by the bureaucratic nature and ethos of the Hong Kong government. The core of this British overseas civil service is its highly efficient administrative service, which is 'conservative, cautious, and with a world view narrowly focused upon' the territory itself.[2] Its *esprit de corps* requires it to act like Plato's Guardians, as the custodian of what it believed to be the best interest of Hong Kong. The reason for its very existence was to provide a good, honest, efficient and effective administration. Its natural response to the challenges of the transition was to continue to run the territory with the same disinterested ability as it has long been conditioned to do.

On signing the Joint Declaration, Britain thought it had considerable latitude to continue to run the territory until 1997 through the Hong Kong government in accordance with established practice. To the British, the transition was to ensure that the pieces would be in place for the Chinese takeover. Little would need to be done apart from a formal handover of sovereignty. This is, after all, what the Joint Declaration states about Hong Kong's supposed future. The British expected the governor to continue to serve as the Crown's personal representative and to exercise his normal authority. The only additional requirement was that he generally be sensitive to the wishes and needs of the PRC, the prospective new sovereign power.

Although it was not immediately obvious and the British did not recognize it at the time, the signing of the Joint Declaration marked the beginning of the end of their pre-eminence in the politics of Hong Kong. Despite the fact that British sovereignty and Britain's right to rule would continue until 1997, by signing this document the British had demonstrated their intention to disengage. The manner and the end product of this withdrawal also differed significantly from the usual process of decolonization elsewhere in the British Empire. As stipulated in the Joint Declaration, Britain would not transfer power to the local people but would relinquish political authority to a new metropolitan power, the PRC. The PRC, in turn, would empower the people of Hong Kong, through the Basic Law, to establish an SAR. Whatever the public rhetoric, this would happen regardless of the local people's wishes.[3]

Despite assessing public reactions to the Joint Declaration, the British government made it 'clear beyond any possibility of misunderstanding' that there was 'no possibility of an amended agreement'. The only alternative was 'to have no agreement' because the Chinese would not reopen negotiations.[4] By its actions, Britain allowed China to become a major factor in Hong Kong's political life during the transitional period.

However, in 1984 the British did not fully recognize the true extent of China's rise as a political factor in Hong Kong.[5] There was a remarkable amount of wishful thinking going on in the British government and parliament, as well as in the Hong Kong government, when the British signed the Joint Declaration. They proceeded on the assumption that they would have a free hand to reform Hong Kong's political system within the framework defined by the Joint Declaration. They attempted to introduce democratization. For a short time they deluded themselves by refusing to recognize that, by signing the Joint Declaration, they had significantly changed the old alignment of power between Britain and the PRC over Hong Kong.

The idea of democratizing Hong Kong's political system was important both to political and public opinion in Britain for accepting the retrocession of Hong Kong. Despite its reformist and pragmatic image, the Chinese regime under Deng was a Communist Party state with a poor record in human rights. The Joint Declaration was the instrument through which Britain would hand over about six million people to this regime. More than half of them were British nationals by birth and the rest had run away from this regime to seek the protection of the British flag. The British parliament and people knew that they had to accept the Joint Declaration because Britain had neither the will nor might to offer Hong Kong an alternative. However, they wanted to feel that Britain was doing right by Hong Kong. They needed to satisfy themselves that adequate safeguards were available to protect the existing way of life in Hong Kong. As a binding international agreement, they saw the Joint Declaration itself as one such defence. There was also a general desire to see this protection strengthened as much as possible.

In a democracy like Britain, people saw democratic institutions as the natural bulwarks with which to ensure that the Joint Declaration's promises were implemented. Thus, in the parliamentary debates over the Joint Declaration in December 1984, most parliamentarians who supported the agreement did so on the understanding that democratization would be introduced as part of the arrangements. Former Prime Minister Edward Heath captured the spirit of the time. He said: 'On the development of representative government within Hong Kong ... we must do our utmost to achieve proper, working representative government there by the time the handover takes place.'[6]

Despite the diversity of views on the pace and scope of reform, the general idea of introducing democratic changes to Hong Kong was not a partisan issue. Foreign Office Minister Richard Luce responded to this outburst by telling the House of Commons that Britain would 'build up a firmly based, democratic administration in Hong Kong in the years between now and 1997'.[7] Baroness Young, Luce's colleague in the House of Lords, likewise confirmed that the reform plan Britain had at hand was 'entirely consistent with the provisions in the draft agreement ... which specified that the Legislature of the Hong Kong SAR shall be constituted by elections.'[8] Britain displayed remarkable confidence in its ability to steer political developments in Hong Kong.

British confidence did not last. Within a year Britain had to admit that, in practice, the PRC could exercise a *de facto* veto over its plan for democratization in Hong Kong. In November 1985, shortly after the Hong Kong government introduced indirect elections to the legislature, the PRC's representative there, Xu Jiatun, openly accused the British of breaching the Joint Declaration.[9] Xu stressed that, in the transitional period, political reforms in Hong Kong must converge with the Basic Law for the SAR, for which the drafting process had just begun.[10] However clumsy Xu may have been, his bold initiative had a major impact.

It challenged the position that Foreign Secretary Howe took in the parliamentary debates of 1984, which was that the Basic Law would be based on the Joint Declaration and its Annexe I.[11] In that the Joint Declaration states that the Chinese NPC will promulgate the Basic Law specifically to implement its terms, the British were justified in taking the Joint Declaration as the basis for ensuring convergence.[12] By insisting that convergence should instead be based on the Basic Law — an entirely Chinese concern — Xu in effect put aside the Joint Declaration and demanded his government's right to exercise a veto. The Chinese government later affirmed Xu's stand when Luce's successor as Foreign Office minister for Hong Kong, Timothy Renton, visited Beijing in January 1986.

As Cradock admits in his memoirs, this meant that the Chinese 'would decide what to put in the Basic Law and the British would converge with it'.[13] The British acquiesced in the Chinese interpretation to ensure that 'major changes in government during the transitional period' would 'remain in force beyond the hand-over'.[14] This marked an important change in the British attitude. Britain finally accepted that a new alignment of power had come into existence in the politics of Hong Kong.

Democratic Debates

The first attempt to introduce constitutional reform to give the people of Hong Kong as a whole, and not just its expatriate European community, a major role in managing their own affairs was made at the end of the Pacific war.[15] Far-sighted Colonial Office officials like Gerald Edward Gent and David MacDougall first examined the idea during the war. It was taken up with zeal when Sir Mark Young resumed his interrupted governorship in 1946. As explained briefly in Chapter

4, Young intended to introduce democratic reforms to encourage local Chinese residents to commit themselves to a local sense of identity to Hong Kong as a British territory. The attempt was abandoned in 1952 after considerable alterations in the interval. This was mainly because Young's successor, Governor Grantham, deemed Young's intention unrealistic and his method dubious. It was also because there was insufficient domestic demand to prevent Grantham attempting a volte-face. Between 1952 and 1982, all suggestions of constitutional reform of a major character were dismissed as 'inopportune'.

In time, a myth developed that democratic changes were not introduced in Hong Kong in the postwar era because the PRC government would reject them. The truth was more complicated. In the early years of the PRC, this interpretation was simply not supported by the available evidence. As quoted at length in Chapter 4, Mao Zedong's main concern about Hong Kong in the late 1940s was that the local Chinese should 'not [be] treated as inferior to others in the matter of taxation and a voice in the Government'.[16]

In the early 1950s, Hong Kong was still actively considering introducing indirect elections to the legislature with a limited franchise. At that stage, however, the Foreign Office rightly assessed the Chinese attitude, for the PRC government was still a revolutionary regime. The Foreign Office's concern was that Hong Kong's reform proposals were 'by no means far-reaching' and would give the Chinese 'ample grounds for charging that the reforms are undemocratic'.[17] The last thing that worried the Foreign Office was the PRC objecting to democratic changes in Hong Kong. In the declassified British archives of the 1950s and early 1960s, there is no record of any British official or diplomat being told that the PRC would not tolerate democratization in Hong Kong.

The first possible indication from the Chinese was a remark reportedly made by Premier Zhou Enlai to Kenneth Cantlie in 1958. Cantlie was a British businessman and was *persona grata* to the PRC. His father, Sir James Cantlie, had rescued Dr Sun

Yat-sen, the 'father of modern China', when agents of the imperial government of China kidnapped him in London in 1896.[18] According to Cantlie, Zhou had said he 'would regard any move towards Dominion status as a very unfriendly act'. Zhou believed that the USA and Chiang Kai-shek intended to use this to turn Hong Kong into 'a base for subversive activities in China'.[19]

There was no specific reference to democratization in Cantlie's account, which failed to provide any link between 'dominion status' and turning Hong Kong into a base for subversion. There are also reasons to doubt the accuracy of the details of his report. To begin with, the British chargé d'affaires who looked after Cantlie in Beijing considered him 'muddle headed' and, for that reason, unfit to use as an intermediary between the two governments.[20] Furthermore, he was not a Chinese speaker so was unable to report Zhou's exact wording. It is impossible to ascertain whether Zhou himself, or for that matter his interpreter, used the term 'dominion status'. Had Zhou done so knowing what it meant, one could infer that the PRC rejected representative government for Hong Kong. It was unlikely, however, for even now Chinese scholars writing on Hong Kong do not usually understand the term 'dominion status' correctly.

In any event, at the end of the 1950s the British government had no plan to democratize Hong Kong or to grant it dominion status. It would have been remarkable for Zhou to have used the term on his own initiative. Moreover, about the same time Zhou also met a number of senior British politicians, including Harold (later Lord) Wilson and Frederick James (later Lord) Erroll. He made strong complaints about Hong Kong, but never once mentioned democratization or dominion status.[21] The thrust of Zhou's remark to Cantlie was probably to warn the British not to let hostile powers use Hong Kong as a subversive base, which was a recurrent theme.[22]

If the PRC changed its views towards democratization in Hong Kong in the late 1950s, it had no impact on British policy makers. There was no discussion on this matter in official circles. It was not until the 1960s that senior Hong Kong officials and relevant British officials came to assume that the PRC would reject democratic reforms in Hong Kong. In time, this idea gained wide currency and was taken as an article of faith.

There were two main reasons for the lack of democratic development in Hong Kong between 1952 and 1982. These were insufficient public demand from below and the existence of a government that largely met public expectations. The two factors mutually reinforced each other.

When Britain abandoned its modest proposals for political reform in 1952, the first postwar recession had hit the territory and Chinese refugees struggling to make a living had swollen Hong Kong's population.[23] Furthermore, most of the new arrivals had just escaped from political chaos and bad government in China. Their top priority was to feed themselves and their families, and they had little incentive to become involved in politics. By the mid-1960s, when there was considerably less destitution and a locally raised generation had come of age, demands for greater participation grew.[24] However, a huge gap separated the government from the governed.

Most people were unaware that the government was actually increasingly prepared to respond to public demands and public frustration was building up. However, fate intervened. In response to the Cultural Revolution in the PRC, local Maoists challenged the authority of the Hong Kong government in the streets. They also disrupted stability, good order and the way of life among the people of Hong Kong in 1967. The local people thus rallied behind the colonial government, though at that time they had little love for it.[25]

After the disturbances, the government took the lead to improve the channels of communication. The most important step was to introduce a network of city district officers 'to receive complaints, representations and personal problems arising from any government activity'.[26] Subsequently, public demands for participation rose. The government responded by opening even more channels, eventually building up a wide network of advisory committees and district boards to provide scope for increasing public participation.[27] The Hong Kong government's approach to meeting its local people's political aspirations has been described as an 'administrative absorption of politics'.[28] This involved 'the co-option of established and emergent Chinese elites into the colonial regime'.[29] In fact, public demands for a greater role in the management of their own affairs were fairly modest. Up to the early 1980s, they could be and were met without democratization.

Three factors were mainly responsible for this extraordinary development:

- the irony of maintaining a colonial administration in an international city in an era when imperialism had become a nasty word;
- the existence of a healthy democracy responsive to world opinion in the metropolitan country that supervised the colonial government. This meant that while the Hong Kong government enjoyed power that could allow it to run the territory like a police state, it could not abuse such power. The watchful eyes of London and the rest of the world were on it.[30] And, finally,
- the presence of a powerful government in the PRC with clear irredentist ambitions, which heightened Hong Kong's vulnerability.

The three factors together produced an 'inhibited political centre' effect.[31] It was a powerful force to ensure good and responsible government because the colonial authority knew that, should it provoke a domestic crisis, it would risk its own survival.

In time, such an awareness became an integral part of the Hong Kong government's ethos. As one retired senior civil servant recounted, between the 1950s and 1980s there gradually emerged a common wish to transform the 'benevolent authoritarianism to wider consultation and a concern with achieving "consensus government".[32] With such an attitude, and the expanding network to collect and to respond to public opinion, the Hong Kong government succeeded in putting off the public clamour for democratization. This was something one would normally have expected as Hong Kong transformed itself into a prosperous and well-educated community in the 1970s.[33] In an important sense, the people of Hong Kong did not demand democratization. They were already enjoying many of the benefits usually associated with a working democracy — freedom, the rule of law, the protection of human rights, stability and the existence of a government responsive to their views.[34]

When the British finally embarked on democratization in Hong Kong during the Sino–British negotiations, the impetus came from within the Hong Kong and British governments. During the latter phase of the negotiations, government officials were conducting a major review. This was part of the British attempt to build as strong a safeguard to Hong Kong's way of life as possible when it became clear that British jurisdiction would end. This initiative from above, as it were, coincided with the emergence of a still small but increasingly vocal public demand for democratization.[35]

The people of Hong Kong changed their opinions about democratization mainly in response to the negotiations. The talks were about their future but they had no elected representatives to speak for them. The Chinese rejection of their participation by dismissing the concept of a 'three-legged stool' — the three legs being Britain, the PRC and Hong Kong — aggravated their sense of powerlessness and frustration.[36] Some of them turned to the idea of democracy because they did not want to be excluded again from being the master of their own fate.[37] Others saw it as a bulwark to protect their way of life from a communist takeover.[38]

In July 1984, two months before the Joint Declaration was

initialled, the Hong Kong government completed its internal review. It published a consultative document, a green paper, and stated its aim clearly. The timing allowed the Chinese an opportunity to see the direction of political evolution under consideration before the terms of the Joint Declaration were agreed.

In this document, the Hong Kong government made the boldest statement for democratic developments in 38 years. (That was when Sir Mark Young declared the British government's intention to give local residents 'a fuller and more responsible share in the management of their own affairs'.[39]) It stated that the government aimed 'to develop progressively a system of government the authority for which is firmly rooted in Hong Kong, which is able to represent authoritatively the views of the people of Hong Kong, and which is more directly accountable to the people of Hong Kong.'[40]

Technically, the British claim that this attempt was built on a principle elucidated in a 1980 green paper on district administration was justified. The principle was: 'The Executive and Legislative councils, the central organs of Government, have evolved, and will continue to evolve as circumstances require, within the imperatives of stability and dependability, which the special circumstances of Hong Kong dictate'.[41] The document failed to mention that, until early 1982, the 'special circumstances' had dictated a rejection of 'fundamental constitutional changes'. However, as expressed in the government's annual report, there was 'in any event little or no popular pressure' for these.[42] In the two years that followed, popular demands had indeed begun to appear, but they were by no means strong enough to require a basic adjustment in policy. The reform proposals were made in anticipation of the retrocession, and emphasis was laid on continuity to make them inoffensive to the PRC.

This was meant to be a genuine review of 'how the central institutions of government in Hong Kong might be made more representative in a way which will make the Government more directly accountable to the people of Hong Kong'.[43] The document not only provided for the introduction of a substantial, albeit indirectly, elective element to the legislature, but also for the introduction of a quasi-ministerial system of government. Nevertheless, it kept to Hong Kong's political tradition by proposing to move forward cautiously. The imperative of maintaining stability and prosperity was fully accepted.

The green paper set off lively debates on both the scope and pace of democratization. There was broad public support for its main objective. On the basis of the consultation, the Hong Kong government published a policy document or white paper on the subject in November — again a month before the formal signing of the Joint Declaration. This document set out provisions for admitting 24 indirectly elected members to the 56-seat Legislative Council in 1985. It also committed the government to review (in 1987) the introduction of directly elected members in the following year, but side-tracked the idea of a ministerial system of government.[44] The British tried to strike a balance between the different views expressed, and between the desire for reform and the need to remain in control of the pace and scope of change. This was not least because of the need to dovetail the Basic Law for the SAR, which the PRC would be enacting in due course.

Though the British presented their ideas about democratization as openly as possible, PRC cadres found it very difficult to grasp what they were attempting. The proposals, and indeed the idea of democracy, were alien to them. They therefore had an inadequate understanding of the real import of the scheme the Hong Kong government proposed. Consequently, the PRC merely reserved its position on the subject and stressed that 'it was a matter for the British, for which it was not responsible'.[45] It was partly for this reason, and partly to meet Deng's deadline for an agreement, that the Chinese negotiators agreed to insert an extra clause into Annexe I of the Joint Declaration. This stated that the legislature of the future SAR 'shall be constituted by elections'. By the Joint Declaration, and by their acts in the summer and autumn of 1984, the PRC government had passively endorsed Hong Kong's democratization scheme. This was provided it did not subvert the objectives and principles laid down in the Joint Declaration. However reasonable such an interpretation, it was emphatically not what the Chinese intended or understood.

In 1985 the Chinese came to see the democratization attempt as an underhand British plot to regain what they had lost in the Sino–British negotiations. From the PRC's point of view, the British attempted to use democratization to ingratiate themselves with the people of Hong Kong in order to build up a pro-British force ahead of retrocession. In short, the British were trying to create a situation that would allow them to continue to run Hong Kong after their formal departure in 1997.[46] Firmly convinced that this was the British objective, Xu Jiatun, the PRC's top man in Hong Kong, organized a counterattack.

This came in November when Xu held his first ever press conference as the *de facto* representative of the PRC. On this occasion he pointedly accused the British of violating the Joint Declaration. In effect, he demanded that they follow the still undrafted Basic Law as the basis for political reform in Hong Kong.[47] Xu and his colleagues in the PRC could not believe that the British had primarily intended democratization to protect the existing way of life in Hong Kong. They never explained how the British could hope to retain control in stealth after 1997 by introducing genuine democracy.

The Chinese also failed to see that much would have to change to preserve Hong Kong's dynamic capitalist system and way of life.[48] This was because, as a leading Hong Kong lawyer put it, its 'political, social, and economic arrangements depend for their efficacy both on strict legal rights and on legitimate expectations habitually upheld by the authorities in accordance with well-established and credible rules of self-restraint'.[49]

With the end of democratic Britain's supervision in sight, introducing democratization was the most effective way to ensure that the local government upheld the existing rules of

self-restraint. This was too alien a concept to be compre-
hensible to the PRC cadres. They took the accuracy of their
own interpretation of Britain's motive for granted. Once Xu's
initiative received Deng's backing, the PRC was set on a new
course. This was to oppose liberal democracy publicly and to
restrict the scope and pace of democratization in Hong Kong.[50]

Convergence

China's strong position over democratization gave the word
convergence a new meaning for Hong Kong. Previously, the
British position was that, while they planned for political
developments, they would 'keep in mind the fact that the
Chinese Government will be considering the future Basic Law
for Hong Kong, and the provisions of the Sino–British agreement, which provides for an elected legislature by 1997 and an
executive accountable to it'. They would therefore do 'nothing
... inconsistent with those aims'.[51] In other words, convergence meant both sides would start on the basis of the Joint
Declaration and meet each other half way.

The British would reform Hong Kong's authoritarian system
as it existed in 1984, and make it dovetail China's plan for
1997. From the British point of view, the two would converge
because the same principles would guide both sides. It was like
laying down new railway tracks from opposite ends and
joining them up in the middle as they met. The Chinese
demand of late 1985 was that the British should stop, or slow
down drastically, their building work. They could recommence
when the Chinese had rethought the plan for laying the track
and had completed work on their own section.

This Chinese view of convergence put the British in an
awkward position. They had publicly stated that the Hong
Kong government would review the progress of reform in
1987, particularly over introducing directly elected members to
the Legislative Council in the following year. They could not
break this promise without gravely undermining the Hong
Kong government's credibility. The British also recognized that

convergence would only happen if their reform plans were acceptable to the Chinese.

Once the Chinese government formally reaffirmed Xu's public position in January 1986, the British basically accepted their interpretation of convergence.[52] They wanted to ensure that whatever was in place by 1997 would survive the hand-over. It was not, however, a complete capitulation. The British reached an understanding with the Chinese that there would be no major reform until the Basic Law was promulgated in 1990, and that nothing the British introduced would breach the Basic Law. The British also expected to make an input into drafting the Basic Law by offering their views as part of the Chinese consultation process. In return, they expected the Chinese to let the Hong Kong government, including its Legislative Council to be formed in line with the Basic Law in 1995, to continue to function after the hand-over in 1997. This became popularly known as the 'through train' arrangement.

It was against such a background that the Hong Kong government proceeded with its political reform review in 1987. In contrast with 1984, when the Hong Kong government boldly stated its objective, in 1987 it tried to obscure the issue and mentioned no objective in the green paper.[53] The government could not, however, avoid stating its objectives in the policy statement or white paper that concluded the review. The document therefore included a list of four 'objectives', though none could properly be called an objective for developing a representative government. According to the white paper, these were:

(a) 'that it should continue to evolve to suit Hong Kong's circumstances;
(b) that its development should be prudent and gradual;
(c) that any reforms should have the widest possible support so as to command the confidence of the community as a whole; and
(d) that the system in place before 1997 should permit a

smooth transition in 1997 and a high degree of continuity thereafter.'[54]

The 1984 objective to develop a government that could authoritatively represent the local people had deliberately been removed. As Foreign Secretary Howe admitted, the exercise was conducted to keep the government's promise to have a review.[55] It was not to explore the way forward for developing a representative government, as suggested in the title of the white paper concerned.

To satisfy members of the general public that their opinions were given due consideration in the review, for a period of four months in 1987 the Hong Kong government set up a Survey Office to collect and collate public responses. The most important question was whether direct elections for the Legislative Council should be introduced in 1988 — an option the PRC rejected. The Survey Office eventually produced a report of over 1500 full pages, but it misrepresented the thrust of the public view.

According to the report, there were 125,833 individual submissions on the question of whether to introduce direct elections in 1988.[56] Of these, 84,202 (or 67 per cent) opposed them, even though most of them supported direct elections in principle. Included among these were 69,557 form letters, most of which were originally handed out to employees by the managements of PRC-owned banks and enterprises in Hong Kong. What the Survey Office did not count as submissions were the results of 21 different signature campaigns, for which individuals were asked to sign and write down their identity card numbers after reading various letters. In all, these contained 233,666 signatures, of which 233,371 supported and 295 opposed direct elections in 1988.[57]

By excluding the signature campaign submissions, but including the form letters, the Survey Office concluded that there was overwhelming support for introducing direct elections to the Legislative Council, but not in 1988. It unjustifiably implied that the people of Hong Kong had changed their minds since 1984. In the white paper of 1984, the Hong Kong government actually correctly reported that 'with few exceptions the bulk of public response from all sources' supported 'introducing a very small number of directly elected members in 1988 and building up to a significant number ... by 1997'.[58]

In the 1988 document, the government claimed, on the basis of the survey report, that public opinion on the subject was 'sharply divided'. However, it admitted that there was strong public support for introducing direct representation.[59] On this basis, the white paper provided for the introduction of ten directly elected members to the 56-seat Legislative Council in 1991. By the time the white paper was published, it was already known that the PRC intended to allow at least ten directly elected members to be admitted to the SAR legislature. The whole exercise was blatantly based on the wish to make Hong Kong's political system converge with the Basic Law, which was in the process of being drafted and would not be finalized until 1990.

Although it might seem improper for the Hong Kong government to have manipulated the results of the opinion assessment, its justification for doing so was on the grounds of Hong Kong's best interests. As Foreign Secretary Howe explained, Britain's key objective was 'to design a structure that will not be temporary or fallible but one that will endure beyond 1997'.[60] Convergence — as defined by the PRC — had become the political imperative. In 1987 and 1988 the British government deemed manipulation the lesser of the two evils. The other was provoking the PRC to commit itself to dismantle whatever reforms the British might introduce. By slowing down the pace of democratization, Britain hoped to persuade the PRC to include provisions in the Basic Law for limited direct representation at the legislature.

The British and Hong Kong governments could get away with manipulating the opinion survey results because the people of Hong Kong did not feel strongly enough about the matter. Had the majority of those who supported holding direct elections in 1988 organized a campaign against the Survey Office report's findings, it would have been gravely discredited. The British and Hong Kong governments would have had to respond. The reality was that there was still public ambivalence about democratization. Not even those most in favour of it were prepared to work for it actively. Equally important, Hong Kong had failed to produce 'a group of popular and organized *indigenous* [italics original] leaders as the guardian of its interests, as confidence-boosters and as guarantors of the success of the vaunted "one country, two systems" approach to Hong Kong's political future'.[61] No political party organized an effective campaign to press the British to stand by their 1984 commitment to democratize. The founding of the first true political party, the United Democrats of Hong Kong had to wait until April 1990.[62]

Because of Britain's acceptance of China's definition of convergence, the Hong Kong government acquired the public image of being a lame duck. This was remarkable for a government that still had a tenure of almost ten years guaranteed by an international agreement. It was particularly remarkable given that this was essentially the same government that had met the requirements of 'as good a government as possible in the Chinese political tradition' only a few years earlier. Two forces were mainly responsible for this.

The first was that the people of Hong Kong had changed. By the late 1980s, they were no longer satisfied, even with an 'ideal' government in the political tradition of China. While they were still reticent about actively campaigning for greater democracy, they expected their government to be increasingly responsive to their wishes. Their most important, though as yet not very vocal, wish was to build up democratic and related institutions to enable them to minimize the impact of the impending PRC takeover.

The second factor, which was closely related to the first, was

Britain's apparent preparedness to accommodate the PRC's wishes. This was so even when these failed to fulfil the common desires of the local people or indeed the terms of the Joint Declaration. The British concession over convergence symbolized this attitude in the public view. The secret diplomacy that the British government conducted to secure Chinese cooperation in other matters in return was generally neither known about nor considered credible. They felt that the British government was betraying them and that the Hong Kong government was letting them down. Their sense of frustration and powerlessness increased and their confidence in the future as 'guaranteed' by the Joint Declaration fell.

An increasing number of Hong Kong residents thus planned and prepared to leave, or at least to seek the security of a foreign passport. Convergence was a double-edged sword for Hong Kong. On the one hand, it harmed the credibility of and public confidence in the Hong Kong government and this reduced its vitality in facing the longer-term challenges of retrocession. On the other hand, convergence provided the best chance to minimize the impact of the Chinese takeover, given the attitude of the Chinese leaders, which is examined in detail in the following chapter.

The alternative — to democratize Hong Kong's political system as permitted in the Joint Declaration — would only have led to the PRC dismantling what it disapproved of in 1997. Obsessed with the idea of sovereignty and 'face', Beijing would deem all political reforms introduced in Hong Kong without the PRC's tacit approval as unacceptable. Ignoring the Chinese completely because their interpretation of the Joint Declaration was ill-based would have been detrimental to Hong Kong's long-term wellbeing. The Joint Declaration would be worth less than the paper on which it was printed if the Chinese should decide not to abide by it because of a difference in interpretation. The British adopted convergence as a policy not because they liked it but because they believed it was, on balance, the lesser of two evils.

In the period of transition, the Hong Kong government needed to steer a course and devise policies that would both be supported by the local people and tolerable to Beijing. Up to 1989, the Hong Kong government tried to find such a course, but appeared to have erred more on the side of accommodating Beijing.

7. China's Policy: 1985–90

Deng Xiaoping laid down the PRC's policy on Hong Kong in the early 1980s. It rests on the principle of exercising maximum flexibility in practical matters but maintaining complete rigidity over sovereignty.[1] It is important to understand this policy, and the rationale behind it, within the context of modern China's history, particularly the history of the communist movement. The PRC's ageing top leaders derived many of their attitudes from their experiences as revolutionaries. The attitudes of younger leaders, however, were mainly shaped by their understanding of modern Chinese history.

Basis of Policy

Once they decided to tackle the Hong Kong question head on in the early 1980s, the ageing top leaders — those roughly of Deng's generation — saw Hong Kong's return as a matter of great import and emotional moment. Although they sincerely regarded themselves as committed communists, they were above all nationalists. As youngsters, most of them had become revolutionaries in order to join the nationalist movement sweeping the country.

In 1919, shortly after the end of the First World War, China attended the Versailles Peace Conference as a member of the victorious Allies. Students and future communist leaders were outraged by what they saw there as the humiliating treatment of China. Several European powers and Japan secretly agreed to transfer to Japan the special privileges Germany had enjoyed in Shandong province before the war. The purpose of this scheme was to induce Japan to join the Allies.

The Chinese government's inability to defend its own sovereign rights, even as one of the victors, provoked the first modern nationalist movement in China, known as the May Fourth Movement.[2] The Communist Party was founded in 1921 against this background, primarily as an instrument for national salvation. The establishment of the PRC in 1949 enabled the communist leaders to remove all traces of a Western imperial presence from mainland China.[3] Hong Kong, the first product of Western incursion in the nineteenth century and still under British rule, increasingly came to symbolise the remnants of China's humiliation by Western imperialists. Until the PRC could re-establish its sovereignty over Hong Kong, the nationalist goal of its top leaders would remain unfulfilled. It was therefore an emotional issue for Deng and his comrades. It formed the basis of the PRC's Hong Kong policy under Deng; and it has remained in place since he died in the spring of 1997. This explains their obsession with matters of sovereignty, over which they refuse to compromise.

The slightly younger generation of China's policy makers, those who joined the Communist Party before 1945, shared the ageing top leaders' nationalist sentiments. Li Hou, who served as deputy director of the Hong Kong and Macao Affairs Office (HKMAO) for much of the 1980s, captures their feelings. As a youngster in the 1930s and 1940s, when China was experiencing Japanese aggression, he recalls how he 'joined the Communist Party to save the nation'.[4] The cadres raised under the red flag did not share the revolutionary experiences of the first and second generation communists. However, they were brought up to believe that Hong Kong was the last major vestige of the nineteenth-century Western imperialism that had humbled China, something that should and would in due course be eradicated.[5] Their understanding of the issue is based entirely on the communist view of modern Chinese history. Without personal experiences, they feel less strongly about the future of Hong Kong than their older colleagues, but they still approach it as an emotional issue. Hence, they share the

intensely nationalistic view that its eventual recovery must be
'an unassailable element' of the PRC's policy — an attitude
essentially unchanged since 1949.[6]

Despite its emotional dimension, Chinese policy makers
have also dealt with Hong Kong as a pragmatic matter. As
explained in Chapter 4, the communists recognized the value
of Hong Kong even before the founding of the PRC. Following
their victory in the Chinese civil war, Mao Zedong and other
top communist leaders deferred the recovery of Hong Kong
because of its economic and other practical benefits to the
PRC. After Deng Xiaoping embarked on economic reform in
1978, Hong Kong's importance increased rather than
decreased. To begin with, it became 'a treasure trove of inspiration and services for the development of Guangdong', the
Chinese province immediately neighbouring Hong Kong.[7]

The communists had no love for condescending Hong Kong
capitalists who profited as middlemen between the PRC and
the rest of the world. However, they knew they 'needed those
capitalists for their knowledge of business and technology,
their access to finance, their skill in managing large projects,
and their control of the transportation and telecommunication
infrastructure'.[8] Within the first decade of the opening of the
Chinese economy, Hong Kong had become the PRC's most
important source of external investment. It was also its largest
trading partner, accounting for 27 per cent of its external trade
in 1988.[9] Increasingly, Hong Kong played 'a crucial role in
China's reform drive, especially in the reform of China's
external sector'. It also exerted 'pressure on China to decen-
tralize its trade, as many localities and enterprises' traded with
the outside world through Hong Kong.[10]

In short, the success of the Dengist reform to modernize the
economy had come to depend on Hong Kong playing the role
of the leading economic locomotive. In response to the conflicting requirements of desiring to recover sovereignty and
needing to utilize Hong Kong for the Communist Party's own
purposes, the PRC devised the policy popularized as 'one

country, two systems'. The Chinese considered it an ingenious idea that would enable the PRC both to have its cake (reclaim sovereignty) and to eat it (retain Hong Kong's economic utility).[11] This was essentially a modification of and, from the PRC government's point of view, an improvement over the policy that Mao had advocated after 1949. The driving force behind it has, however, remained essentially the same. It is to further the interests of the PRC as defined by the Communist Party. This is the most powerful factor in inducing PRC leaders to keep their promises to Hong Kong as enshrined in the Joint Declaration.

Despite the PRC leaders' commitment to make a success of Hong Kong, there are good reasons to doubt that they will fully honour their 1984 promises.[12] Despite their public rhetoric, the real purpose of the 'one country, two systems' formula is to serve the interests of the PRC and the Communist Party rather than those of Hong Kong. Capitalist Hong Kong will be permitted to enjoy a high level of autonomy only so long as it enhances, rather than undermines, the party's interests. Indeed, as ministerial level PRC cadre Lu Ping explained, if Hong Kong should 'be of negative value instead of positive value to China', it 'would be disastrous for Hong Kong'.[13]

A basic problem is that capitalist Hong Kong can only run its own affairs with 'a high degree of autonomy' within the framework of a socialist PRC if the latter feels confident enough to allow an *imperium in imperio* to practise a system fundamentally hostile to its survival. In the mid-1980s, Deng had the necessary confidence. He believed that the PRC's Communist Party dominated system was superior to Hong Kong's capitalist system.[14] However inherently self-contradictory this might sound, he also conceded that it would be advantageous to let Hong Kong capitalism supplement the superior PRC system. It was in any event for a limited period only. Deng never intended to let Hong Kong be the catalyst to set off a chain reaction to change, let alone subvert or supplant, the socialist system in the PRC.[15]

As it will be explained in Chapter 8, if or when the communist leaders feel threatened, they will either pre-empt or eliminate such a threat, regardless of the cost. This was how they dealt with the student movement in Beijing in spring 1989. If Hong Kong were to be deemed the source of such a menace, it would be dealt with accordingly. One should not underestimate the PRC leadership's willingness to resort to extreme measures to maintain Communist Party rule. Deng expressed such preparedness to the British prime minister, Margaret Thatcher, at the beginning of the Sino–British negotiations. He emphatically stated that if, in trying to protect its sovereignty over Hong Kong, the PRC should bring about catastrophic results, he would face them.[16] But then Deng felt confident that the PRC would take over Hong Kong successfully.

The PRC's approach to the recovery of sovereignty severely restricts whatever 'high degree of autonomy' Hong Kong might expect to enjoy. A Westerner may see the idea of 'Hong Kong people administering Hong Kong' within the framework of 'one country, two systems' as implying that, so long as the PRC's sovereignty is acknowledged, after 1997 Hong Kong will be free to run its own domestic affairs without interference from Beijing. This interpretation is unacceptable to Beijing. The PRC will only regard its sovereignty over Hong Kong as fully recovered when it has actually exercised authority and stationed troops in the territory.[17]

Deng himself told the drafters of the Hong Kong Basic Law that they 'should not think Hong Kong affairs should all be handled by Hong Kong people': 'this was impossible, and such an idea was unrealistic'.[18] He added that, should it become necessary for Beijing to interfere, 'it would in the first instance be done through the executive branch without involving the Chinese garrison'. This would only need to be called out in the event of disturbances.[19] Deng obviously spoke on the assumption that, as from July 1997, the SAR government would act on directives from Beijing. Behind its rhetoric about autonomy, the PRC's policy is to allow the SAR government to run its own affairs only so long as the Communist Party or its leaders do not see its actions as contrary to their interests.

The very nature of the Communist Party state influences its Hong Kong policy. Organized along Leninist lines, the Chinese Communist Party is interventionist in its ethos. When he re-emerged from political oblivion after the Cultural Revolution, Deng reaffirmed the basic principle that the party must play a leading role in all matters.[20] As he put it, 'one should never depart from the leadership of the party and praise the initiative of the masses'.[21] Deng's directive was very much in character with the party tradition that transformed 'what Sun Yat-sen described as a "sheet of loose sand" into one of the most highly organized societies in the world'.[22]

Deng then instructed his party to go against its tradition and make an exception of Hong Kong. While he was undoubtedly sincere, he gave the party a very tall order. The party–state was to keep the promises it made in the Joint Declaration. In principle, this was an easy task to perform — all it required was to do nothing and let the Hong Kong government continue as before after retrocession. In reality, the Chinese Communist Party was being asked to contradict its very nature — the most difficult task for any individual or organization.

The PRC's Hong Kong policy is also influenced by a basic distrust of the British and of their supporters in the territory. This derives from China's tendency to adopt a doctrinal and nationalistic view of the British colony. It colours their judgement of Britain's intentions there and the nature of British rule. PRC leaders and officials remain convinced that the British engaged in a conspiracy, at the expense of the territory and its future sovereign, to spirit wealth from Hong Kong to Britain before 1997.[23] They cannot believe that the public tender system and oversights by various public bodies, including the Legislative Council's Finance Committee, would not allow Britain to do so.

Their view is partly explained by Hong Kong and the PRC having very different bureaucratic cultures and practices. PRC cadres assume that British imperialists have always exploited Hong Kong and have done with the cooperation of local civil servants. They do not realize that, after the Pacific war, the Hong Kong civil service developed a very strong commitment to the territory and has at times fought London in defence of local interests.[24] They would have understood the true nature of the Hong Kong government if they had tried to find out why, for the last four decades, the undemocratic colonial administration consistently enjoyed such strong public support. In other words, they should have adopted a dispassionate rather than a doctrinal and nationalistic approach.

In reality, they could not accept that, by the 1980s, the Hong Kong government had become as good a government as possible in the Chinese political tradition — efficient, honest, paternalistic yet non-intrusive. The PRC's failure to grasp this is an indication that it really does not understand what makes Hong Kong tick.[25] It can interfere out of good though also selfish intentions — in this case, to prevent the British 'stealing' from Hong Kong's Treasury and its large reserve prior to the handover in July 1997.

Structure of Policy Making

The PRC's Hong Kong policies create bureaucratic complications because Hong Kong is neither a wholly foreign nor a wholly domestic matter. It is both at the same time. It qualifies as a foreign policy matter because it is under British rule and its status cannot be altered without British cooperation. However, because it is regarded as Chinese territory, it also falls within the domain of domestic policy. The PRC therefore has to adjust its bureaucratic structure to make and implement its Hong Kong policies.

As a matter that involves sovereignty, national dignity and the future of economic reform within the PRC, their Hong Kong policy is of great importance to Chinese leaders. There can be no major policy decisions or changes over Hong Kong without the top leaders' approval. In structural terms, this means the approval of the Communist Party Politburo's Standing Committee. In practice, questions about Hong Kong policy are usually first referred to the party's Central Foreign Affairs Leading Small Group (*zhongyang waishi lingdao xiaozu*).[26] This is the main organization for collecting, collating and coordinating the views of the principal party and government leaders involved in the conduct of foreign relations.[27] Placing Hong Kong policy under this group thus reflects the importance of its foreign policy dimension.

A leading small group usually consists of all the senior cadres 'with responsibility for different aspects of a comprehensive functional arena'.[28] In the mid-1980s, President Li Xiannian headed the Central Foreign Affairs Leading Small Group. Its chief members included Premier Zhao Ziyang, first vice-premier Wan Li, state councillor and HKMAO director Ji Pengfei, as well as vice-premier and foreign minister Wu Xueqian.[29] In the mid-1990s, President Jiang Zemin became its head. He also serves as a member of the Politburo's Standing Committee and general secretary of the party. The official head of this group is not, however, always the ultimate arbiter of policies over Hong Kong. When he was alive and physically fit, paramount leader Deng Xiaoping retained the final say.[30] In other words, the top leaders make all major decisions about Hong Kong. As Sir Percy Cradock observed during the Sino–British negotiations, this restricts the amount of flexibility senior PRC cadres or diplomats are able to exercise.[31]

Below the top leadership, three ministerial level offices are directly involved in working out policies for Hong Kong:

- the HKMAO of the State Council;
- the Foreign Ministry in Beijing; and
- the Hong Kong and Macao Work Committee of the Chinese Communist Party in Hong Kong.

The latter attained full provincial status in 1983,[32] and thus holds the same bureaucratic rank as a ministry.[33] Its head or secretary holds the public office of director of the Hong Kong branch of Xinhua News Agency and is the PRC's *de facto* representative in Hong Kong. Although the three institutions have the same bureaucratic rank, their relative importance in the policy-making process has varied. This is partly because a department's political clout also depends on the personal standing of its head.

The foreign minister and director of HKMAO are usually more senior than the secretary of the Hong Kong and Macao Work Committee. They are often concurrently either a vice-premier or state councillor, and are at least members of the party's Central Committee. They are also usually members of the Foreign Affairs Leading Small Group, which places them higher up the chain of command than the secretary of the Work Committee. Furthermore, it is a convention in the Chinese Communist Party for the head of a central organ to take precedence over a regional cadre of the same rank.[34] The formal line of command requires the secretary of the Work Committee to answer to the director of HKMAO.

The personal relationships of the senior cadres concerned complicate the whole policy-making process. For example, Xu Jiatun was unusually powerful when he headed the Work Committee from 1983 to 1990. Sometimes he bypassed the HKMAO and reported directly to the Politburo, with the latter's encouragement.[35] Xu was a special case because of his seniority in the party, but, more importantly, because he had access to Premier Zhao and Deng Xiaoping. In the latter case, this was due to his close personal connections with Deng's eldest son, Deng Pufang. Making use of his special access to the top and to Beijing's fluid power relations, Xu at times outmanœuvred the others. He and the Work Committee thus became even more influential than the HKMAO, which had played the pivotal role when Liao Chengzhi headed it from 1978 to 1983. This happened despite Liao's successor Ji Pengfei actually holding the higher bureaucratic rank of state councillor, and Foreign Minister Wu being a Politburo member.

They did not have the same personal access to the paramount leader.

The relative power of the Work Committee clearly fell when Zhou Nan succeeded Xu in 1990. Some claim that the bureaucratic rank of the secretary of the Work Committee was downgraded one level when Zhou, a mere deputy foreign minister at that time, was appointed.[36] This is unlikely to be true, for Hong Kong is at least on a par with Shanghai and Tianjin, which enjoy full provincial (that is ministerial) status.[37] Furthermore, after his appointment to Hong Kong, Zhou was promoted to the Communist Party's Central Committee. The decline of the Work Committee has more to do with Zhou not enjoying the same standing, personal connections and consequently clout among the top leadership as his predecessor. Since the mid-1990s, the most powerful figure at the ministerial level has been Foreign Minister Qian Qichen, who is concurrently a vice-premier and a member of the Politburo.

In Hong Kong itself, the Work Committee, which functions under cover of the Xinhua News Agency, is in principle the coordinating umbrella organization for party and state organs in the territory.[38] The need for the Communist Party to operate underground is a legacy of 1949 when the Hong Kong government outlawed all political parties with an affiliation to a foreign government.[39] As a coordinating body, the Work Committee's membership includes the local heads of various offices representing PRC agencies. Among these are the Bank of China, the China Resources Corporation, the China Merchants Group and the China Travel Service.[40] The Ministry of Public Security (*Gongan Bu*), which is responsible for the security of PRC offices in Hong Kong, the Ministry of State Security (*Guojia Anquan Bu*), which is charged with intelligence work, and various branches of military intelligence also operate under the cover of the Xinhua News Agency.[41]

In practice, however, different ministries, agencies, provinces and regions have set up their own offices or stationed intelligence officers in Hong Kong. In other words, they belong to different *xitongs*, for which there is no equivalent word in English. A *xitong* is essentially a grouping of bureaucracies and cliques organized vertically from the top down and is usually led by a senior leader in the Politburo's Standing Committee.[42] According to Xu Jiatun, cadres who came from different *xitongs* in the PRC did not necessarily follow his directions in Hong Kong, despite the great influence he generally enjoyed in the policy-making process.[43]

In discharging its responsibilities, the Work Committee relies on the Xinhua News Agency, not only as a cover but also to function effectively in its officially accredited capacity as a PRC-owned news agency. In organizational terms, the Xinhua News Agency in Hong Kong is divided into two parts. One functions as a genuine news agency and the other handles the non-clandestine work of the Work Committee. Since the main thrust of the latter is to persuade the general public to support the PRC, this means effective united-front work.[44] It involves using propaganda and other means to consolidate the support of the sympathetic, win over the wavering and neutralize those opinion leaders hostile to the PRC.

Such an operation requires the news agency to coordinate and direct the propaganda work of the so-called pro-PRC Hong Kong newspapers. The most important of these are *Wen Hui Pao* (*Wenhuibao*) and *Ta Kung Pao* (*Dagongbao*). Whatever legal position these newspapers and other publications may enjoy under Hong Kong law, they are subject to the Work Committee's control.[45] For example, when the head of *Wen Hui Pao* refused to toe the party line in the immediate aftermath of the Tiananmen massacre in 1989, the Work Committee ordered his removal in the name of the Xinhua News Agency.[46]

Apart from spreading propaganda through the media, the main thrust of united-front work in Hong Kong involves building up networks of personal contacts. These contacts are then used to neutralize some of the Communist Party's critics. In the 1980s, Xu Jiatun himself took the lead in dining, wining and charming Hong Kong's community leaders, intellectuals and opinion makers.[47] Even those who declined dinner invitations received rare fruits from the Chinese interior, presented with a handwritten message from Xu. As one local academic admitted, he could not send the fruit back without being offensive, so he accepted it. He also understood the message — 'to be kinder to the Communists' in his writings.[48]

To extend the party's reach and the effect of its united-front work, in 1985 Xu set up three Xinhua News Agency regional offices — on Hong Kong island, in Kowloon and in the New Territories.[49] They all work for the same goal among the lower-level community leaders. Though its existence was an open secret by the 1980s, the Work Committee continues to discharge its clandestine duties surreptitiously. These include recruiting local members, intelligence work and coordinating and supervising friendly labour unions. The exact strength of the communist presence in Hong Kong is unknown. Xu, who gives the most reliable figure, reported a network of 6000 party members in Hong Kong and Macao in the mid-1980s, of whom half had been sent from the PRC.[50]

The proliferation of PRC organizations in Hong Kong and their practice of reporting directly to Beijing means that the Work Committee cannot always function effectively as the coordinating umbrella body. This lack of a clear chain of command has created confusion, friction and often rivalries among various agencies and officials at different levels.[51] In his memoirs, Xu recalls that his deputy secretary, Li Jusheng, who belonged to a different *xitong* but officially represented the Work Committee in the Sino–British negotiations of 1982–4, kept him in the dark about the negotiations.[52] Xu had to get the information from meetings in Beijing and through his own *xitong*. His memoirs confirm that rivalries among cadres responsible for Hong Kong could be intense, bitter and, in his case, actually instrumental in bringing about his own downfall in 1990. Policy recommendations for Hong Kong thus sometimes reflect the senior cadres' rivalries and power struggles rather than their best advice.

The lack of an effective central coordinating body in Hong Kong makes it possible for individual cadres to work for several agencies separately without informing their superiors in Beijing. Thus, what the PRC government believes to be collaborative evidence from different intelligence sources sometimes comes from the same informant who 'supplies intelligence to different offices and takes money from them separately'.[53] Competition and rivalries among various agencies and senior cadres mean that they are reluctant to contradict views held by their superiors unless their own interests are at stake and this makes the problem worse.[54] As illustrated in Chapter 5, top leaders in Beijing, including Deng himself, tend to dismiss honest reflections of public opinion by the few Hong Kong visitors who dare to speak the truth. With little or no first-hand experience of present-day Hong Kong, the top leaders are generally a lot less well informed than they realize.[55] Given the concentration of decision-making power in their hands, top leaders with an insufficient or poor understanding of the situation in Hong Kong sometimes make policies on the basis of patchy information.

Drafting the Basic Law

Whatever importance one may lay on the Sino–British Joint Declaration as an international agreement to protect Hong Kong's way of life, its implementation requires the promulgation and enforcement of the Basic Law for the Hong Kong SAR. According to the terms of the Joint Declaration, this new constitutional instrument should simply stipulate the terms of its Annexe I in an appropriate legal form.[56] The PRC leaders had no intention of breaching the Joint Declaration. However, when they started to work on the Basic Law, they did not accept, in a metaphorical sense, that it was the son of the Joint Declaration. In the light of its rigid view of sovereignty, the PRC deemed the Basic Law a subsidiary of its own constitution.[57] Its drafting was consequently entirely a matter for the PRC itself to decide. The only concession Beijing was willing to make was to accept that the British government could offer constructive comments about what it would handle as it saw fit. To the Chinese leaders, the real issue was how to make the Basic Law serve their best interests rather than fulfil the commitments made in the Joint Declaration.

Both Hong Kong and the PRC regarded the drafting of the Basic Law as a matter of great importance. To the people of Hong Kong, for whom it was the litmus test of the PRC's sincerity, it was about how to preserve their 'system' and way of life for 50 years. To the PRC, it provided an opportunity to lay down the perimeters of Hong Kong's autonomy after retrocession. It also gave them a chance to win over the support of the local residents. Indeed, it was pivotal to the PRC's united-front work towards resuming sovereignty and retaining Hong Kong's utilities. It was for this reason that the PRC devoted considerable human resources to it and set aside a period of over four years in which to complete the process.

The PRC leaders realized that, in the mid-1980s, the people of Hong Kong were sceptical about their sincerity and ability to take over Hong Kong and preserve its way of life. However, in the light of Hong Kong's importance, they were prepared to go a long way towards persuading the local people of their sincerity. To allow their cadres sufficient time to do the united-front work properly, they set aside a long period for drafting. They tried to enhance public confidence by arranging for the National People's Congress (NPC) to appoint a committee of specially co-opted Hong Kong members to draft the Basic Law for the SAR.[58] The Basic Law Drafting Committee (BLDC) came into existence on 1 July 1985 with 59 members.[59] To ensure that it would be seen as having been drawn up 'democratically', the PRC also appointed a consultative committee of local residents.

The composition of the BLDC was carefully worked out. It had to contain a sufficiently large representation of Hong Kong residents to give it a democratic façade, but not large enough to oppose the PRC's will. In accordance with usual Communist

Party practice, the Hong Kong and Macao Work Committee compiled the list, which the top leaders approved before the individuals in question were invited to serve.[60] On the Work Committee's recommendation, 23 of the members, or just under 40 per cent, were selected from among Hong Kong's residents. This gave what was deemed an appropriate representation from different sectors of the local community.

The PRC chose this percentage because it only just provided the two-thirds majority needed if united Hong Kong members were to control more than two-thirds of the votes. This was what they needed to oppose the mainland members on important matters.[61] However, at least two of the 23 Hong Kong members could not be counted as free agents because they represented organizations under Communist Party control. They were the publisher of *Ta Kung Pao* and the deputy head of the Federation of Trade Unions.[62] In other words, on matters of importance only 21 members could not always be counted on to vote for the Communist Party. The members also disagreed with each other on many issues, which was partly why they were selected. In some cases, their backgrounds and political persuasions were so different that it was more difficult for them to work with each other than with PRC cadres.[63]

The PRC's concern to sustain Hong Kong's economic utilities also influenced its choice of local members. Ironically, of the 23 Hong Kong members the Communist Party nominated, only two were union leaders. The party preferred to give the business tycoons a stronger say. After all, it needed to secure their investments. Furthermore, in line with united-front practice, the Communist Party also offered membership to one of its most vocal local critics, Martin Lee. Xu Jiatun of the Work Committee was confident that including Lee would be preferable to excluding him.[64] It would be easier to contain his criticisms inside than outside the BLDC's confidential working atmosphere. Making Lee a party to the drafting process would also make it easier to persuade the rest of the Hong Kong community that the Basic Law was good for them.

Ultimate control of the BLDC rested in the hands of senior PRC cadres normally responsible for Hong Kong policies. This was despite the fact that, strictly speaking, the BLDC was an NPC and not a State Council special committee. Ji Pengfei, the director of the HKMAO, chaired the committee and his deputy, Li Hou, headed the BLDC secretariat. The other members of the secretariat were also senior cadres from the HKMAO and the Work Committee. Not surprisingly, the head of the Work Committee, Xu Jiatun, was a deputy chairperson of the BLDC. In other words, among the three ministerial-rank cadres responsible for Hong Kong policy, all except the foreign minister occupied leading positions on the BLDC. Their dominance was unquestionable, however much they claimed to be willing to listen to other members. This of course did not eliminate the rivalries among various PRC cadres and their respective *xitong*s. In any event, they had the numerically superior backing of the mainland drafters. These were mostly members of the Communist Party and, as such, had to observe party discipline. There was no danger of errant Hong Kong drafters violating them over matters that threatened the basic interests of the Communist Party or PRC.

The guiding hand of PRC cadres was also behind the form-ation of the Basic Law Consultative Committee (BLCC). Like the BLDC, it too was intended to be a major instrument for united-front work. The Work Committee therefore carefully planned its size and composition.[65] As a purely consultative body, the Communist Party could afford to fill its 180 seats with Hong Kong residents only. For example, the Work Com-mittee invited prominent local citizens it could not trust on the BLDC to join the BLCC. The BLCC also provided a means of reaching out to Hong Kong's so-called pro-British and Kuomin-tang elements. Although the Work Committee's attempt to neutralize their open opposition failed, those who were invited found it difficult not to soften their stand towards the BLCC.

Despite the Chinese cadres' deliberate efforts to give the selection of the BLCC a democratic façade, the true nature of the exercise was revealed in December 1985. This occurred during a meeting to prepare for the inauguration of the committee. To counter the impression that communist cadres ran the whole process, they entrusted the Hong Kong vice-chairman of the BLDC, Sir Y. K. Pao, to chair the preparatory meeting. Its purpose was to elect an executive board of 19 from among members; they considered Pao to be sound. Their strategy backfired. To begin with, Pao was not a member of the BLCC and therefore, according to its charter, had no authority to chair the meeting.[66] His high position in the BLDC was completely irrelevant because, as Jei Pengfei put it, 'there was no question of one [committee] being subordinate to' the other.[67] Furthermore, Pao ignored the agreed procedures and proceeded to read out a list of 19 names and directed the meeting to elect them with a round of applause.[68]

The process revealed the invisible hand of the Communist Party. The list had been agreed beforehand and, as was usual practice inside the PRC, those elected had already been consulted. They unwittingly ignored the due process because, as Xu Jiatun admitted in retrospect, those concerned, including himself, lacked any appreciation of the democratic procedure.[69] They later rectified the problem by holding another meeting during which they produced the same list and duly elected those whose names appeared on it. While this showed the PRC leadership's willingness to respond to the public outrage, it also demonstrated the extent of the Communist Party's influence. Once they had publicly invested their reputation, albeit unintentionally, on their choice of the BLCC Executive Board, members of the BLCC felt they had no choice but to acquiesce.

To ensure that the BLCC behaved responsibly and did not damage the vital task of recovering Hong Kong, the Communist Party kept it under its guidance, though not always directly. The first instrument was the BLDC, despite Ji's public statement that the BLCC was not subordinate to it. Notwithstanding its rhetoric, the PRC tried to ensure that leading BLDC figures would strongly direct the BLCC's leadership. The

PRC expected the former to steer the BLCC towards supporting the Basic Law and to become personally involved in its formulation. Hence, six of them were appointed to the BLCC's Executive Board, one of whom (Dr T. K. Ann) was even 'elected' chairperson.

The vital task of handling the paperwork was first entrusted to Mao Junnian, a member of the Work Committee and deputy secretary-general of the BLDC. The intention was clearly that the BLCC should support rather than be independent of the BLDC. Once the Communist Party felt more confident of its ability to direct the BLCC's work, it allowed a non-communist to replace Mao. Although the new secretary-general of the BLCC, Leung Chun-ying, was born in Hong Kong, he had by then built up a reputation as a staunch opponent of democratic change.[70] Leung's own political conviction was such that the Communist Party regarded him as a safe pair of hands in which to entrust the Basic Law.

The principle behind the procedure for drafting the Basic Law, the so-called 'two ups and two downs' approach, was based on Mao Zedong's idea of 'from the masses to the masses'. The Maoist axiom requires the Communist Party to 'take the ideas of the masses (scattered and unsystematic ideas) and concentrate them (through study turn them into concentrated and systematic ideas), then go to the masses and propagate and explain these ideas until the masses embrace them as their own, hold fast to them and translate them into action'. It then needs to repeat the process 'so that the ideas are persevered in and carried through'.[71]

By combining this principle with that of the united front and adapting the end product to Hong Kong's circumstances, the PRC leaders devised a basic policy for drafting the Basic Law. This entailed having the local people conduct the drafting process with the invisible hand of the Communist Party guiding them. They would produce a draft for submission to Beijing, which the PRC would then send back to Hong Kong for public consultation. The local people would then complete the drafting work and resubmit the Basic Law to Beijing for formal promulgation.

The communist cadres did, however, considerably adapt their work style to make the whole drafting process acceptable to their Hong Kong colleagues. In the early stage of the drafting process, the BLDC secretariat, which communist cadres controlled, followed standard PRC procedure. They prepared an important document about the structure of the Basic Law and circulated it among leading BLDC members. When this came to the attention of a Hong Kong member (Dorothy Liu), who had no such privileged access, she openly criticized the practice as undemocratic. In response, the communist cadres agreed to change the procedure and appoint two co-convenors to each of the BLDC task groups, one of whom would always be a Hong Kong person.[72]

This accommodation to the specific demands of Hong Kong members did not mean that the PRC cadres were prepared to relinquish control. What they did was to give the impression that both co-convenors were equal. The Hong Kong convenors might even be seen as the more dominant, for they were expected to be more activist than the PRC ones, particularly in public. The relationship between the two co-convenors was similar to that between a military commander and a political commissar in the People's Liberation Army (PLA).[73] In this analogy, the Hong Kong convenor is the military commander and the mainland convenor the commissar. While both have the same institutional status, the first is expected to 'command', whereas the latter is there to ensure that political mistakes are not made.

For the actual drafting of the Basic Law, the BLDC was divided into five task groups. To the PRC, the two most important of these were the ones responsible for the political system and for working out relations between the central government and the SAR. The BLDC members allocated to these specific task groups were also senior communist cadres. Li Hou, Lu Ping, Zhou Nan and Ke Zaishuo, who were of deputy ministerial or at least ambassadorial rank, were all assigned to these two groups and not to any of the others.[74] The remaining three groups dealt respectively with the rights of the residents of the SAR; economic and financial matters; and education, science, technology, culture, sports and religion. These groups were also important, but since they did not deal with matters of sovereignty, the PRC leaders could afford to be more relaxed about them. Indeed, the main issue for them was how to ensure that existing policies in these areas were preserved in a constitutional document.

The task groups working on central government–SAR relations and on the political system had to define the exact scope of the autonomy Hong Kong was to enjoy. This was a testing task for all the Hong Kong members, who had to play the more active role. It was particularly demanding of the two Hong Kong co-convenors, Dr Rayson Huang and Dr Louis Cha. There was a tacit understanding that Hong Kong would have relatively little room for manœuvre in relations between the central government and the SAR. There was no such understanding over the question of political developments. Thus, as co-convenor of the political system task group, Cha had the most difficult and sensitive job. He and his group had to function while the Hong Kong government was introducing an element of representative government and then reviewing the progress of its reforms. This was also the time when the rest of Hong Kong was openly debating democratization. Cha and his group needed to balance local demands against what Beijing would actually tolerate.

The torrent of public criticism levelled at Cha when he tried to steer the BLDC towards accepting a compromise, illustrates how difficult his task really was. This was before the Tiananmen massacre in Beijing in 1989, over which he resigned from the BLDC. In many ways, for both Hong Kong and the PRC, Cha was the best possible choice for the position. He is a distinguished novelist, intellectual and billionaire, whose vast fortune has given him a strong vested interest in making sure that the transition succeeds. He learned about communist ways of doing things when he worked as a young journalist for the communist-dominated *Ta Kung Pao*. By the early 1980s he had already built up a formidable reputation as an independent journalist who had been highly critical of the PRC under Mao, but enjoyed access to senior Chinese leaders under Deng.

When he joined the BLDC, he was someone who commanded great respect, both as an individual and for his judgements on Chinese and Hong Kong politics. His commitment to Hong Kong was also well known. If anyone could find a compromise political system acceptable to both Hong Kong and the PRC, it would be Cha. When the Hong Kong members of the BLDC were unable to resolve their differences over the pace and scope of democratization in late 1988, it was Cha who attempted to find a compromise solution. He did not aim to resolve the Hong Kong drafters' differences. The compromise he sought was one that would give Hong Kong sufficient democratization to sustain its existing way of life and yet prove acceptable to Beijing. As a realist, he saw the latter as of primary importance, since Beijing would never permit the SAR to introduce a system of which it disapproved.

Consequently, he produced a set of proposals that included as many democratic elements as possible but touched the PRC bottom line, which he ascertained from senior PRC cadres, including Xu Jiatun.[75] His proposals would not give democracy to Hong Kong until at least 2011, when a referendum would be held to decide the matter.[76] Meanwhile, they would allow Hong Kong's existing system to become more representative and would commit the PRC to respect such a development. Although the BLDC adopted his proposals — with an amendment to make the conditions for the referendum more restrictive — they provoked vehement attacks from the Hong Kong media.[77] By the late 1980s there was already a strong undercurrent favouring democracy in Hong Kong.

Though the majority of local people remained silent, they undoubtedly shared the broad sentiments of the media's opinion leaders, who generally supported democracy. They felt that Cha had let them down badly. An important difference divided them from him. They saw democracy as a goal permitted in the Joint Declaration and were less sensitive to what Beijing would allow. They simply wanted democracy for Hong Kong and expected Beijing to tolerate it. Cha believed Hong Kong's best interest lay less in developing full democracy (which he judged intolerable to Beijing) than in tying down the PRC to respect a political system in the SAR that would permit at least some democratic representation. The public's criticism of Cha reflected the great gap that lay between the PRC leadership and Hong Kong people's wishes.

The political crisis that erupted in Beijing in the spring and early summer of 1989 briefly interrupted and significantly affected the drafting process. The Tiananmen incident and its general ramifications for Hong Kong are examined in the next chapter. Suffice to stress here that it badly shook the PRC leadership's previous confidence in the 'one country, two systems' model. When Communist Party rule in China became threatened, the PRC expelled Martin Lee and Szeto Wah from the BLDC. These two men were the BLDC's leading advocates for a faster pace of democratization. The Communist Party linked their calls for democratization in Hong Kong to their other role as leaders of the Alliance in Support of the Patriotic and Democratic Movement in China. This organization supported challengers to the party's supremacy within the PRC. The Communist Party responded to the blow to its confidence by tightening its control over the drafting process and by adding provisions to enhance the PRC's control over the SAR in the Basic Law.[78]

The president of the PRC promulgated the Basic Law after the NPC adopted it in April 1990. According to the Basic Law, Article 31 of the PRC constitution of 1982 provided the basis for its enactment. This permits the state to 'establish special administrative regions when necessary' and to do so 'by law enacted by the National People's Congress in light of the specific conditions'.[79] Strictly speaking, whether this can provide the necessary constitutional authority is at best doubtful. Article 1 of the constitution states that 'the People's Republic of China is a socialist state' and adds that 'sabotage of the socialist system by any organization or individual is prohibited'.[80] Article 5 further stipulates that 'the state upholds the uniformity and dignity of the socialist legal system' and 'no law or administrative or local rules and regulations shall contravene the Constitution'.[81]

In the common law tradition, the three articles together suggest that the NPC can establish an SAR, but that the SAR must nevertheless practise and uphold the socialist system. Article 4 of the Basic Law, which stipulates that 'the socialist system and policies shall not be practised in the Hong Kong Special Administrative Region', must therefore be unconstitutional. However, since the PRC is still a Communist Party state and thus considers the Hong Kong question above all a political issue, such a legalistic view is merely of academic importance. Indeed, none of the PRC's four constitutions since 1949 contains an effective procedure for independent review of a law's constitutionality.[82] More important, the entire PRC establishment holds that the Basic Law is completely in line with the constitution.[83] Since Hong Kong wishes to minimize interference from the PRC, it does not serve its best interests by challenging the legality of the Basic Law.

The Basic Law's drafting process is a good illustration of how the PRC's approach to allowing maximum flexibility within a rigid framework works in practice. While much of the thinking behind the PRC's approach originated in communist practices, these were adapted whenever possible to meet Hong Kong's demands. This was done so skilfully that most people, including politicians and political analysts in Hong Kong, do not realize that the guiding principles behind the drafting process are based on Mao's ideas of the mass line and the united front. The PRC's bottom line was that it could not allow its ultimate control to be undermined: it was a matter of sovereignty. Once it was satisfied on this front, the PRC was prepared to consider all other demands made by the local people.

By and large, the PRC commits itself in the Basic Law to recreate in the SAR a Chinese version of the British Crown Colony system of government that existed in Hong Kong in the 1980s. This may have fallen short of public expectations, for by then the people of Hong Kong wanted a more democratic system of government. There are also specific provisions in the Basic Law that are problematic. However, the drafting process has demonstrated the amount of flexibility Beijing is willing to exercise to ensure a successful takeover of Hong Kong.

8. The Tiananmen Factor: 1989–91

D
evelopments north of the border, in the PRC, made 1989 a traumatic year for Hong Kong. Deng Xiaoping's post-Mao reforms, encapsulated in the four modernizations—agriculture, industry, science and technology, and national defence — had entered a critical stage.

Turmoil in Beijing

The four modernizations were first announced in 1975, when Mao Zedong was still alive, but they only became the key policy when Deng emerged as paramount leader towards the end of the 1970s.[1] Deng and his comrades in the Chinese Communist Party planned to modernize these four specific sectors. However, they had no such intentions for the country as a whole. They recognized they had much to learn from the advanced West, but did not wish to import anything they considered undesirable, particularly ideas about democracy, human rights and freedom. In short, they wanted to introduce 'economic improvement without systemic change'.[2] It was one thing to import capitalist methods to help enrich the PRC and entrench party rule; it was a totally different matter to allow Western ideas to infiltrate the PRC and challenge the party–state and their own power.

Their attitude notwithstanding, like any other country, the PRC is an organic entity. It is impossible to modernize specific parts of it without this having some impact on the rest of the structure. By the beginning of 1989, enough reforms had taken place in the PRC, particularly economic ones, to generate a demand to see political reform put on the national agenda. This essentially was at the root of the crisis that faced the PRC and its leadership in that momentous year.

More specifically, with the introduction of Deng's economic reforms, the Communist Party's control became more relaxed. A money-oriented mentality developed in the party and in the society at large. Corruption spread rapidly and, despite anti-corruption campaigns, even implicated leaders holding responsible positions.[3] Those who were widely believed to be corrupt included not only senior cadres like Chen Xitong, mayor of Beijing, but also Zhao Ziyang, who was general secretary of the party at that time. The intellectuals, who resented the rise of a new privileged class openly flaunting its ill-gotten wealth, were the first to protest, albeit gingerly. Their writings were censored and a few were also expelled from the party, but they were not subjected to the full rigour of the Maoist totalitarian terror.[4] They became bolder.

At this point Deng's economic reforms ran into difficulties. The most serious of these were high unemployment and high inflation. Unemployment in the major cities rose to between 14 and 25 per cent; and in the first half of 1989 prices increased by 25.5 per cent.[5] The Dengist reforms had created huge inequalities, which contrasted sharply with the apparent egalitarianism of the Maoist era. As the economy slowed down, this put an undue burden on the poor. As 1989 dawned, the PRC was 'a tinderbox of suppressed anger, mounting despair and corrosive envy'.[6]

Hu Yaobang had been Deng's right-hand man when he had launched his reforms a decade earlier. However, when he urged Deng to step down in 1987, he was sacked as general secretary of the Communist Party. When he died, disaffected elements decided to take advantage of his funeral to test party–state reactions to a protest movement.[7] University students were among those who felt alienated: they were dissatisfied with their living conditions.[8] To many students, Hu stood out as the last of the non-corrupt top communist leaders. His death on 15 April thus symbolized the loss of what they saw as 'their last hope for a good leader'.[9] Although the students were initially driven primarily by self-interest, they acted within the perimeters of Chinese political culture and used high sounding, moralistic slogans to support their cause. Their appeals elicited the support of the general public in Beijing and Tiananmen Square, where their demonstrations were centred, became a major political theatre.[10]

Once it developed its own momentum, the student movement quickly underwent a transformation. Public endorsement made student leaders feel they were following in the footsteps of the May Fourth Movement of 1919. This was when, on 4 May some 70 years earlier, Beijing university students organized China's first modern mass student demonstration against the then government's failure to defend China's national interest at the Versailles Peace Conference. Ever since, it has been hailed as a selfless movement of national salvation by young intellectuals. Seeing themselves as successors to the May Fourth generation, students acted to 'proclaim their superior moral righteousness', but in so doing stripped the communist leadership of its claim to probity.[11] They thus turned their efforts to improve conditions on the campuses into a challenge to the legitimacy of the party–state.

The challenge mounted in seriousness when ordinary citizens rallied behind the student demonstrators. They then raised the stakes by staging hunger strikes and calling for top leaders to step down, including Deng Xiaoping.[12] The communist leadership's self-control during the early stage of the protest had unwittingly heartened the protesters and the whole process escalated further.[13] The party–state's restraint was mainly the result of being paralysed for a short time by an intense power struggle at the top. The upshot of this was that, by 20 May the relatively moderate general secretary of the party, Zhao Ziyang, had been ousted and martial law was imposed. With more than a million demonstrators peacefully resisting the army and some dissent within the military leadership over the use of force, the enforcement of martial law was attempted, but only half-heartedly. However, it was only a matter of time before the party–state would unleash the full force of its might against the protesters.

Not only the so-called hard-liners, but Deng himself, firmly believed that the protesters 'had two objectives — to overthrow the Communist Party and to topple the socialist system'.[14] In other words, the top communist leadership had come to see the protest movement as 'a life and death' struggle for the party.[15] Thus, towards the end of May, as President Yang Shangkun told the Central Military Commission, the only matter of real importance was to make sure the army would stand solidly behind the leadership and obey orders for which individual commanders were held personally responsible.[16] Senior cadres who understood the nature of the party–state had by then realized a forceful suppression was in the making.[17]

'Today Beijing, Tomorrow Hong Kong'

When the student movement erupted in Beijing, an increasing number of people in Hong Kong came to identify with what the media soon portrayed as a 'democracy movement'. The people of Hong Kong had come to feel increasingly frustrated and helpless about the PRC side-tracking the Sino–British Joint Declaration and restricting democratic developments. As a result, public confidence was falling steadily and ordinary people were losing trust in the governments of Hong Kong, Britain and the PRC.[18] Many had wanted to do something positive and recognized that the key to their future lay in Beijing. However, being unfamiliar with and somewhat intimidated by PRC politics, they did not know how to go about doing it or indeed what to do. Thus, when the student demonstrations in Beijing started, they watched with keen interest.

As the students took their initial bold steps, many people in Hong Kong held their breath and prayed for them. When the students and citizens of Beijing gained ground, interest in

Hong Kong heightened — it raised their own hopes. By then, there was a widespread belief that 'as long as freedom, human rights, and democracy cannot be guaranteed in the PRC, they cannot be protected in Hong Kong after 1997'.[19] Consequently, an unspoken common front emerged between the people of Hong Kong and the Beijing demonstrators. Admiration and support, including generous donations, built up quickly. The Beijing protesters were in a sense also fighting Hong Kong's battle with the feared communist party–state. There was so much emotion and hope invested in the movement that most Hong Kong residents simply took it for granted that the student leaders were courageous, dedicated, honest, selfless and democratic. Their journalists reporting from Beijing not only shared this sentiment but reinforced it.

Some had become too emotionally involved to see the reality. Others chose to ignore the many serious shortcomings various student leaders exhibited. Wang Dan was one of the more thoughtful and honest student leaders. He admitted retrospectively that, although they had 'been called "soldiers of democracy" and "stars of democracy"', they did 'not have a "working" knowledge of real, operating democracy'. They also did 'not understand how to establish and implement democracy'.[20] On the whole, they used communist methods to organize the movement. Even the mendacity that characterized communist rule in the PRC found an echo in the student leadership. It was known at the time that 'a lot of students were cheating during the hunger strike'.[21] Wu'er Kaixi, for example, a student leader who became the darling of the Hong Kong and Western media, ate noodles at night during his hunger strike 'because as a "leader" he needed to conserve his strength'.[22]

Chai Ling, who together with Wu'er Kaixi topped the communists' most wanted list after the crackdown, was at least as equally defective as a leader. A few days before the massacre she admitted that 'what we actually are hoping for is bloodshed'. As she put it, 'only when the Square is awash with blood will the people of China open their eyes' and 'really be united'.[23] She had no idea how this could promote democracy and no plan for leading the movement once her wish for blood turned into reality. She was also emphatic that under no circumstances should her own blood be shed. She was 'not going to be destroyed by this government' and she 'wanted to live'.[24] Neither Wu'er nor Chai saw any contradiction in their public attacks on the communist regime's lack of probity and their own readiness to compromise their own integrity. They seemed quite prepared to sacrifice their supporters for no greater cause than to make a political point.

The behaviour of these and other, though not all, student leaders, should have cast a long shadow of doubt over whether they represented the sort of future Hong Kong wanted. However, in the heady days of the early summer of 1989, the people of Hong Kong did not want to hear about the dark side of the student movement, or indeed of anything else. They, along with their reporters and most of their international colleagues, chose to turn a blind eye.[25] They wanted to believe in a bright future for the PRC and thus for Hong Kong too.

When the movement in Beijing came under serious threat, the already strong support of the people of Hong Kong suddenly mushroomed. Premier Li Peng's imposition of martial law on 20 May galvanized them into action. On the following day, the people of Hong Kong showed their solidarity with the Beijing protesters. They staged an unprecedentedly massive sympathy demonstration of up to 500,000 residents (out of a total population of fewer than 6 million at that time).[26] Even communist cadres and their close supporters in Hong Kong gave their backing to the student protesters, seeing the unfolding events as a great patriotic movement.[27] In Hong Kong, there was a general feeling that what was happening in Beijing would have major (though as yet not clearly defined) implications for its own future.

On the night of 3/4 June 1989, the PLA executed the orders of the top communist leaders (led by Deng) and carried out a massacre. It used excessive and indiscriminate force to suppress the Beijing protest movement centred on Tiananmen Square. The communist leaders intended not only to disperse the demonstrators, but to teach them and the rest of the nation a lesson. Their message was that the party–state had the might to maintain power and the will to use it. It was a classic case of applying the old Chinese proverb of 'killing a cock to warn the monkey'. This public and bloody suppression was designed to pre-empt any similar protest movement in the future.

The brutal way in which army tanks mowed down peaceful protesters' tents and soldiers with automatic weapons opened fire on unarmed civilians were extraordinarily harsh measures to use to quell a civil demonstration. It was obvious that the armoured units were there for the rest of the nation to notice. The PLA's ferocity was captured on film and immediately relayed around the world, particularly by the electronic media. A large number of foreign correspondents had by then congregated in Beijing. Some had originally come to cover the state visit in mid-May of the Soviet Union's president, Mikhail Gorbachev. The whole world was stunned and dismayed by the massacre they saw on their television sets. The people of Hong Kong were utterly devastated.

As soon as they recovered from the initial shock, horror and disbelief, over half a million people went on a march in Hong Kong to mourn the dead and to express their anger at the PRC regime.[28] The spirit of the time was captured in the editorial of a local newspaper: 'In supporting the Beijing student movement, the people of Hong Kong had identified themselves completely with it. The recent marches, [fund-raising] concerts, sit-ins, and hunger-strikes have reflected the Hong Kong people's yearning for liberal-democracy—both for China and for Hong Kong.'[29]

If the earlier successes of the Beijing students had given the people of Hong Kong a ray of hope for the future, the tanks that rolled down Changan Avenue to Tiananmen Square shattered it. The brutal military crackdown raised the spectre that what happened in Beijing could well be the future for Hong

Kong in less than a decade down the line after the PRC's resumption of sovereignty.

Identity Crisis

It is important to understand Hong Kong's feelings about the Tiananmen incident in the context of the people's changing sense of identity. This has a bearing both on how they reacted to the massacre and what they saw as its implications for Hong Kong. When a peaceful demonstration in Beijing ended in a savage tragedy, it forced the people of Hong Kong to confront the problem of who they really were.

Prior to 1950, Chinese people were free to enter Hong Kong from China without restriction.[30] Until the communists came to power on the mainland, there were free and regular movements of people between the two places. Most ethnic Chinese residents of Hong Kong were either sojourners, economic migrants or refugees, and they were not noticeably different from their fellow inhabitants elsewhere in China.[31] The situation changed after 1949. The PRC and Hong Kong followed different routes as they developed. The movements of people between the two territories were reduced to a trickle, except for short periods when a relaxation of border controls by the PRC led to an influx of people into Hong Kong. This happened in 1962 and in the latter half of the 1970s. Communist rule in China had for the first time in its history turned the Chinese population of Hong Kong into a settled one. Those born and bred in Hong Kong since 1949 on the whole had no experiences of the PRC until the latter opened up in the late 1970s. By then, they had developed an identity and a political culture of their own. The older generations who had arrived as economic migrants or refugees also shared the experiences of the younger generations and became noticeably different from their mainland compatriots. As Hong Kong entered the 1980s, a local as distinct from a PRC identity clearly emerged.[32]

This Hong Kong identity rested on a shared outlook and a common popular culture. This blended traditional Chinese culture with overseas imports, with the influences of the USA, Britain and Japan being particularly noticeable. A Hong Kong person of the early 1980s would therefore identify with Hong Kong and, at the same time, feel at ease with both his Chinese heritage and his British nationality document.[33] Social anthropologist Hugh Baker described 'Hong Kong Man' as 'not British or western (merely westernized)'. At the same time, he was 'not Chinese in the same way that citizens of the People's Republic of China' were Chinese.[34] He belonged to Hong Kong and was intensely proud of it.

In the mid-1980s, with the signing of the Joint Declaration and the imminence of the retrocession, 'Hong Kong Man' began to change. In 1997, all Hong Kong residents of Chinese origin would become Chinese nationals. Since only a select few would be granted British citizenship, many of them began to feel they had no choice but to identify with China. The upshot was the gradual emergence of a dual identity—they belonged both to Hong Kong and to China. When a 'Hong Kong Man' referred to 'China' he was not always clear what he had in mind. Sometimes it meant China in a geographical or cultural sense, for which Hong Kong, Taiwan and Macao were deemed as much a part as the PRC. Sometimes 'China' meant the PRC. The average Hong Kong Man did not make a clear distinction between the two concepts and did not refer to them consistently.

In the realm of wider politics, this lack of clarity in their minds had important implications. On the one hand, as Hong Kong citizens, they wanted to preserve their own way of life under the 'one country, two systems' formula. This should have implied non-intervention into each other's affairs by both the PRC and Hong Kong. On the other hand, feeling that they were Chinese too, they believed they had a right to have a say in vital matters affecting the future of the nation, which in practice meant PRC politics. Few Hong Kong people could see the inherent contradiction between asserting their right to have a say in the politics of the PRC and their demand that the PRC should not interfere in Hong Kong's domestic affairs under the 'one country, two systems' principle.

The confused identity of most Hong Kong people and their resultant schizophrenic view of Sino–Hong Kong relations made it easy for them to make a vital transition in the first half of 1989. They swiftly shifted from a position of wanting to minimize any political dealings with the PRC—to forestall PRC interference in Hong Kong affairs—to wanting to play a meaningful though essentially supportive role in the Chinese 'democracy movement'. They became emotionally committed. When they stood behind the students they felt they were not just Hong Kong citizens, but Chinese ones as well. This is important because it made them feel righteous about demanding changes within the PRC in 1989.

Most Hong Kong people's identification with the 'democracy movement' turned them, in their own minds, into the student protesters' instant comrades. When tanks rolled into Tiananmen Square and PLA soldiers machine-gunned protesters in Beijing, on their televisions many people in Hong Kong saw *their* comrades fall. They felt just as anguished and outraged as Beijing citizens. They felt frustrated that there was little they could do to help: they could only watch in agony. However, they were also thankful that the Union flag flying over their heads in Hong Kong had saved them from their comrades' fate. This security and protection, which they craved, also gave them what one may perhaps call survivor's guilt. Consequently, they were prepared to do anything that might ease their conscience. In their scramble to donate blood, they overwhelmed the collection centres in Hong Kong. They also tried to force a run on PRC-owned banks in Hong Kong by withdrawing their deposits.[35] None of these actions could help the hapless protesters in Beijing or save the movement from being ground to dust. However, to an extent, they eased the intense pain brought about by their own failure to stand by their comrades under fire.

Their emotional commitment and sense of guilt also affected

their ability to put matters in perspective. Most people in Hong Kong found it difficult, if not impossible, to envisage that the PRC government could justifiably see their support for the 'democracy movement' as subversive.[36] It was clearly wrong and monstrous to suppress a peaceful demonstration so brutally. However, the communist party–state was the PRC's legitimate government and the Beijing protesters aimed to topple it by means other than those stipulated in their constitution. Perhaps such an approach was unavoidable in a power hungry and ruthless dictatorship.

For those living under the protection of the British flag, giving material support to people across the border to overthrow their legitimate government was clearly subversive. The PRC government could justifiably take it as an attempt to interfere in its domestic affairs—against the principle of 'one country, two systems'.[37] Technical definitions of 'subversion' apart, self-interest should have encouraged the people of Hong Kong to insulate themselves from volatile PRC politics to avoid provoking the wrath of big brother. The communist party–state had shown its true colours in Tiananmen Square. It should have been obvious to Hong Kong that the PRC would deal with it equally ruthlessly if it in any way threatened the continuation of the party–state after retrocession. Hong Kong's best chance of maintaining its system after 1997 lay in persuading the PRC leadership that it neither intended to nor would try to become such a menace. In the event, the people of Hong Kong were far too emotionally involved to consider such an option calmly.

The Tiananmen incident both brought the Hong Kong people's identity problem to a head and destroyed their confidence in their future. The political atmosphere was affected as a result. It did not mean the Hong Kong government or its people intended to abandon convergence as a policy but there was a general toughening in their attitude towards the PRC, particularly among the latter.

Rise of Confrontational Politics

While the Tiananmen massacre captured the world's imagination and had the greatest impact, the events leading up to it
were equally instrumental in making relations between the
PRC, Hong Kong and Britain more confrontational than at any
time since the Joint Declaration was signed in 1984. Although
the massacre created the crisis situation and forced the Hong
Kong and London governments to take remedial action, the
protest movement in Beijing was the critical factor affecting
PRC government policy. Though different parties saw the crisis
in Hong Kong differently, they all shared a common desire to
limit the damages. The main differences were between Beijing
and the two British administrations, but Hong Kong and
Britain also did not see everything eye to eye.

The crux of the matter for Britain was that the Tiananmen
massacre had created a confidence crisis in Hong Kong. In its
inquiry into the implementation of Britain's Hong Kong policy,
the House of Commons Foreign Affairs Committee noticed a
visible collapse of public confidence when the Tiananmen
incident unfolded. The incident made such an impact on Hong
Kong society, the committee reported, that there were 'calls to
tear up the agreement, reneging on the Joint Declaration and
breaking off all negotiations with China', but this was 'simply
not an option'.[38] Whatever had happened in Tiananmen
Square, the political reality for Britain was that it had neither
the resources nor the will to defend Hong Kong against a
Chinese attempt to take the territory. It was also unrealistic to
think that the PRC regime would make more concessions to
Britain or Hong Kong if the Joint Declaration were to be
annulled, especially so shortly after the military crackdown.

However, the Foreign Affairs Committee asked for a change
in the policy of convergence. The aim of this was to secure a
'through train' in the handover by conceding to the PRC's
demands to limit the pace and scope of democratization in
Hong Kong. Mindful of the need to restore public confidence,
it recommended 'that the Hong Kong Government must . . .

seize the initiative so as to establish in Hong Kong in advance of 1997 the institutions and systems best designed to guarantee Hong Kong's future autonomy and stability within the terms of the Joint Declaration'.[39] The committee also made other recommendations, all of which aimed to restore public confidence.

It based its calculations on the fact that there was no alternative to the Joint Declaration for British policy and that the PRC still wished to ensure a successful transition. It was therefore likely to cooperate and allow the British to do what would be necessary to restore confidence.[40] The committee did not advocate abandoning convergence as a policy. Rather, it wanted to push the clock back to before November 1985 when, at least to the British, convergence meant the two sides meeting in the middle. It belatedly challenged the British government's policy since that date, which was to allow the Chinese to define the scope and pace of political developments in Hong Kong before converging to meet the Chinese position.

In Hong Kong the confidence crisis was real. According to newspaper opinion surveys, 75 per cent of respondents were optimistic about the future in January 1989, but this had dropped to 52 per cent by September, three months after the massacre.[41] Another survey conducted a month later suggested that 70 per cent of the respondents had no confidence in the PRC honouring its pledge not to interfere in Hong Kong affairs after 1997.[42] A general view quickly emerged that three measures were needed to prevent the crisis deepening.

The first and most important was for the local people to have an opportunity to leave should the Chinese takeover turn out to be a disaster.[43] The idea was to provide the people of Hong Kong with a home of last resort in what came to be known as the 'Armageddon scenario'. This involved asking Britain to restore full citizenship, including the right of abode in the UK, to Hong Kong's 3.25 million British subjects and help the remaining 2.5 million secure a chance of settlement elsewhere if necessary.[44] The thought was that with an escape route provided, the people of Hong Kong who did not really want to leave could have the confidence to stay and the exodus of individuals essential for the territory's wellbeing could be reduced.

Moreover, the purpose of the proposal was to discourage the PRC government from importing Tiananmen-style solutions to Hong Kong. The departure of more than 3 million non-Chinese passport holders from Hong Kong amid the major international crisis it would inevitably provoke, would render such a gesture worthless.[45] Various Hong Kong groups lobbied for such a policy in London.[46] A group of economists led by Professor Bernard Corry of London University also carried out an independent study of the impact of mass emigration from Hong Kong to the UK. Its main conclusion was that 'such a migration is essentially manageable for the British economy, and in certain circumstances the outcome might be favourable to Britain'.[47]

Whatever the economic case or importance of this matter to Hong Kong, the British government rejected it firmly.[48] This was not because the arguments for such a measure were considered unconvincing. It was because of the powerful resistance led by Norman Tebbit, a political heavyweight in Margaret Thatcher's ruling Conservative Party, and opposition from the Labour Party.[49] The upshot was therefore a classic British compromise. It was to give UK citizenship to 50,000 key people holding essential positions in Hong Kong and their dependents to provide sufficient reassurance to persuade them to stay.[50] The British government's handling of the citizenship issue demonstrated the limit of its commitment to Hong Kong.

The second requirement, which this time the British adopted, was to accelerate the process of democratization.[51] Over this matter, Hong Kong's interests did not contradict those of Britain. As a leading democratic country in the modern world, Britain had no objections to promoting democracy in Hong Kong. Its hesitation before the Tiananmen incident was due to the perceived need to accommodate the PRC in exchange for the 'through train' arrangement. The real obstacles to democratization since the mid-1980s had been the PRC's attitude and the lack of a strongly expressed common view among the people of Hong Kong. Indeed, divisions between the so-called conservatives and democrats over the pace and scope of democratization characterized the general political situation in Hong Kong in the winter of 1988/9. A compromise between the two was out of the question.

This situation changed during the student movement in Beijing. The strong public emotions expressed in support of democracy generally and the highly responsible manner in which local people expressed their support for the Beijing movement, left their marks on local politicians. Any lingering doubt about whether the people of Hong Kong were ready for democracy was removed.[52] The turn of events persuaded both conservative and pro-democratic politicians to reach a compromise. Under the leadership of Lydia (now Baroness) Dunn, the Executive Council's most senior unofficial member, the unofficial members of both local councils (Legislative and Executive) reached a consensus.

They asked for direct elections for half the Legislative Council by 1997 and for the whole council by 2003. They also asked for the chief executive of the SAR government to be popularly elected no later than 2003.[53] They hoped that the common front they had obtained through reaching a consensus might persuade the PRC government to revise the draft Basic Law to accommodate their strongly expressed wish. The people of Hong Kong who gave general support to this consensus proposal did not intend to use it to confront the PRC authorities. However, the Chinese leadership viewed their firm stand on a matter Beijing had rejected earlier with suspicion.

With the swing of public opinion in Hong Kong and the British media encouraging Britain to give Hong Kong as much democracy as possible before handing over to the PRC, the British government raised the matter with the Chinese government. It did not, however, push very hard. While sympathetic to Hong Kong's case, Prime Minister Thatcher thought instinctively 'that this was the wrong time'.[54] Her top official adviser on Hong Kong, Sir Percy Cradock, shared this astute view. They believed a powerful push 'could have provoked a strong defensive reaction that might have undermined the Hong Kong Agreement'.[55]

Consequently, Thatcher secretly sent Cradock to Beijing to try to get the best deal possible within the framework of convergence in December 1989. The House of Commons Foreign Affairs Committee's recommendation that Hong Kong be given full democracy before 1997 did not change the British government's policy.[56] In Beijing, Cradock pleaded for 'sufficient flexibility in the Basic Law to accommodate the new situation'. In Hong Kong 'there was now a widespread desire for a substantial proportion of the legislature to be directly elected'.[57] The Chinese were tough, unyielding and deeply mistrustful of the British. All Cradock could secure was the possible prospect of 20 Legislative Council seats for direct elections in 1997.[58]

The British government pressed to turn this prospect into a specific commitment. By February 1990 it finally reached an understanding with the PRC government. It was for the British 'to limit to 18 the number of directly elected seats to be introduced in 1991'. In return, China would agree to extend to '20 directly elected seats in the SAR legislature in 1997, 24 in 1999, and 30 in 2003'. It would also 'observe the 1991 legislature in operation' and on that basis consider a faster pace of democratization.[59] This understanding fell significantly short of the consensus reached among Hong Kong's legislative and executive councillors, but represented a step forward. The net gain for Hong Kong was to increase the number of directly elected seats in the Legislative Council from 10 to 18 (out of a total membership of 60) in 1991. Its terms were duly incorporated into Annexe II of the Basic Law.

The third measure to restore confidence was non-controversial between London and Hong Kong. It was to introduce a bill of rights to enhance the legal basis for the protection of human rights in Hong Kong. The Joint Declaration requires the SAR government to 'protect the rights and freedoms of inhabitants and other persons in the Hong Kong Special Administrative Region according to law'.[60] However, the collapse of confidence meant that such a provision was generally deemed no longer adequate. The Hong Kong government therefore introduced a bill of rights 'to incorporate provisions of the International Covenant on Civil and Political Rights as applied to Hong Kong into the laws of Hong Kong'.[61] The objective was to strengthen the legal framework for protecting human rights before the takeover by the PRC. As a safeguard against Tiananmen-style repression, the bill of rights is no more effective than a glazed door against a determined intruder. Nevertheless, the need to restore confidence was so acute that this was a welcome gesture in Hong Kong.

In the immediate aftermath of the massacre, the PRC government also tried to stop Hong Kong's confidence crisis deepening. HKMAO director Ji Pengfei stated: 'I, on behalf of the Chinese government, solemnly declare that the Chinese government's policies towards Hong Kong and Macao, which have been formulated in line with the conception of "one country, two systems," will not change.'[62] This public reaffirmation of its basic policy did not alter the fact that the PRC leadership was very angry at and resentful of the support the people of Hong Kong had given the student protesters. From the communist leaders' point of view, the reality was that the

> student movement, turmoil and counter-revolution rebellion was orchestrated by a small number of people both inside and outside the Communist Party of China (CPC) who stubbornly clung to their bourgeois stand and engaged in political conspiracy in collaboration with some anti-communist and anti-socialist forces in the West, Taiwan and Hong Kong with the aim of overthrowing the leadership of the CPC, subverting the socialist People's Republic of China, and establishing in China a completely Westernized bourgeois republic.[63]

Even when he tried to dispel the fear among the people of Hong Kong, Ji could not resist reminding his audience that they had 'done something that is impermissible by the state Constitution and law and has in fact added fuel to the flames of turmoil'.[64] Chen Xitong, the mayor of Beijing who officially summed up the party–state's verdict on the incident, was particularly bitter about the money Hong Kong donated to the protesters, and the support the Hong Kong media gave to the students and to Zhao Ziyang.[65] In other words, the PRC leadership believed the people of Hong Kong attempted to subvert it even though, in line with the united-front approach, it only accused a small group of 'reactionaries' within Hong Kong of having done so. After the massacre it wanted to restore public confidence in Hong Kong, not because it thought the local residents there deserved help but because it was in the party–state interest to do so—Hong Kong was still the goose laying badly needed golden eggs.

The Chinese leadership was also bitter about Britain being the first to impose sanctions in response to what it saw as a purely internal affair.[66] It remained unconvinced by British claims that Hong Kong support for the protest movement was not part of a Western conspiracy. And, it did not believe that Britain had no intention of allowing Hong Kong to be used to subvert the PRC.[67] It could not understand the feelings of the people of Hong Kong.[68] Deng Xiaoping himself decided that the PRC should take a tough stand towards the British.[69] The PRC leadership therefore only gave limited cooperation to British attempts to restore confidence in Hong Kong.

Two other basic problems dampened the PRC leadership's willingness to cooperate with the British. First, to endorse any of the three British confidence boosting initiatives would have been an admission on its part that its actions in Tiananmen caused fear in Hong Kong. The communist leadership insisted on seeing the Tiananmen incident as the right and proper suppression of a counter-revolutionary movement. It would have been embarrassing for it to admit that such a justifiable and righteous defence of the communist 'revolution' could have destroyed public confidence in Hong Kong.

Second, and more fundamentally, the popular challenge to its authority in Beijing gravely weakened its self-confidence, which was further undermined as communism collapsed in eastern Europe in the winter of 1989/90.[70] As explained in Chapter 7, the PRC government was hitherto willing to exercise maximum flexibility towards Hong Kong, albeit within a rigid framework, because it had tremendous faith in the superiority of its own system. Now that this confidence was seriously undermined, it reduced the scope of flexibility and looked at Hong Kong with suspicion.

In policy terms, after the military crackdown, PRC leaders sought to neutralize anyone in Hong Kong who posed a challenge to them during the protest movement. On the other hand, they also tried to prevent any further loss of confidence there. Their first task was to rectify the communist organizations in Hong Kong, which had wavered in their support for the top leaders. Another urgent task was to destroy the main Hong Kong organization that had supported the Beijing protesters. Because the Communist Party's Work Committee still operated mainly underground, the rectification work was on the whole carried out secretly. However, it did eventually result in the removal of Xu Jiatun as its head. Xu was seen as having been too soft during the Tiananmen incident and too close to Zhao Ziyang.[71]

Of the Hong Kong organizations, the main target of attack was the Alliance in Support of the Patriotic and Democratic Movement in China, which Szeto Wah and Martin Lee had founded. The Chinese asked the British government to proscribe it, but the latter politely refused on the grounds that there was no legal basis for such an action.[72] The PRC leaders then tried to intimidate the organization's supporters into abandoning it, and attempted to isolate Szeto and Lee by naming them as subversives.[73] The two were also expelled from the BLDC. The intimidation backfired, for it actually encouraged many local people to rally around the two men and their organization. When work on the Basic Law was resumed, the PRC leaders introduced new provisions, including a clause on subversion, to strengthen their ability to control events in the SAR before they finalized the Basic Law.[74] In the interests of maintaining confidence, the PRC authorities decided not to punish Hong Kong any harder for its involvement in the Tiananmen incident.

In terms of Sino–Hong Kong relations, the Tiananmen incident gave rise to more confrontational politics. The British confidence boosting measures continued to remind everybody of the massacre. For a couple of years, they turned the PRC into a pariah in the international community. The PRC government responded to these measures by becoming more confrontational than at any time since 1984. The PRC nullified the British scheme to give 50,000 Hong Kong families the right of abode in the UK. The Chinese response to Britain's announcement of a bill of rights was that they would disregard it after 1997.

The only exception was over the composition of the legislature, which was not a unilateral British action but the result of secret diplomacy. As the British avoided a public confrontation, the PRC government did not feel it had to react defensively and therefore negatively.[75] The compromise, which was to add eight directly elected seats to the legislature in 1991 and a further two by 1997, was also acceptable to the Chinese because its effect was marginal. Since Hong Kong's legislature had 60 seats, allowing 20 rather than 10 to be directly elected was of little import. It would neither bring democracy to Hong Kong nor decisively reduce the PRC's scope to manipulate the SAR legislature if necessary.

Moreover, with the Basic Law not yet finalized, the PRC could disguise the limited concession it had made. It could do this by incorporating the changes into the Basic Law and then claim credit for its willingness to accommodate public opinion in Hong Kong. Sino–Hong Kong relations became more confrontational in the aftermath of Tiananmen, but this was not something either side wanted. It happened because the British side needed to rebuild public confidence in Hong Kong and the Chinese were suspicious of British intentions and defensive of their own record over Tiananmen.

Status Quo Ante?

Once the dust had settled over the Tiananmen incident, British officials handling Hong Kong affairs were keen to restore Sino–British relations. Sir David Wilson, the governor of Hong Kong, stressed in his first post-Tiananmen state of the territory address that Hong Kong and the PRC 'need to restore mutual trust as the necessary cornerstone for the unprecedented political experiment that will begin in 1997'.[76] Wilson's approach was very much in line with the thinking of Cradock, who remained the most senior official coordinating Britain's Hong Kong policy on a daily basis in London.[77]

Although there were difficult problems between Britain and the PRC over Hong Kong even before 1989, they were largely resolved through negotiations and compromises, albeit mainly at Hong Kong or Britain's expense. Apart from the decline in public confidence over the Joint Declaration, which predated the Tiananmen incident, the state of Sino–British cooperation provided a framework for discussing the future of Hong Kong that was satisfactory for both the British and the Chinese governments. The PRC authorities at first acquiesced in Britain's attempt to put the clock back in their relations to before 1989. However, the scars of the Tiananmen incident on the people of Hong Kong were too deep for them to accept a restoration of the *status quo ante*.

Rightly or wrongly the people of Hong Kong were known not for their political activism but for their apathy.[78] The massive sympathy demonstrations staged in Hong Kong during the Tiananmen incident were often seen as an aberration. There was therefore a lingering view that once the memories of the horror of the Tiananmen crackdown receded the people of

Hong Kong would return to political apathy. This was put to the test in the first ever direct elections to return 18 of the 60 legislative councillors in September 1991.

The elections dissipated any hope of the Hong Kong people putting the Tiananmen incident behind them. The single most important electoral issue was the so-called '1997 issue', which in practice meant the candidate's attitude to the PRC and the Tiananmen incident.[79] All the candidates who campaigned on a pro-PRC platform were defeated for this reason.[80] The pro-democracy parties and groups had a landslide victory. They won 58 per cent of the votes and 15 of the 18 seats.[81] The United Democrats of Hong Kong, which Martin Lee and Szeto Wah had organized into a political party only a little over a year earlier, did particularly well. It alone won 12 seats.

Ironically, by being branded 'subversives', Lee and Szeto's party gained a reputation for being a champion for democracy. It could not have delivered democracy to Hong Kong even if it had won all 18 seats. The election results were indicative of the mood of the local people, for an unusually high 48 per cent of eligible voters cast their ballots.[82] This is considered high for Hong Kong, for, unlike democratic countries, the election results there have no bearing on who constitutes the next government.

The message Hong Kong's voters delivered was that they were still emotionally committed to the causes championed by the Tiananmen protesters. Indeed, some of the victors in the elections 'campaigned on the "platform" that democracy in Hong Kong and in China were inseparable, thus implying that they would work for the end of communism in China'.[83] By exercising their first ever democratic rights, albeit on a limited scale, the people of Hong Kong had voted against the restoration of the *status quo ante*. While they dare not confront the PRC government publicly, their strong negative feelings were disclosed. The elections demonstrated the political maturity of the Hong Kong people and proved beyond any reasonable doubt that they could make a democracy work. The Chinese leadership emerged convinced that democratic developments in Hong Kong were against their own interests and should not be allowed to spread uncontrolled. The electoral fiasco of the pro-PRC forces had destroyed any hope of the PRC agreeing to any British proposal to quicken the pace of democratization in Hong Kong after 1991.

The Tiananmen incident left another important legacy that made the idea of restoring the *status quo ante* meaningless. In October 1989, Governor Wilson announced the Hong Kong government's plan to build a massive infrastructural project known as the Port and Airport Development Strategy (PADS). The entire project was scheduled to be completed in 2006 at a cost of HK$ 127 billion, but the first phase, including the building of a new airport, would be finished in 1997. Wilson stressed that it was 'to show clearly how, despite the shocks we have experienced during the year, your government is continuing to plan for the long-term future of Hong Kong'.[84] Whatever the strength of the economic case put by the governor, it was primarily intended as part of the British effort to rebuild public confidence in Hong Kong.[85]

Although the PRC government did not object to it at first, it became increasingly suspicious of the British intention once it had time to reflect on the matter. Since neither the proposed new airport nor the main port expansion would be completed much before the scheduled British departure in 1997, Chinese cadres could not understand the British rationale. The British notion of 'good intention' was simply deemed too fanciful to be true. Chinese cadres looked at PADS with the suspicion that Deng Xiaoping first expressed when the Joint Declaration was being agreed in 1984. He thought the British would conspire to use Hong Kong's financial resources to buy goodwill from the local people, and to spirit Hong Kong's wealth to Britain before the handover.[86]

As Communist Party General Secretary Jiang Zemin saw it, PADS was a British plot to host a lavish dinner party and leave the Chinese to pay the bill.[87] It is indicative of the PRC mentality that Jiang already considered that Hong Kong's financial resources belonged to the PRC seven years before retrocession. When the Hong Kong government granted the contracts to build and run two of the four berthing places for a new container terminal to a leading British Hong Kong company but not a PRC consortium, the PRC leadership found confirmation of their suspicion.[88] Plagued by suspicion of corruption in their own bureaucracy, Chinese leaders doubted the integrity of Hong Kong's public tender system. Driven by self-interest and a conviction that the British —being imperialists—must have ulterior motives, the PRC blocked PADS. Since such a massive project required public borrowing on a large scale, the PRC's hostility meant it could not be built without its blessings.

When the PRC government took a public and high profile stand to block PADS, it changed the nature of the dispute. The crux of the matter was no longer about whether new infrastructures were needed for economic or confidence rebuilding purposes. It had become the assertion by the PRC to exercise 'the right to be consulted on all matters that straddled 1997'.[89] The PRC position in fact amounted to exacting the power to veto major Hong Kong economic policies or public projects if they should have significant implications for the SAR.[90] Conceding this demand would have reduced the Hong Kong government to a lame duck. The Hong Kong government therefore resisted it.[91] The deadlock in negotiations was finally broken during a visit by Cradock to Beijing in June 1991. The PRC finally indicated a willingness to compromise because it was eager to break the diplomatic quarantine imposed by major western powers following the Tiananmen incident.[92] Premier Li Peng, whose reputation was particularly badly tarnished by the Tiananmen incident, was personally keen to have a summit meeting with the British prime minister in Beijing.[93] For such a British concession Li and the PRC government were willing to reach an agreement over building the proposed new Hong Kong airport.

John Major, who had taken over as prime minister from Margaret Thatcher less than a year earlier, duly visited Beijing in September 1991 and signed a memorandum of understanding over the airport. The British tried to limit the scope of the veto demanded by the PRC. On major projects relating to the new airport, the British had to concede the principle that the PRC could exercise a veto. However, they sought to diffuse the Chinese claim for the same power over other issues. On other matters, the British merely agreed 'to intensify consultation and cooperation' with the Chinese by having their foreign ministers meeting 'twice a year to discuss matters of mutual concern' and for the director of HKMAO and the governor of Hong Kong to meet regularly.[94]

Despite British efforts to limit damages to the authority of the Hong Kong government, arrangements over the new airport 'created precedents for Chinese intervention on all issues straddling 1997'. This gave the PRC grounds to demand prior consultation on other major policy matters.[95] By its actions over PADS, the PRC government actually asserted for itself a far greater say over Hong Kong affairs than it had enjoyed prior to 1989. The British were keen to restore the *status quo ante* because it was the lesser of two evils, but the Chinese wanted more. British efforts since the Tiananmen incident were all part of a rearguard operation. This was to minimize the damage the incident could do to Hong Kong, preferably without putting any of the UK's own interests at risk.

9. End of Cooperation: 1992–7

The countdown to Hong Kong's historic appointment with the PRC entered a new phase in 1992. The year started with Prime Minister Major deciding to retire Sir David Wilson from the governorship. Given the centrality of the role usually played by governors of Crown colonies, any change in the governorship is significant. The removal of Wilson is particularly important. He was given a life peerage in the British new year honours' list, but it was a smoke screen to disguise the prime minister's dissatisfaction with him. In January 1992, Wilson was not yet 57. Major had asked him to leave Hong Kong more than three years before reaching the retirement age for the diplomatic service. Also, no arrangements were made for him to serve out his career as a professional diplomat elsewhere. That the prime minister made his decision public before he had made up his mind about exactly when Wilson should go and who would take his place, was even more indicative of his thinking. The British government merely announced that Wilson would leave sometime in 1992 after the British general election, for which no date had yet been set.[1]

With Hong Kong still recovering from the trauma of the Tiananmen incident, this was a bad time to introduce any uncertainty. The prime minister would not have decided to remove Wilson without naming a successor unless he had a strong reason. Equally important, Major also quietly retired Sir Percy Cradock, his most senior official adviser handling Hong Kong affairs on a day-to-day basis. This was the position

Cradock had been persuaded to take up after reaching the mandatory retirement age in the diplomatic service in 1982. He had thus devoted ten years beyond the normal call of duty to serve his country. His service went unrecognized when he left office. The prime minister's decision to pension off two key Hong Kong officials at about the same time was an indication of his dissatisfaction with the way in which they were handling Hong Kong policy.

Unlike his predecessor Margaret Thatcher, who demonstrated a commitment to Hong Kong, Major took very little personal interest in it. Furthermore, since he was not directly involved in the arduous and often unpleasant negotiations with the Chinese over Hong Kong, he may have misjudged the limits of British diplomacy.[2] When he visited Beijing in September 1991, it was undoubtedly on the advice that a British gesture to rehabilitate the PRC in the international community would resolve the important dispute over the PADS. However, the PRC remained difficult and obstructive over various matters relating to the financing of the PADS, despite the exchange of a memorandum of understanding.[3] Although such behaviour by the Chinese would not have startled the best of the old China hands, it must have taken Major by surprise. He came to see the Cradock–Wilson approach of giving ground steadily to the PRC, after engaging in tough secret negotiations to minimize British concessions, as a failure. This thinking must have underlined Major's decision to remove them. The prime minister probably made the premature announcement of Wilson's retirement because he had not thought through its implications for Hong Kong.[4] Major unwittingly reduced Governor Wilson to a lame duck until he could replace him.

In other words, by late 1991, when Major decided to change his top policy advisers, he and his government had already decided to take a tougher stand towards the PRC over Hong Kong. Major did not, however, seem to have a clear idea of what to do. All that was decided at this stage was that Wilson's successor would have to be a senior politician, and therefore the choice would have to wait until after the forthcoming general election. As long as the Conservative Party remained in power, whoever was appointed as Hong Kong's last governor could be expected to review and adjust, if not overhaul, Britain's Hong Kong policy. It could only have meant stiffening up Hong Kong and Britain's posture when dealing with the PRC. The only questions were the extent and the manner of such a change.

A New Governor

The results of the 1992 British general election caught many people by surprise. Chris Patten was one of them. As chairperson of the Conservative Party, he had played a crucial role in steering the party from a widely expected defeat to an electoral victory. Ironically, he lost his own seat in Bath, which was 'a devastating shock' to him.[5] Fresh from his electoral triumph, Prime Minister Major showed his gratitude by trying to 'find a proper job for someone who had, in effect, laid down his constituency for the party'. He offered him Hong Kong, 'an obvious plum'.[6] Patten's appointment as the last governor of Hong Kong could not have been more of an accident of history.

With no meaningful experience of Hong Kong or in dealing with the Chinese, Patten prepared himself before heading east by talking to a range of China experts from the political, diplomatic and academic worlds. Among the many issues he explored was the question of what the PRC would do if Britain granted democracy to Hong Kong. He was advised on at least one occasion that, while the communist leaders would prefer not to have to do it, they would undo any political reforms in Hong Kong that challenged what the PRC saw as its sovereign authority. When he took up the governorship in July, Patten was aware of the delicate and difficult position in which Hong Kong found itself. However, he either misunderstood or rejected the advice he received about the PRC's policy.

Patten wanted to do better than his diplomatic predecessor

and to leave his own mark. Arriving in Hong Kong, where Wilson was unkindly but widely denigrated for his alleged readiness to yield to pressure from the PRC, Patten intended to restore credibility to the governorship in the eyes of the local people.[7] He did not set out to antagonize the PRC, but he knew that his standing would be gravely undermined if he were to be seen to kowtow to Beijing, particularly in his early days. He had to balance the PRC leadership's expectation that he would pay homage to it in Beijing and the wish of the Hong Kong people that he would represent them and stand up for them. A skilful politician, Patten tried to finesse a compromise between these conflicting requirements, but he placed the greater emphasis on securing the support of the local people.

Patten was a political heavyweight in British politics. He was a friend and close political ally of Prime Minister Major and Foreign Secretary Douglas (now Lord) Hurd. As governor of Hong Kong, he enjoyed more leverage than any of his predecessors this century.[8] Though he enjoyed direct access to the prime minister and foreign secretary, the Foreign Office continued to handle most contacts between the Hong Kong and British governments through its normal channels of communication. He had a mandate from the prime minister to review Britain's Hong Kong policy, and played the pivotal role in revamping it as he saw fit. As he admitted to an old journalist friend from his Balliol College days, he 'pretty well had a free hand right the way through'. This allowed him to 'make decisions very quickly' and to 'adjust and manoeuvre much more rapidly'.[9]

Apart from his close personal and political links with the prime minister, there were other reasons for vesting so much power in him. There was a general feeling in British political circles that the last governor would need political clout to handle what everyone expected to be particularly difficult and delicate matters in the final stage of the transition. This consideration underlined the original idea that the last governor should be a senior politician rather than a career diplomat. An important effect of this change was to shift the locus of policy making for Hong Kong from the old China hands or career diplomats versed in Chinese idiosyncrasies to their political masters, who delegated it to Governor Patten. After the summer of 1992, the governor of Hong Kong became the most powerful factor in formulating Britain's policy towards the PRC with reference to Hong Kong.

In October 1992, in his first policy address to the Legislative Council, Patten announced his agenda as governor. He attempted a finesse. He produced a political reform package that would give the local people as much democratization as possible without breaching the terms of the Basic Law. To sweeten the deal for the PRC, he adroitly removed a major political irritant to Beijing. To appreciate the ingenuity of Patten's proposals, we need to understand the nature of the political demands the PRC government and the people of Hong Kong had put on the governor earlier that summer.

More than anything else, the people of Hong Kong expected their new governor to speed up the pace of democratization.[10] Although the details were not clearly defined, they included expanding the representativeness of the Legislative Council and appointing a couple of directly elected legislative councillors to the Executive Council. Martin Lee, leader of the United Democrats, which won most of the directly contested seats in the election the previous September, was at the top of the short list of potential legislative councillors.[11] However, this was not what Beijing wished to see. The PRC could tolerate Patten tinkering with the political system so long as this did not undermine its plans and it was consulted beforehand. It disapproved of any attempt by the Hong Kong government to appoint one or more elected legislators to the Executive Council. However, it would not necessarily refuse to discuss or even tolerate this provided Martin Lee and Szeto Wah were excluded. The finesse the governor attempted had to reconcile these contradictory expectations.

Patten came up with an extremely cleverly devised set of

proposals. These, at least from a British or purely rational Western viewpoint, would reconcile most of the requirements outlined above. First, by claiming that the existing overlap of membership between the Executive and Legislative Councils would 'inhibit the effective development of the Legislature as an independent check on Government', he proposed to separate the two bodies completely.[12] It was a masterstroke that diffused the intractable problem over the appointment of Martin Lee to the Executive Council. It also did the PRC a favour by delivering what it wanted — a strengthening of the executive branch at the expense of the legislature. (If Hong Kong had followed the more usual process of democratization in a British colony, it would develop towards a Westminster model with parliamentary supremacy.) To compensate somewhat for the severing of links between the two councils, the governor gave up the presidency of the legislature. Instead, he introduced a question time during which he would, as head of the executive branch, answer questions from legislators.[13] He supplemented this by establishing a 'Government-LegCo Committee' through which to maintain 'an effective working relationship between' the administration and the legislature.[14] All the above proposals were deemed unlikely to be objectionable to Beijing and were implemented without delay.

Patten also suggested introducing changes to electoral arrangements for the Legislative Council in 1995. He stressed that, as far as possible, he wanted the 'reforms to be compatible with the Basic Law and, accordingly, to transcend 1997'.[15] There were seven recommendations in this package:

- to reduce the voting age from 21 to 18, which was the voting age in the PRC as well as in Britain;
- to increase the number of directly-elected seats from 18 to 20, which was the number laid down in the Basic Law for the first SAR legislature in 1997;
- to change multiple-seat geographical constituencies into single-seat ones;

- 'all forms of corporate voting should be replaced by individual voters' in the 21 existing functional constituencies.[16] This meant giving a vote to the individuals working in professions or specified business sectors rather than their companies. It would make this archaic type of representation more in tune with modern times, and its voting less susceptible to manipulation;

- to add nine new functional constituencies so that people who did not belong to existing categories would be represented in the new functional constituencies. This was needed to enable the Legislative Council of 1995 to dovetail the arrangements laid down in the Basic Law, which provided for 30 functional constituencies in the SAR legislature in 1997;[17]

- to devolve some power over local matters and give more financial resources to district boards. Also, direct elections would replace all appointments to these boards and to the municipal councils; and

- finally, he suggested that the Basic Law's requirement for ten members to be elected by a selection committee of 400 should be chosen in a different way as a stopgap measure in 1995.[18] In Patten's conception, instead of having the governor appoint a similar committee — the composition of which would probably be objectionable to Beijing — he would ask all the directly-elected members of the district boards to elect ten among themselves as a one-off arrangement.[19]

In making his proposals for electoral reform, Patten pushed the grey area in the Basic Law to its outer limit, but did not actually violate its terms. The Basic Law does not specifically prohibit anything in his scheme. This is very much in line with the common law tradition whereby anything not prohibited is permitted. In this sense, the Patten scheme was a masterstroke. It did not contravene the constitutional position to which the PRC had committed itself in the Basic Law. Yet, it nonetheless delivered to the people of Hong Kong the largest possible step in the direction of democracy. In reality, this largest possible step remained a modest one. However, Patten did a first-class job in packaging and marketing it as a major step forward. He claimed it 'would give every single worker in Hong Kong the opportunity to elect to the Legislative Council a Member to represent him or her at the workplace'.[20] Though technically true, this was misleading. In 1991, every single worker already had a vote on a geographical basis, albeit to return only 18 legislators. Patten played down the fact that, even if his scheme were implemented *in toto*, Hong Kong would not be turned into a democracy. It would still only have one-third of its legislature returned by direct elections. His scheme was seen as a major step forward because the people of Hong Kong and PRC cadres accepted his democratic rhetoric at face value.

While it was obviously important to persuade the people of Hong Kong that his plan was a major democratic reform, Patten should have also ensured that the Chinese cadres understood what it really entailed. This was vitally important, for the Chinese cadres were notoriously bad at understanding how the system in Hong Kong worked. They were therefore likely to misinterpret the real thrust of the proposals. Patten should have realized this and not tried to surprise the Chinese, which could only provoke them into overreacting.

Before finalizing his plan, Patten was aware that the PRC government was unhappy about it. Two weeks before announcing his proposals, Foreign Secretary Hurd had given his Chinese counterpart an outline of the scheme when they met in New York.[21] Patten was told that the PRC considered that his idea of extending the number of directly elected members from 18 to 20 'would be incompatible with the Basic Law'.[22] The governor must have calculated that, despite being dissatisfied with his electoral proposals, the PRC would not jeopardize confidence and stability in Hong Kong by refusing to discuss them. He himself openly stated that he expected to hold 'serious discussions with Peking' over his proposals.[23] For this purpose, he planned to visit Beijing after they were announced. He could not have expected the PRC to accept them in full, but he must have intended to make the PRC justify the rejection of any of his proposals in public. Had he been operating within the framework of British politics, this would have been a clever pre-emptive manœuvre to seize the moral high ground and force his political opponent to negotiate publicly from a weak moral position. However, as a means of neutralizing PRC objections, Patten's adroit move turned out to be as clever as waving a red flag at a bull one is trying to induce to leave a china shop.

Confrontation

The PRC leaders looked on with suspicion at the appointment of this politician who, from the very beginning, expressed his interest in furthering Hong Kong's freedom.[24] They wondered whether the new man — who had no understanding of Chinese thinking and was probably primarily concerned with British interests — would introduce any basic changes to Britain's Hong Kong policy. They reserved judgement during Governor Patten's settling in period. However, as the summer progressed, their original suspicions were confirmed. To begin with, unlike their 'old friend' Wilson, who from a Chinese point of view duly paid his respects upon assuming the governorship five years earlier, Patten did not plan to visit Beijing before announcing his political agenda. Furthermore, Patten did not get along with the PRC's top cadre in Hong Kong, Zhou Nan, which exacerbated their misunderstandings. When Hurd outlined Patten's proposals to Foreign Minister Qian Qichen in New York, it caught the PRC by surprise. To Beijing, Patten's Legislative Council address suggested that a sinister plot was being hatched, either by him personally or by the British as a whole.

The PRC found Britain's handling of Patten's plan at least as objectionable as its contents. The Chinese believed they had had an understanding with the British since late 1985 over the meaning of convergence. As they saw it, they would define the scope and pace of the democratization in Hong Kong towards which the British would converge. After 1989 the Chinese made what they believed to be a major concession in allowing the number of directly-elected seats to the Legislative Council to be increased from 10 to 18.[25] This was achieved by secret diplomacy, which to the Chinese meant their 'sovereign authority' over Hong Kong was respected. Since the Patten plan was being hailed as a major political reform, the Chinese expected the British to have consulted them first and to have provided them with an opportunity to reject any unacceptable elements. However, the British merely informed them on this occasion and, according to the director of HKMAO, Lu Ping, completely ignored the Chinese comments.[26]

The Chinese also believed that, by announcing the plan publicly, the British intended to present them with a *fait accompli*. They considered it at best a deliberate affront and at worst a sly move to undermine Chinese sovereignty. The Patten plan looked like a conspiracy to extend British influence beyond the handover. The Chinese felt that by creating a Legislative Council that was beholden to them in 1995, the British would expect the PRC to allow it to continue in 1997 under the 'through train' arrangement. The British handling of the Patten plan also raised a serious doubt in the Chinese mind. Did it mark a fundamental change in British policy? Since convergence had worked well for PRC interests, Beijing was eager to nip in the bud any change in British policy.[27] Hence, they made a very strong and swift negative response to warn the British to return to the policy of convergence.[28]

The skilful way in which Patten made his modest proposals look as if they were a major democratic reform also backfired. It so confused the Chinese cadres that they gave Patten much more credit than he deserved for 'democratizing' Hong Kong. The Chinese saw the plan to fill the ten Legislative Council seats by means of elections among elected municipal coun- cillors and district board members as direct elections in disguise. They mistakenly equated them with the electoral colleges in US presidential elections. Following this logic, Patten would indeed have taken a major step towards democratization through the back door, for half the Legislative Council seats would for all practical purposes be open to direct elections. The Chinese failed to understand the subtle yet vital differences between Patten's proposal and the US electoral college system. In the USA, electoral colleges have no function other than to elect the president and each delegate is by convention returned on the basis of his or her declared choice of presidential candidate. In the Hong Kong case, the local-level elections would have to be contested on the whole range of issues handled by the municipal councils and district boards. Furthermore, there would be a year between the local elections and the Legislative Council elections. During the 1994 local elections, no one could know who the candidates for the 1995 Legislative Council elections would be, and the latter therefore could not be an issue in the local elections. Hence, turning the municipal councils and district boards into an electorate for 1995 was not a direct election in disguise, but this was something the Chinese did not understand.

The Chinese further exaggerated the effect of Patten's proposed reform. They also counted the nine new functional seats as if they were direct election seats.[29] They therefore wrongly thought that 'the number of directly and in effect directly elected legislative councillors would amount to 40 [sic]'. This was two-thirds of the council's total membership — a percentage that could allow the United Democrats (the predecessors of the Democratic Party) to win a majority.[30] They saw the Patten plan as 'an attempt to let the "anti-Chinese democratic party" which represents British interests to win, and enable it to take "the through train" into the first Legislative Council after the return of Hong Kong's sovereignty in 1997'.[31]

The Chinese also raised serious objections to other aspects of the Patten proposals. These included:

- substituting corporate voting with individual voting in the functional constituencies;
- ending appointments to (or more realistically gubernatorial patronage in) municipal councils and district boards; and even
- ending overlapping membership in the Executive and Legislative Councils.[32]

They failed to understand that the last proposal was a sweetener for them. They did not realize that it removed the public pressure on the Hong Kong government to appoint Martin Lee to the Executive Council. They also failed to understand that it took away the most powerful influence the Legislative Council traditionally exercised over the Executive Council in Hong Kong. For more than a century, the Executive Council had tended not to push a controversial policy if its unofficial members, who also sat on the Legislative Council, could convince it that such a policy would be unacceptable to the legislature.

Patten's uncoupling of the two councils therefore turned the Hong Kong system into a much more 'executive-led' one.[33] It was exactly what the PRC wanted, but the Chinese cadres failed to grasp it. It reflected their inadequate understanding of how the political system in Hong Kong actually worked. It was also because they started from the assumption that Patten had ulterior motives. By focusing on every conceivable negative implication, they overlooked those that were positive to the PRC. As Lu Ping saw it, because the Chinese had already set out their plan in the Basic Law, they even found Patten's appeal to produce counterproposals offensive.[34] The PRC government's basic objection to Patten's plan lay in the belief that it intended to introduce democracy to Hong Kong in open defiance of its stated policy.

Since Chinese cadres at first misread the nature of Patten's plan, their inaccurate assessments became the basis for decision making at the top. Seeing it essentially in terms of a British challenge to Chinese sovereign authority, the reaction was to take a tough stand.[35] The PRC leadership felt that if the British would correct their mistake and promptly return to convergence, they would only need to be punished slightly. Should the Patten plan prove to be the spearhead of a wider or sustained challenge, however, then the British must be made to pay for it. The PRC decided to face this British confrontation squarely and win at all costs.[36] The Chinese were convinced that the British would try to further their interests by seeking a confrontation over Hong Kong. The old mistrust expressed by Deng was revived — 'someone would not implement in full' the Joint Declaration.[37] Building on such a suspicion, the Chinese even saw it as part of a wider conspiracy.[38] As Zhou Nan explained, the British mistakenly believed that 'after the dissolution of the Soviet Union, China would also face the same kind of changes'. They thus wanted to 'use proxies installed with their help to extend British colonial rule, turn Hong Kong into a semi-independent political entity, and unrealistically wish to influence political developments in China'.[39] As the dispute developed, the PRC position hardened.

If the PRC had at first had doubts about whether or not the new governor wanted a confrontation, they were cleared after Patten visited Beijing in the latter part of October. This was the only occasion when Governor Patten was received by senior Chinese leaders like the foreign minister and the director of HKMAO. To the governor it was an occasion when he could have serious talks with the Chinese about his proposals. To the PRC leaders it was an opportunity for Patten to admit his mistake and return to convergence.[40] There was no meeting of minds. The PRC leaders felt they had confirmation that the British were attempting a *volte face* and consequently prepared for confrontation.

The PRC leadership was still keen to make a success of the retrocession under the 'one country, two systems' principle. It thus decided to apply its well-tested united-front tactics to divide the British–Hong Kong camp and neutralize the Patten initiative. Used for this purpose, united-front tactics require one to isolate one's principal antagonist and destroy it by rallying one's supporters, winning over those wavering and neutralizing the opponent's natural supporters. Once this is completed, one moves on to the next target and repeats the exercise until one establishes full control. In the winter of 1992/3, the Chinese saw Governor Patten as the principal target. The people of Hong Kong were the wavering elements, and the British government and Hong Kong civil service were the opponent's natural supporters. Hence, despite seeing the Patten plan as a wider British conspiracy, the PRC propaganda machine singled out Patten for attack. In public, the PRC argued that one person, who was the cause of all the troubles, was destroying Hong Kong's interests and Sino–British cooperation. Its message to both the British government and Hong Kong was that once Patten had been removed, the *status quo ante* could be restored and Hong Kong would not have to see its stability and prosperity threatened.

This virulent attack on Patten provoked the British to close ranks. The British government felt that if it replaced Patten under overt heavy-handed PRC pressure, it would lose all credibility and authority over Hong Kong matters in the run up to 1997. Hong Kong would become ungovernable. It was simply not an option. The barrage of verbal abuse the Chinese heaped on Patten also made him appear like a great champion for democracy in Hong Kong. Some people there were intimidated and many wealthy capitalists asked the governor to defuse the crisis for the sake of stability and prosperity. The majority of ordinary folk, however, rallied around him for standing up for them. When the PRC propaganda campaign intensified in the winter, his popularity ratings rose to their highest point during his governorship.[41] To most Hong Kong people, strong Chinese hostility was sufficient proof that Patten's plan must be a major democratic reform. The world media, which was still influenced by the legacy of the Tiananmen massacre, shared the same sentiment. Ironically, through the eyes of the international media, the high profile PRC propaganda attacks quickly turned Patten into Hong Kong's English hero. The PRC had badly miscalculated the reactions of Britain, the people of Hong Kong and the international media. Its united-front tactics had backfired.

The confrontation between Britain and the PRC over the Patten plan was a tragedy, for neither side wanted it at heart. The changing of guards and the new team's well-intentioned though naïve wish to recover some of the lost ground on the British side, led to its failure to anticipate the likely responses from the Chinese side. It was a sad mistake, which would prove to be very costly for Hong Kong, but was not the result of malevolent scheming. The PRC, for its part, grossly over-reacted and dramatically raised the stakes. The escalation hardened attitudes on both sides. Patten was the key figure in setting off this chain of events. He made a serious error of judgement, but it was one that was understandable in the light of his background.

Failure of Conciliation

In April 1993, the Chinese finally but reluctantly realized that their united-front divide-and-rule tactics had failed and that the British would not be replacing Governor Patten. At that point they agreed to enter into negotiations with Britain. Deputy Foreign Minister Jiang Enzhu represented the Chinese in the negotiations with the British ambassador Sir Robin McLaren. Throughout the 17 rounds, the PRC kept up the pretence that the governor was not a party to the talks. Patten was of course fully informed and involved as the key figure behind the scenes on the British side. The negotiations were tough and there was little significant progress in the first six months.[42] Though both sides had entered the talks partly to secure popular support in Hong Kong, they also wanted to reach an agreement so as to ensure a successful transition. However, they remained suspicious of each other's intentions.

The Chinese starting position was that Patten's plan violated the Joint Declaration, the Basic Law and various understandings over political developments reached after the Tiananmen incident. They were particularly unhappy about Britain's denial that Patten's plan breached the Basic Law. Since the Basic Law was a piece of Chinese legislation, they believed only they could interpret it and that the British had no right to tell them whether or not their interpretation was correct.[43] General Secretary Jiang Zemin defined their basic stand on the dispute. He said that the PRC 'would not make any concession on matters of principle'. It would be 'guided by the one country, two systems' policy and would 'take into account the basic interests of the Chinese people, who include the Hong Kong and Macao compatriots'.[44] In other words, he reaffirmed the policy of exercising maximum flexibility within a rigid framework.

An acceptable compromise would require considerable back-peddling on the part of the British to bring Patten's plan into line with the PRC's interpretation of the two documents and of various understandings. While Chinese sincerity was not in doubt, it was unclear whether they were keen to reach an agreement quickly. As the Chinese knew only too well, time was on their side. To introduce the changes proposed in the Patten plan, the Hong Kong government would need to pass one or more new laws. From Beijing's point of view, this was largely a British problem, for it was they who had provoked the dispute in the first place. The Chinese were unsympathetic to the time pressures the British side faced.

Governor Patten essentially defined the British position. As he himself put it, the crux of the matter was 'not about the pace of democratic development', which was 'set out in the Basic Law'.[45] The British sought to secure two basic principles. The first was to ensure that 'election arrangements in Hong Kong should be fair, open and acceptable to the community'.[46] The other 'was to agree on arrangements which would provide continuity through 1997', or, in local parlance, to keep the 'through train'.[47] The British were therefore willing to reach a compromise by revising the 1992 proposals. In October 1993, the governor publicly stated the main thrust of the concessions the British were willing to make:

> First, we have devised a new proposal for the nine new functional constituencies, based on organizations as the Chinese have argued and with a total eligible electorate of about a third of that in my original proposal. We continue to insist that electors should vote individually, not corporately. Secondly, we have tried to meet China's preference for a four-sector Election Committee of the kind set out in the Basic Law for the post-1997 Election Committee. We continue to argue that all members of the Election Committee should themselves be elected.[48]

The governor also made clear, however, that 'there is a point beyond which I do not believe that we could justifiably go, even in pursuit of an agreement to which we genuinely aspire'.[49] The limits of the British concession were not only about the substance of the plan, but also about the timing for concluding the negotiations. The British had to set a time limit because the necessary legislation had to be introduced to put into effect the proposed electoral changes.

Britain's time limit for introducing the bill governing local elections the following autumn ran out in late November 1993. The Hong Kong government gave the PRC a few days' warning before gazetting the draft bill it later introduced into the Legislative Council. The British stressed their wish to continue negotiations,[50] but the Chinese, as they warned they would, responded strongly and declared the talks terminated.[51] They were only prepared to resume negotiations if the British discontinued their unilateral action. They saw the British move as confirmation of their insincerity in the talks and held them fully responsible for all the consequences.[52] Conciliation had failed. The point of no return was reached in June 1994 when the Hong Kong Legislative Council passed into law in full the remaining reform proposals of Governor Patten's 1992 plan.

There is little doubt that Governor Patten was mainly behind this momentous decision, though he clearly enjoyed the backing of the Cabinet in London.[53] He appeared to have felt a sense of frustration and perhaps even resentment over the PRC's heavy-handed approach and verbal abuse of him personally. Because such a move would be so obviously against the PRC's own interests, he seemed reluctant to believe that the PRC would honour its own threat to demolish his reforms. Patten's assessment revealed his own ignorance and misunderstanding of the PRC's Hong Kong policy. From Beijing's point of view, the British move amounted to a return to challenging its sovereign rights over Hong Kong. It could not back down and its reaction was predictable. Whatever reasons the governor had for recommending such a course, they could not be justified in terms of safeguarding Hong Kong's interests.

Patten's handling of his proposals in October 1992 showed a serious but understandable error of judgement. His decision to implement the plan in full despite clear warnings from the PRC was a major and inexcusable policy blunder. Though the gap separating the two sides in the talks was still wide in December 1993 and the prospect of an early agreement questionable, a complete break was not inevitable. The Chinese decision to open negotiations, after having insisted on their withdrawal in March 1993, demonstrated their preparedness to exercise maximum flexibility, albeit still within a rigid framework.

When the time came for the British to introduce the bill on the Legislative Council reforms, they should have based it on the governor's revised proposals announced in October 1993. Instead, they based it on his 1992 plan. In terms of slowing down the pace or scope of democratization, this concession amounted to very little. If properly managed, it would have been possible to have persuaded the people of Hong Kong that it was necessary to safeguard their long-term future. It would unquestionably still have failed to satisfy the PRC, but it would at least have sent a different signal. To the PRC, by returning to the 1992 plan the British showed their true colours — they had

abandoned convergence and cooperation in favour of confrontation in order to undermine the Chinese takeover of Hong
Kong. Although their assessment was wrong, the Chinese had
good grounds for thinking along these lines. After all, if
Governor Patten had meant what he said in October 1992
about discussing his plan with the Chinese, he could not have
expected to implement the plan without modifications.

To the Chinese, implementing the plan in full was conclus-
ive proof of the existence of a British conspiracy. By contrast,
implementing the revised October 1993 proposals would have
suggested that the British genuinely wanted to compromise.
The PRC would still have attacked it in public. In private, however, the Chinese would have seen it as a British face-saving
move and, more important, not as a deliberate challenge to the
PRC's sovereign authority over Hong Kong. Unsatisfactory as it
remained, the PRC could have chosen on this basis to respond
with flexibility rather than rigidity. It would then have had the
option of not committing itself to demolishing whatever the
Patten plan established before 1997. As it was, Patten's
decision to push for his original plan once the talks had led
nowhere, confirmed all the PRC's worst fears. It also removed
any possibility of the Patten reforms surviving the transition.
The concept of a 'through train' had been rendered irrelevant.

However well intentioned and broadly supported by the
local people, the decision to implement the Patten plan in full
was the British government's biggest and most unjustifiable
policy mistake since it decided to open negotiations with the
PRC over the future of Hong Kong. The Patten reforms were
too little too late, but this was not the issue. The problem was
that the highly moralistic stand that Patten and the British
government took in 1994 merely covered up their failure at the
expense of Hong Kong's interests. In principle, the British
government's assertion that 'Hong Kong's best interest lies in
making electoral arrangements for 1994 and 1995 which carry
forward the already agreed and established process of democratic development, which are themselves open and fair' cannot

be faulted.[54] In reality, this is true only if such a reform has a reasonable, or at least a fighting, chance of success. This would have been the case if the same policy had been introduced before, say, 1984. At that time democratization was on the political agenda, but the PRC had not yet committed itself to reversing any changes that were introduced.

When the British finally took a stand a decade later, in 1994, the situation was completely different. By then, a decision to introduce the Patten plan in the face of PRC objections would definitely provoke the latter into undoing its reforms and thus badly undermine Hong Kong's chances of surviving the handover. Once Hong Kong's future had been decided by the Joint Declaration, its basic interest lay in persuading the PRC to uphold all its promises enshrined in it. Admittedly, the PRC had a poor record in keeping what it saw as other people's interpretations of its promises. However, it believed it took its own promises seriously and the Joint Declaration remained the cornerstone of a set of Sino–British understandings. The failure of conciliation in 1994 and China's certainty that Patten's plan violated the Joint Declaration, seriously weakened the PRC's sense of commitment to it and 'provided a perfect pretext for tinkering by the Chinese'.[55]

While Patten's error of judgement in 1992 was regrettable, it was forgivable because he had taken up the governorship with no previous experience of handling the PRC. Furthermore, although a serious mistake, its damages were not irreparable. The 1994 blunder, however, was inexcusable. By then Patten had served a third of his term as governor: he should have acquired sufficient knowledge of the PRC's Hong Kong policy to avoid an obvious mistake with such predictable and disastrous consequences. His failing was comparable to that of a jumbo jet pilot not bothering to learn to read weather charts properly and then flying a fully loaded plane into a typhoon, despite clear warnings on the charts. Patten's mistake was an error for which the Hong Kong community would have to pay very dearly.

Building a 'New Kitchen'

The most important activity in a Chinese community is feeding the people and, in this respect, families function as the basic unit. The family kitchen is therefore the hub — the vital place in which to turn raw materials into nutritious food to sustain the family and enable it to prosper. Building a new kitchen symbolizes the splitting of a family or the assertion of independence. When the PRC realized that it could no longer count on the British to adhere to convergence as a policy, it first threatened and later started to build a 'new kitchen' for Hong Kong. The implication was that, with a 'new kitchen' in place, it would not need to rely on the existing one. This would remain under British control and be modified according to Patten's rather than the PRC's specifications until the appointed date in 1997.

The threat was first made by HKMAO director Lu Ping in October 1992 when Patten was visiting Beijing in a disastrous attempt to resolve the dispute over his reform proposals.[56] Lu merely meant to warn Patten to abandon his scheme. The PRC government had not yet committed itself to building a 'new kitchen'. The idea only developed and became really attractive after the PRC's initial attempts to force the removal of Governor Patten had failed. In March 1993, the PRC seriously contemplated opening negotiations with the British over the Patten plan. However, it also decided to plan for the worst and to strengthen its hand in the talks by preparing the ground for a 'new kitchen'. It announced its intention to set up a preliminary working committee (PWC) as a first step towards the eventual appointment of a preparatory committee for the Hong Kong SAR.[57] This was a clever move and in a sense was in retaliation against Britain's claim that the Patten plan had not breached the Basic Law. Although there is no provision for a PWC anywhere in the Basic Law, one of its appendices does require the forming of a preparatory committee sometime in 1996.[58] Since the Basic Law does not prohibit the setting up of a PWC, its creation did not strictly violate the terms of the law.

The PRC had two objectives in forming the PWC in July 1993. The first was to put pressure on the British to make concessions over the Patten plan. The possibility of the PWC becoming an alternative centre of authority generated a certain amount of concern in Hong Kong. Its creation by slow but steady steps gave the PRC a useful additional bargaining chip.[59] Should the British decide to abandon the Patten plan, the PRC could then make a grand symbolic gesture. It could either suspend the appointment of the PWC or, if already formed, give it purely honorific functions. Such considerations lay behind the PRC's decision, while talks were underway over the Patten plan, to allow a long interval — three months — between announcing its intention and actually naming the committee.

The other, and at first secondary, objective was to provide the infrastructure to build a 'new kitchen'. All its 57 members were either senior cadres from relevant departments within the PRC establishment or Hong Kong residents who had taken a pro-PRC stance over the Patten plan. If it should prove unnecessary to build a 'new kitchen' the PWC could still serve as a useful interdepartmental coordinating body. Hence, it was headed by vice-premier and foreign minister Qian Qichen. It was represented at the vice-ministerial level by the Ministry of Public Security, the PLA, the Communist Party's United Front Department, and various economic, trade and financial ministries in addition to the Foreign Ministry and HKMAO. To make it non-offensive to Hong Kong opinion, 30 of its 57 members were carefully selected from among Hong Kong's residents.[60] With a membership on which the PRC leadership could count to safeguard its interests, it became a useful organization in case a 'new kitchen' really needed to be built.

Until the Sino–British talks collapsed in December 1993, the PRC kept its promise not to make the PWC into an 'alternative centre of authority or a shadow government'.[61] On its inauguration earlier in July, the PRC gave the PWC rather general terms of reference, with no specific instructions to build a 'new kitchen'. It was only after the talks were terminated that the

PRC asked the PWC to carry out serious and specific research into what could actually be done to prepare the PRC to resume sovereign authority.[62] By then, the PRC believed that conciliation had failed. The originally secondary purpose of the PWC, which was to build a 'new kitchen', had become the primary one. The point of no return was reached when the Hong Kong Legislative Council passed into law the last tranche of the Patten plan. Jiang Zemin then directed the PWC to 'rely on our own resources as the basis and staunchly follow the directive of upholding our interests to ensure the stable transition' in Hong Kong.[63] Construction work for a 'new kitchen' had started in earnest.

This change in PRC policy in 1994 was very important. Marked by Jiang's directive on self-reliance, the PRC acted as if the British had irretrievably abandoned convergence as a policy. It ceased to count on Sino–British cooperation to ensure a stable transition and minimized making public references to 'Hong Kong people ruling Hong Kong'.[64] Instead, it emphasized relying on itself to implement the 'one country, two systems' policy. Beijing accepted that Patten's reforms would be introduced, but was determined to reverse them and to destroy any goodwill they were generating for him. Through its commitment to undoing Patten's reforms, the PRC was ensuring that Hong Kong would enjoy no more democracy in 1997 than it had before Patten's arrival in 1992. Furthermore, by preparing to nullify all legislative changes implemented through the bill of rights during Patten's tenure, the PRC aimed to counteract the impression that he had improved Hong Kong's human rights situation. Once conciliation failed, the PRC sought to destroy Patten's reforms and to lay the blame entirely on him for causing the retrogression.

The British, for their part, had not abandoned convergence as a policy in 1994. They still wanted a smooth and successful transition and therefore continued to cooperate with the PRC over practical arrangements. After their spectacularly unsuccessful stand over the Patten plan, the British conceded that

'further contests with China' on most other matters had
become 'a thing of the past'.[65] Although the British did not
capitulate on all issues, they accepted that, by July 1997, the
PRC would be able to do whatever it wanted. If they believed
that the PRC was misguided over some issue, they were
prepared to argue and try to persuade it otherwise. However,
apart from the Patten plan, they did not take a stand on other
issues — such as the Court of Final Appeal, which is vital for
maintaining judicial independence. Since the PRC mistakenly
thought the British had abandoned convergence and no longer
expected almost automatic British cooperation, their public
disputes became relatively less acrimonious. An ironical situation was thus created in which Sino–British cooperation
appeared to improve after the talks over the Patten plan
collapsed.

In September 1995, Hong Kong elected a new Legislative
Council along the lines of the Patten plan. Although the
elections proved beyond any reasonable doubt that it was
possible for fair, open and democratic elections to flourish
there, Hong Kong was not turned into a democracy. Martin
Lee's Democratic Party failed to gain power, despite its
electoral successes. Contrary to the PRC's understanding, there
was simply no scope for such a development in the Patten plan
or in Hong Kong's political system. The PRC allowed its
supporters to take part in the elections, but they did badly at
the polls. They won only 16 seats from different types of
constituencies in a council of 60. It was a slap in the face for
the PRC. It removed what residue of hope there was that the
Chinese leadership might allow the last Legislative Council to
continue basically as it was after retrocession.[66] This led to a
difficult problem. Arrangements had to be made either for new
elections in 1997 or for an interim measure to be taken.

In the light of the shift in PRC policy from seeking Sino–
British cooperation to relying on itself to implement the 'one
country, two systems' directive, and the electoral defeat of pro-
PRC forces, the PRC leadership decided to keep a tighter rein

over the first SAR legislature. It thus resolved not to hold new elections but to form a provisional Legislative Council by appointments. Such an arrangement breached the Basic Law and the Joint Declaration, both of which required the first SAR legislature to be elected. Justifying its creation on the grounds that this had become unavoidable following the British violation of these two documents by implementing the Patten plan, the PRC turned the provisional Legislative Council into a key feature of the 'new kitchen'.

In the meantime, the PRC also proceeded to form a preparatory committee chaired by Qian Qichen in January 1996. This was 'responsible for preparing the establishment of the Selection Committee for the First Government' of the SAR.[67] The selection committee itself was duly constituted in November 1996. It was entrusted with selecting the provisional Legislative Council and with electing the chief executive for the SAR.

As the PRC had by then committed itself to dismantling Patten's reforms, it did not depend on British cooperation to build the 'new kitchen'. Britain had become irrelevant to its endeavours to set up the SAR's political institutions. In its own way, however, the PRC did try to assuage public opinion in Hong Kong. The provisional Legislative Council finally appointed in December 1996 was constituted with this requirement in mind. Hence, of its 60 members, 33 were in the existing Legislative Council.[68] Allocating more than half the seats to incumbent legislators was meant to suggest that, had the British not implemented the Patten plan, Hong Kong could have had a 'through train'. In other words, the 1995 legislature could have served out its four-year term until 1999.[69] Though the 60 did not include anyone from Martin Lee's Democratic Party, which condemned the selection process, four members of the Association for Democracy and People's Livelihood, one of the smaller pro-democracy parties, were included.[70] This was supposed to suggest a balanced representation of the local community's different political persuasions.[71]

The above two arrangements were designed to reassure the more sceptical elements of Hong Kong society. Seats were allocated both to reward groups closest to the PRC and to guarantee the PRC's ability to dominate the council. Ten of those who campaigned (but were defeated) on pro-PRC platforms in the 1995 Legislative Council elections were appointed, and 85 per cent of all appointees were themselves members of the selection committee.[72] With an appointed council making a mockery of the 1995 election results, the PRC had forced democratization in Hong Kong to take a step back. Also, because Governor Patten was held to be responsible for derailing the 'through train', it was he who received the blame.[73] The composition of the provisional Legislative Council suggested that, for the PRC, the more important consideration had remained the safeguarding of its interests.

In December 1996, before the appointment of the provisional Legislative Council, Premier Li Peng appointed Tung Chee-hwa — a local shipping magnate whose company was financially beholden to the PRC — chief executive of the SAR. He was to take office formally on 1 July 1997.[74] A chief executive would probably have been selected around this time even without the dispute over Patten's plan. Given the decision to build a 'new kitchen', however, the PRC's needed to handle the whole matter differently. When convergence was still in place, there was a general expectation that, to ensure continuity, the British would appoint the chief executive elect as a lieutenant-governor or in a similar position in the months leading up to the handover. This prospect was removed when conciliation failed. In picking Tung, the PRC again ignored the British as a factor. This was in sharp contrast to the drafting of the Basic Law, when British comments were taken into account. In other words, although the idea of electing the chief executive predated that of building a 'new kitchen', Tung's appointment turned him into the most important part of this new creation.

Once appointed, Tung proceeded to name his Executive Council in early 1997. In so doing he had to defer to the PRC's wish to reverse Patten's 1992 initiative to separate the Executive Council from the legislature. Apart from two members of the SAR Executive Council being chosen from members of the provisional Legislative Council, the same rationale governing the formation of the provisional Legislative Council applied. Tung and the PRC government tried to appoint an Executive Council that would enjoy credibility among the people of Hong Kong, provide a degree of continuity and, most important, safeguard the PRC's interests.

To satisfy the first two requirements, Tung nominated two members of Governor Patten's Executive Council to serve on his 11-member SAR Executive Council. They would provide continuity. Furthermore, Tung appointed Sir Sze-yuen Chung as convenor of the SAR Executive Council. Chung had been the senior member of the Hong Kong Executive Council for much of the 1980s, particularly during the negotiations for the Joint Declaration. He had become acceptable to the PRC because he opposed Governor Patten's reforms. Although Chung has continued to put Hong Kong's interests before all others, the PRC regards him as a repentant 'patriot'. As a highly respected elder statesman, his appointment was meant to lend credibility to the SAR Executive Council. To meet the requirement of safeguarding the PRC's interests, Tung allowed the PRC's invisible hand to guide him. He dropped two of his original choices and appointed a few whose names had been gently suggested to him.[75] It was not purely accidental that four convenors of various subgroups in the preparatory committee were appointed. Three of the 11 members are believed to belong to the Chinese Communist Party.[76] The composition of the SAR Executive Council reflected the PRC wish to strike a kind of balance between reassuring the local people and protecting its own interests.

By the spring of 1997, with the chief executive, his Executive Council and the provisional Legislative Council in place, the PRC had completed the 'new kitchen'. It had been built largely without taking British views into account. Now the

PRC had an institution with which to take over Hong Kong on the appointed date, with or without British cooperation. The transition had reached a point at which the British had only limited room for manoeuvre. Foreign Secretary Malcolm Rifkind admitted in early 1997 that 'both the British Government and Hong Kong people were realistic about the scope for action by Britain at this stage in the transition period'.[77] Although the British government continued to discharge its responsibilities, it had accepted that the Patten reforms would not survive retrocession.

10. Happy Ever After?

At midnight on 30 June 1997 Hong Kong's historic appointment with China, made 99 years earlier, will take place. The Crown colony of Hong Kong will become a Special Administrative Region (SAR) of the PRC. The Chinese idea of 'one country, two systems' will be put to the test. The rule of law, civil liberties and human rights are routinely upheld in capitalist Hong Kong, whereas these same ideas are not respected in the socialist PRC. Will Hong Kong be able to live happily as part of the PRC?

To answer this question one needs to look at several factors and their interaction over the past decade. These include the driving forces behind the PRC's policy, the resilience of the local society, and what influences the outside world, including Britain, can exert. A balanced analysis of these factors will provide a reasonable framework within which to assess what the future holds for the Hong Kong SAR.

'One Country, Two Systems' in Perspective

The starting point of the PRC's Hong Kong policy is to protect and enhance its own interests. This was why it adopted the 'one country, two systems' model. It allows the PRC to exercise as much flexibility as possible on practical matters without having to compromise its sovereignty. Two factors have influenced how much flexibility it has felt able to exercise since the drafting of the Joint Declaration in 1984. First, is the question of whether the PRC sees a particular issue as having implications for its sovereignty. This applies even to the thorny issue of political reform or democratization, which the PRC government does not wish to see in Hong Kong. When the

British raised the matter, it was dealt with through secret diplomacy in the 1980s. At that time Beijing was willing to accept
the need to satisfy to an extent the local demands for greater
democracy in Hong Kong. In such a context the PRC did not
see its sovereignty involved and was thus prepared to be
flexible for the sake of stability and prosperity. By contrast,
when the issue came to be seen as a British challenge to PRC
sovereign authority, as happened over the Patten reforms in
the early 1990s, the PRC was unyielding.

The other variable is how confident the Communist Party
feels about its position in both the PRC and Hong Kong.
Generally, the greater the communist leadership's confidence
in the superiority of its system or its grip over the country
(including Hong Kong), the more relaxed it is when dealing
with Hong Kong. The boost in public support for the PRC
leadership the Dengist reforms brought in the early 1980s,
allowed Deng to take this bold initiative over Hong Kong. By
contrast, the Tiananmen incident and the collapse of communism in eastern Europe almost a decade later made the
Chinese communist leaders feel vulnerable and they took a
harder and harsher line towards Hong Kong. If Hong Kong
wants the PRC to adhere to the 'one country, two systems'
policy, it has to reassure the latter that there will be no
challenge to the PRC's sovereignty over the SAR or, for that
matter, to the continued dominance of the Chinese Communist Party. The fact that adhering to this policy serves its
own interests is the most powerful incentive for the PRC
leadership to keep the status quo in Hong Kong.

However strong the self-interest argument, it must be set
against the interventionist ethos of the communist party–state.
It is unrealistic to expect the PRC not to interfere with the
running of Hong Kong after June 1997. The building of the
'new kitchen' during Patten's later years, and the friendly
advice the chief executive elect was offered in constituting his
Executive Council, suggest a degree of meddling is unavoidable. Nevertheless, it is important to recognize that the PRC

stressed the retaliatory nature of the 'new kitchen' and kept its influence over the formation of the first SAR government within bounds. While Beijing insisted on safeguarding its interests in terms of membership of the Executive Council, the chief executive elect won the day by keeping all the serving top ethnic Chinese civil servants in place. Despite its inclination to intervene, the PRC government is aware that it must try to restrain itself, for it has no wish to kill the goose that is laying golden eggs.

To make 'one country, two systems' work, it will be imperative to build on this awareness of the PRC leadership. The PRC and SAR governments will need to develop a *modus operandi*. They must be able to understand each other fully and develop a degree of trust over the vital issue of defining their fundamental interests, which must be upheld. The SAR will have to take the lead in reassuring the PRC that it has no intention of undermining its basic interests, which include maintaining the existing political system. It must also explain to the PRC, in a way the latter can follow, the nature of the basic forces that have made Hong Kong develop into what it is. These essential features of the Hong Kong system must be defended and upheld, but this can only be done successfully if Hong Kong's case can be put to the PRC leadership dispassionately and non-provocatively.

This will be an uphill struggle because many such features, such as the rule of law and judicial independence, are alien to the PRC. Since they relate to notions of human rights and democracy, which the PRC view with acute scepticism and suspicion, they must be handled with sensitivity. The PRC is not only hostile to these ideas because they are alien Western concepts. It is also hostile to them because they are seen as tools with which the West is trying to subvert the party–state in a conspiracy called 'peaceful transformation'.[1] Hong Kong has to persuade Beijing that these concepts are essential for its well-being and for maintaining its vitality. To do this, however, it must also convince Beijing that allowing them to flourish within the SAR will not result in them being exported across the border into the PRC. The emergence of a *modus operandi* is by nature a dynamic process involving many interactions. Following retrocession, the SAR government must develop a rapport with the PRC government that will provide the basis for such a *modus operandi*.

In this connection, the biggest problem for the SAR is the growing activism of Hong Kong's pro-democratic forces. Admirable as they are in campaigning for democracy, they have often advocated their cause in a counterproductive way. By pitching their case for democracy against the PRC, they are reinforcing the latter's suspicion that ultimately they are trying to subvert its system. Consequently, Beijing looks upon Hong Kong being allowed to develop democracy as giving hostile forces a beachhead to work against the party–state's survival. Such an assessment induces the PRC leadership to move away from flexibility. This is a major problem with which Hong Kong's democratic activists will need to come to terms very quickly.

They do not yet have enough political wisdom to understand that the cause of democracy there has been and will continue to be harmed if they take a stand that Beijing sees as menacing. This is partly attributable to the ironic situation in which they find themselves. In other words, they can afford to be irresponsible because they have no chance of forming a government or being held politically accountable for their programmes and actions. They should have learned a powerful lesson from seeing how painfully counterproductive was the so-called confrontational approach of the Patten reforms. Regrettably, Martin Lee and his colleagues have so far failed to grasp the moral of the recent events. They still refuse to accept the political reality that Hong Kong has no choice but to set its own democratic development against the wider context of and restraints imposed by PRC politics.

The 'anti-PRC slant' of Martin Lee and his closest political allies is a delicate political issue the SAR government will need to handle carefully. On the one hand, the SAR must uphold the principle that unless a person has broken a law, he or she should enjoy the usual freedoms that have been taken for granted for a long time in Hong Kong. On the other hand, it must try to persuade Lee not to precipitate an open confrontation with the PRC in court over a matter the latter sees as having implications for its sovereign authority. In such a situation, the PRC would destroy Hong Kong's judicial independence in order to face the challenge, and thus ruin one of British Hong Kong's most valuable legacies. It could even set off a chain reaction leading to a general tightening of the degree of autonomy the SAR is allowed to enjoy. It is therefore imperative for Lee and his colleagues to learn to operate above the bottom line for SAR politics as laid down by the PRC.

Given the rigidity of the PRC's Hong Kong policy over what it defines as sovereignty related issues, there is no alternative to self-restraint if Hong Kong is to minimize political interference from the PRC. The other side of this depressing reality is that if, by their actions, the local democrats demonstrate a commitment not to challenge the PRC's sovereign authority, a *modus operandi* for further democratic developments along the lines set out in the Basic Law will be possible. Otherwise, the provisions in the Basic Law will be little more than paper promises. The task of steering the various parties concerned to reach such a *modus operandi* falls primarily on the shoulders of the SAR government, particularly on those of its chief executive.

Resilience of Hong Kong

Modern Hong Kong is a product of the entrepreneurship, pragmatism and resourcefulness of its people who have made the most of the political and legal framework provided by the British administration. While both sets of factors have been equally important in contributing to Hong Kong's spectacular success, the political and legal infrastructures are the most vulnerable to interference from the PRC.

Hong Kong society has shown remarkable resilience in facing the momentous changes implied by its historic appointment with China. The quality and ethos of the local people, who are predominantly but not exclusively Chinese, is what has made this possible. The resourcefulness and pragmatism of its business persons and entrepreneurs have enabled Hong Kong to respond adroitly to adversity and to prosper, particularly over the last 50 years. Before 1949, Hong Kong was primarily an entrepôt built mainly on the re-export trade with China. The China trade collapsed when the USA and UN imposed trade embargoes on the PRC after it joined the Korean war in 1950. On their own initiative, Hong Kong's traders then turned to manufacturing light industrial goods. When the embargoes ended and the PRC opened its economy in the 1970s, the Hong Kong business community promptly revived the entrepôt trade. In the 1980s, when local manufacturing costs soared and the investment environment in the PRC improved, Hong Kong business people again rose to the challenge. They moved their manufacturing facilities to the PRC and turned Hong Kong primarily into a financial and other tertiary servicing base. Since they received no help or subsidy from the Hong Kong government, they have demonstrated remarkable flexibility in adapting to the changing environment — whether economic, social or political.[2] This is a crucial element of local resilience.

The cruel fact that none of the big business conglomerates, whether locally based or multinational, can afford to lose confidence and try to pull out of Hong Kong is another reason for Hong Kong's economic resilience. Local business and financial circles are compact and tightly interwoven. Should any one of them make even a hypothetical attempt to sell off its assets in a big way, everybody would know about it within hours. This would provoke a panic rush by others to do the same and cause the economy to crash. Because people are very conscious of this hypothetical trigger effect, it is improbable that any of the big conglomerates will ever test it. The big capitalists of

Hong Kong have no option but to profess confidence in its future and try to dismiss specific acts of PRC interference as having no direct relevance.

The economy's resilience is vital for two reasons. First, Hong Kong's economic values underline the PRC's rationale for allowing the capitalist system to survive there. Second, realistically one has to expect a degree of economic meddling by the PRC. The irrelevance of the sovereignty issue to the economic sphere does not mean there will be no interference. One must realize that PRC cadres have always believed that the British colonial administration habitually tilted the economy towards favouring British capitalists. PRC leaders are therefore likely to assume that the SAR government will do the same for Chinese investors. They are even more likely to assume this if such investors happen to be their own relatives, or state-owned institutions such as China Resources or Everbright. The Hong Kong government's ethos, which is to leave the economy to the free market and to private entrepreneurs rather than to civil servants, is anathema to PRC cadres. Beyond the short term it is unrealistic to suppose that all PRC leaders will resist the temptation to put pressure on the SAR government to manipulate the local economy. This is likely to happen either for private gain or to help the PRC meet as yet undefined short-term economic needs. Interference of one kind or another will happen, but Hong Kong's economic resilience will allow it to take a considerable amount of such intervention in its stride.

The same qualities that have given the local economy its resilience also apply more generally. Pragmatism, resource-fulness and the entrepreneurial spirit are human qualities that flourish under pressure. They will enable Hong Kong society to come to terms with whatever political interference may occur. While there is no question that local Hong Kong people have reached the stage of strongly desiring democracy, it is reasonable to expect them to continue to get on with life even if the promises of further democratization in the Basic Law are not implemented. Under such a scenario, there would be public protest and some agitation, but the overall reaction is more likely to be one of pragmatism. In much the same way as the people of Hong Kong adjusted to the prospect of retrocession, their pragmatism is likely to steer them away from open confrontation with Beijing and towards tolerating a degree of political interference.

The International Dimension

Hong Kong is a major international city and, in this capacity, it will have a key contribution to make to the PRC. It is the most cosmopolitan and vibrant metropolis in the PRC and is its gateway to the rest of the world. Given that Hong Kong handles more trade than the rest of the PRC together, the SAR will be even more important to the PRC than New York is to the USA. The crisscrossing contacts and relations Hong Kong people and businesses have with the rest of the world and with the overseas Chinese communities are invaluable to the PRC. No other city in the PRC could replace Hong Kong for the foreseeable future. For all its glories before 1949 and its spectacular rejuvenation in the last decade, Shanghai is still merely a shadow of Hong Kong. Hong Kong's international contacts will remain priceless for as long as the PRC remains committed to economic reform. This commitment is likely to continue because the survival of the communist party–state now relies on the reforms bringing steady improvements to living standards. The PRC leadership, however, also views these international contacts, including Hong Kong's historical links with Britain, with suspicion and concern.

The PRC's main concern in this connection is to ensure that Hong Kong is not a western capitalist Trojan Horse handed over by the British to bring down its political system. Despite dramatically increased contact between the PRC and the capitalist west since Mao's death in 1976, the PRC remains mistrustful of its old adversaries' intentions. Outstanding disputes between itself and the USA, particularly over Taiwan, but including other issues like human rights, constantly remind the PRC leadership of the adversarial nature of the relationship. Since the collapse of Soviet military power and its threat to the PRC, the USA has again become the PRC's leading potential enemy. In Beijing, it is taken for granted that the ultimate objective of the USA's China policy is to bring about the collapse of the communist system in the PRC. Failing that, it is to prevent the PRC from matching the USA in wealth and power, if not also in importance in the world.

From Beijing's point of view, the purpose of US support for Taiwan is to divide China and to keep it weak, or at least preoccupied with this thorny issue. Following the same line of thinking, Beijing also doubts US intentions towards Hong Kong. It believes that the USA must have certain ulterior motives in passing a Hong Kong Act. Under this act the US government has to report to Congress on the progress of Hong Kong's transition to PRC sovereign rule. Since Beijing sees the Hong Kong question as a purely bilateral issue between itself and London before July and as a domestic affair afterwards, it is resentful of the USA's interest. One explanation the PRC cadres find credible is that the British have sought US help over Hong Kong by building on the Anglo–American 'special relationship' and appealing to the hidden US agenda for the PRC. However fanciful it may be, it links Hong Kong to an international conspiracy. The USA is seen as the leader of this conspiracy, with Britain playing second fiddle. Hong Kong is the bait or catalyst with which to start a process of transformation in the PRC without resorting to war. This is essentially what the PRC sees as the 'peaceful transformation' conspiracy. It underlines the PRC's sensitive and hostile responses to Governor Patten or Martin Lee's appeal to the USA for support over democratization and related issues in Hong Kong.

Given the PRC's complex view of Hong Kong's international contacts, it would obviously like to enjoy the advantages of Hong Kong's outside links without their negative implications. What this means in practice is that Hong Kong should maintain its attraction to the multinationals, either as a place for investment or as a gateway for investing in the PRC. It should not, however, be part of any Western conspiracy. The PRC would prefer to see a cooling off in Hong Kong's relations with Britain and, for that matter, with the USA as well. It would, however, want this to happen without any adverse effect on these countries' investments in the SAR or PRC. The PRC would be upset if the SAR government, or even Hong Kong's political activists, appealed to the USA or the international community to support any activity it deemed infringed on its sovereign authority over Hong Kong. While Hong Kong must maintain its international links, it needs to be circumspect about enlisting the open support of the outside world in any Hong Kong versus PRC issue. This applies particularly to the USA and, to a slightly lesser extent, Britain. Hong Kong would have a better chance of securing concessions from Beijing if the latter did not see this as yielding to international pressure and thereby allowing a wider international conspiracy to hatch.

The Future

The political imperative governing the PRC's policy towards the SAR will define the framework for Hong Kong's future. This means that the PRC will not permit any development in the SAR that it deems threatening to its sovereignty or to the communist party–state's survival. Despite all the promises and documents, such as the Joint Declaration and the Basic Law, the PRC will interfere in Hong Kong's affairs. There is as yet no clear definition of the degree and scope of this intervention. That will depend on the process of dynamic interaction between the SAR and the rest of the PRC. This is not a simple bilateral affair between the SAR and the PRC governments. Other major actors within Hong Kong include various political parties of different persuasions, the civil service, the Communist Party's Hong Kong and Macao Work Committee, the media, leading investors and, to a lesser extent, even the ordinary people as a whole. In the PRC, various central government ministries and Communist Party departments, provincial governments (particularly that of Guangdong), and the PLA all have a role to play.

The SAR government will need to help other players in Hong Kong understand the PRC's bottom line and to persuade them not to cross it. It will also need to enlist the PRC government's support to ensure that the various actors in mainland China abide by the guidelines the PRC government had itself laid down. Ultimately, exactly how much autonomy the PRC allows the SAR to enjoy will depend on how Beijing interprets the actions of the various actors in Hong Kong, rather than what they actually do. The less Beijing feels its sovereignty over the SAR challenged, the more autonomy it will allow the SAR to enjoy and the more closely it will follow the Joint Declaration and the Basic Law.

This is one of the ironies of Hong Kong politics. To minimize the erosion of its own system and way of life, the SAR must exercise enough self-restraint to make sure that its continuance does not threaten the socialist system in the PRC. This is inherent in the 'one country, two systems' model of allowing a free and non-interfering capitalist system to exist within the wider framework of a restrictive and interventionist socialist system. There is a basic contradiction between the need for self-restraint and the forces behind the economic and social developments in postwar Hong Kong that have given rise to a demand for democratization. The popularity of Martin Lee and his Democratic Party reflects this pattern of evolution. The tragic reality is that if Lee and his colleagues fail to rein in their own activities to within the limits defined by Beijing, they will probably provoke a reaction from Beijing that will reduce the scope of autonomy for the SAR. While such a scenario will have a strong negative impact on morale, it is unlikely to destroy Hong Kong because of the resilience of the local community. The same applies to limited meddling in the economic spheres by the PRC. However, there is a limit to how much interference Hong Kong can take and it is imperative for the SAR to cut down, if not completely avoid, provoking the PRC.

Hong Kong's international links will also affect the scope of its autonomy. The SAR will need to do two things:

- preserve and enhance its network of international contacts; and
- persuade its supporters and well-wishers in the rest of the world to watch its developments but, unless absolutely necessary, to avoid putting overt pressure on the PRC.

High-profile pressure, particularly from the USA, would only prove counterproductive and convince the PRC that Hong Kong is colluding in a worldwide conspiracy against it. This applies less to Britain, for it is bound by the Joint Declaration to ensure that Hong Kong's system remains basically unchanged after the handover. Hong Kong must, however, be realistic about the limits of British influence after the retrocession. Believing that the British still want to resurrect their influence in post-colonial Hong Kong, the PRC is hardly likely to respond positively to British recommendations it strongly dislikes.

Generally, the guarantees enshrined in the Joint Declaration and the Basic Law for Hong Kong's future will merely provide a guide to what will happen. How closely they are followed will depend on the working out of a *modus operandi* between the SAR and PRC governments. There are two main reasons for adopting a basically optimistic view of Hong Kong's future:

- the PRC's own self-interests will impose restraints on how much it interferes in the SAR; and, equally important,
- through its resilience, Hong Kong will be able to accommodate to much of the interference and will, it is hoped, allow some of the damage to be repaired.

Hong Kong's prospects of surviving the handover are fair, though it is unlikely to be able to continue exactly as before.

Keeping Hong Kong's historic appointment with China has some features in common with an arranged marriage. It is entered into without the bride being allowed any say and there is no possibility of a divorce. In this analogy Hong Kong is the bride. After the official celebrations, the bride's choices are to learn to live with the reality, to make her life a misery, or to provoke a confrontation that will certainly lead to dire consequences. Although her husband is prone to bullying, he wants to make a success of the marriage and thus provides a glimpse of hope. It may be unrealistic for the wife to hope that her married life will be 'happy ever after', but it does not have to end in utter disaster.

Notes

Chapter 1

1. Ronald Robinson and John Gallagher, *Africa and the Victorians: The Official Mind of Imperialism* (London and Basingstoke, 1981) p.8.
2. Steve Tsang (ed.) *A Documentary History of Hong Kong: Government and Politics* (Hong Kong, 1995) p.32.
3. Robinson and Gallagher, *Africa and the Victorians*, p.17.
4. Philip Bruce, *Second to None: The Story of the Hong Kong Volunteers* (Hong Kong, 1991) p.4.
5. Peter Wesley-Smith, *Unequal Treaty 1897–1997: China, Great Britain and Hong Kong's New Territories* (Hong Kong, 1983) p.11.
6. PRO CO537/34, Enclosure from Robinson to Ripon, secret dispatch 24, 14 November 1894.
7. PRO CO537/34, Robinson to Ripon, secret dispatch 23, 9 November 1894.
8. Quoted in Wesley-Smith, *Unequal Treaty*, p.17.
9. Frank Welsh, *A History of Hong Kong* (London, 1993) p.318.
10. Quoted in ibid., p.320.
11. John E. Schrecker, *Imperialism and Chinese Nationalism: Germany in Shantung* (Cambridge, Massachusetts, 1971) p.23.
12. Quoted in ibid., p.320.
13. Philip Joseph, *Foreign Diplomacy in China 1894–1900* (New York, 1971).
14. Pamela Atwell, *British Mandarins and Chinese Reformers: The British Administration of Weihaiwei (1898–1930)* (Hong Kong, 1985) p.215.
15. L. K. Young, *British Policy in China 1895–1902* (Oxford, 1970) p.71.
16. *House of Lords Debates*, 56 (1898) pp.165–6.
17. Quoted by H. Z. Schiffrin, *Sun Yat-sen and the Origins of the Chinese Revolution* (Berkeley, 1970) p.132.
18. Wesley-Smith, *Unequal Treaty*, p.28.
19. Young, *British Policy in China*, pp.85–7.
20. PRO FO17/1340, MacDonald to Salisbury 122, 4 April 1898.
21. Hong Kong Government, *Xianggang yu Zhongguo: Lishi Wenxian Ziliao Huibian* (Hong Kong and China: Collected Historical Writings) (Hong Kong, 1984) pp.181–2 (Tsungli Yamen to Emperor Guangxu, 14 April 1898).
22. Schrecker, *Imperialism and Chinese Nationalism*, p.251.
23. Yu Shengwu and Liu Cunkuan (eds) *Shijiu Shiji de Xianggang* (Nineteenth Century Hong Kong) (Beijing, 1994) p.115.
24. Wesley-Smith, *Unequal Treaty*, p.38.

25. Ibid., pp.136–8.
26. Ibid., p.41.
27. Minutes of Bertie, cited in ibid., p.44.
28. PRO CO882/5, Chamberlain to Blake, confidential dispatch, 6 January 1899.
29. PRO CO537/34, Enclosure from Robinson to Ripon, secret dispatch 24, 14 November 1894.
30. PRO CO882/5, Report by Stewart Lockhart on the Extension of the Colony, 8 October 1898.
31. PRO CO19/494, Convention of Peking.
32. Liang Binghua, *Chengzhai yu Zhongying Waijiao* (The Fort and Sino–British Diplomacy) (Hong Kong, 1995) p.4.
33. PRO CO19/494, Convention of Peking.
34. PRO CO882/5, Report by Stewart Lockhart on the Extension of the Colony, 8 October 1898.
35. PRO FO17/1334, MacDonald to Salisbury, dispatch 102, 27 May 1898.
36. PRO CO882/5, Report by Stewart Lockhart on the Extension of the Colony, 8 October 1898.
37. PRO FO17/1335, MacDonald to Bertie, letter of 28 July 1898.
38. Wesley-Smith, *Unequal Treaty*, p.35.
39. PRO CO19/494, Convention of Peking.
40. PRO CO882/5, Royal Order in Council 1898.
41. Ibid.
42. Wesley-Smith, *Unequal Treaty*, p.33.
43. Quoted in Mary H. Wilgus, *Sir Claude MacDonald, the Open Door, and British Informal Empire in China, 1895–1900* (New York and London, 1987) p.82.
44. Atwell, *British Mandarins and Chinese Reformers*, p.62.
45. Ibid., pp.62–3.
46. Ibid., pp.155–6.
47. Sir Eric Teichman, *Affairs of China* (London, 1938) pp.196–7.
48. Mao Zedong, *Mao Zedong Waijiao Wenxuan* (Mao Zedong's Selected Writings on Foreign Affairs) pp.77–8.
49. Ibid., pp.89–91.
50. S. N. Goncharov, J. W. Lewis and Xue Litai, *Uncertain Partners: Stalin, Mao, and the Korean War* (Stanford, 1993) p.40.

Chapter 2

1. Liang Binghua, *Chengzhai yu Zhongying Waijiao* (The Fort and Sino–British Diplomacy) (Hong Kong, 1995) pp.29–32.
2. PRO CO882/5, Colonial Office to Foreign Office, confidential letter, 30 November 1898.
3. PRO CO882/5, GOC in China and Hong Kong to the Governor, letter of 20 April 1899.
4. PRO CO882/5, Blake to Chamberlain, dispatch 123, 27 May 1899.
5. Liang, *Chengzhai yu Zhongying Waijiao*, pp.55–62.

6. Joseph W. Esherick, *The Origins of the Boxer Uprising* (Berkeley, 1987) p.xiii.
7. Mary C. Wright, *China in Revolution: The First Phase* (New Haven and London, 1968) p.1.
8. Ibid., p.4.
9. Chou Tse-Tsung, *The May Fourth Movement: Intellectual Revolution in Modern China* (Stanford, 1967) p.20.
10. Edmund S. K. Fung, *The Diplomacy of Imperial Retreat: Britain's South China Policy, 1924–1931* (Hong Kong, 1991) p.36.
11. Martin Wilbur, *Sun Yat-sen: Frustrated Patriot* (New York, 1976) pp.141–7.
12. Harumi Goto-Shibata, *Japan and Britain in Shanghai 1925–31* (Basingstoke, 1995) p.11.
13. Martin Wilbur, *The Nationalist Revolution in China, 1923–1928* (Cambridge, 1983) p.68.
14. Goto-Shibata, *Japan and Britain in Shanghai*, p.15.
15. Chan Lau Kit-ching, *China, Britain and Hong Kong 1895–1945* (Hong Kong, 1990) p.177.
16. Fung, *The Diplomacy of Imperial Retreat*, pp.42–3.
17. Jiang Jieshi, *Zongtong Jianggong Sixiang yanlun Zongzi* (Collected Works of President Chiang Kai-shek) (Taipei, 1984) (hereafter, Chiang Kai-shek, *Zongzi*) vol. 36, p.146.
18. Norman Miners, *Hong Kong Under Imperial Rule, 1912–1941* (Hong Kong, 1987) p.17.
19. Donald A. Jordan, *The Northern Expedition: China's National Revolution of 1926–1928* (Honolulu, 1976) p.81.
20. Ibid., p.85.
21. PRO CO129/503/2, draft telegram to Clementi, undated, January 1926.
22. PRO FO371/11662, Statement of British Policy in China, approved by Cabinet on 1 December 1926, dated 2 December 1926.
23. Fung, *The Diplomacy of Imperial Retreat*, p.114.
24. PRO CO129/503, Clementi to Amery, paraphrase telegram of 19 January 1927.
25. Ibid.
26. PRO CO129/355, Lugard to Crewe, 26 May 1909.
27. PRO CO129/323, May to Lyttelton, 17 June 1914.
28. Zhang Yongjin, *China in the International System, 1918–20: The Middle Kingdom at the Periphery* (Basingstoke, 1991) pp.104–5; and Wesley-Smith, *Unequal Treaty*, pp.150–4.
29. PRO CO129/503, Clementi to Amery, telegram of 19 January 1927.
30. PRO CO129/503/2, draft telegram to Clementi, undated February 1927.
31. Ibid.
32. Wesley-Smith, *Unequal Treaty*, p.158.
33. Quoted in ibid.
34. PRO CO129/503/2, Minutes by Gent, 3 July 1928.
35. In Hong Kong the war formally started on 8 December because of the time zone difference.

36. Ch'i Hsi-sheng, *Nationalist China at War: Military Defeats and Political Collapse, 1937–45* (Ann Arbor, 1982) p.56.

37. Aron Shai, *Origins of the War in the East: Britain, China and Japan 1937–39* (London, 1976) p.162.

38. Michael Howard, 'British Military Preparations for the Second World War', in David Dilks (ed.) *Retreat from Power: Studies in Britain's Foreign Policy of the Twentieth Century. Volume One 1906–1939* (London and Basingstoke, 1981) p.116.

39. Shai, *Origins of the War in the East*, pp.156–8.

40. Peter Lowe, *Great Britain and the Origins of the Pacific War: A Study of British Policy in East Asia 1937–1941* (Oxford, 1977) p.2.

41. Martin H. Brice, *The Royal Navy and the Sino–Japanese Incident 1937–41* (London, 1973) p.148.

42. S. Woodburn Kirby, *The War Against Japan Volume I: The Loss of Singapore* (London, 1957) p.56.

43. Oliver Lindsay, *The Lasting Honour: The Fall of Hong Kong 1941* (London, 1978) p.2.

44. Waijiaobu, *Zhonghua Minguo Zhongyao Shiliao Chubian: Duijih Gangzhan Shichi* (A First Selection of Important Historical Material of the Republic of China: The Period of the War of Resistance against Japan) series III, *Zhanshi Waijiao* (Wartime Diplomacy) vol. II (Taipei, 1981) (hereafter, *ROC Documents: Wartime Diplomacy*) pp.171–2 (records of meeting on 6 August 1941) (ROC Foreign Ministry, Taipei).

45. Zeng Sheng, *Zheng Sheng Huiyilu* (Memoirs of [General] Zeng Sheng) (Beijing, 1991) p.209.

46. Wang Fu, *Jihjun Qinhua Zhanzheng 1931–1945* (The Japanese Army's Aggressive War Against China) (Shenyang, 1990) vol. 3, pp.1621–2.

47. Winston S. Churchill, *The Second World War Volume III: The Grand Alliance* (London, 1950) p.563.

48. Quoted in Christopher Thorne, *Allies of a Kind: The United States, Britain and the War against Japan, 1941–1945* (Oxford, 1978) p.157.

49. *ROC Documents: Wartime Diplomacy*, series III, vol. 3, agreement between Chiang Kai-shek and Mountbatten, October 1943.

50. *ROC Documents: Wartime Diplomacy*, series III, vol. 3, Roosevelt to Chiang, telegram of 31 December 1941.

51. PRO FO371/46251, 'The Political Issues between Great Britain and China regarding Hong Kong', Far Eastern Department paper, 7 July 1945.

52. Barbara Tuchman, *Sand Against the Wind: Stillwell and the American Experience in China 1911–45* (London, 1985) p.299.

53. Chiang Kai-shek, *Zongzi*, vol. 31, p.310 (statement of 7 July 1942).

54. Xu Kangming, *Zhonghuo Yuanzhengjun Zhanshi* (A History of the Battles of the Chinese Expeditionary Force) (Beijing, 1995) p.56.

55. Li Dongfang, *Xishuo Kangzhan* (Explaining the War of Resistance in Detail) (Taipei, Yuanliu Chubenshe, 1995) p.193. China's commitment was very considerable, for its armed forces had no more than 1 million rifles in total in 1942. Artillery was rare.

56. Ch'i Hsi-sheng, 'The Military Dimension, 1942–1945', in James Hsiung and Steven Levine (eds) *China's Bitter Victory: The War with Japan 1937–1945* (New York, 1992) p.159. In the event, China defeated the Japanese in Changsha, which was the only significant Allied victory in early 1942.

57. Gu Weijun, *Gu Weijun Huiyilu* (Memoirs of Wellington Koo) vol. 5 (Beijing, 1987) pp.14–15.

58. PRO CO825/42/55104/2, Gent's minutes, 14 February 1942.

59. Martin Gilbert, *Road to Victory: Winston S. Churchill 1941–1945* (London, 1986) p.18.

60. PRO CO825/35/55104, Secret note by MacDougall, March 1942.

61. PRO CO825/35/55104, Minutes of 35th meeting of the committee on postwar problems, 2 April 1942.

62. PRO FO371/31804, Clarke to Eden, report of 11 June 1942.

63. PRO CO825/35/55104, Minutes by Gent (on interdepartmental meeting of 30 June 1942) dated 1 July 1942.

64. PRO CO825/35/55104, Gent's minutes of 17 June 1942.

65. PRO FO371/31777, Cranborne to Eden, letter of 18 August 1942.

66. PRO CO825/35/55104, Gater's minutes (for Cranborne) 31 July 1942.

67. PRO CAB65/28, WM171(42) 21 December 1942.

68. *ROC Documents: Wartime Diplomacy*, series III, vol. 3, p.707, Guo to Wang, telegram of 29 April 1941.

69. *ROC Documents: Wartime Diplomacy*, series III, vol. 3, pp.758–61, Song to Chiang, submission of 7 November 1942.

70. *Wellington Koo Papers*, Butler Library, Box 56, Sino–British Treaty 1942–4, record of Sino–British negotiation conference on 28 December 1942.

71. Gu Weijun, *Gu Weijun Huiyilu*, vol. 5, pp.16–18.

72. PRO FO371/31662, Seymour to Eden, no. 1552, 13 November 1942.

73. PRO FO371/31662, Cadogan's minutes of 21 November 1942.

74. PRO FO371/31662, Eden's minutes, 22 November 1942.

75. Gu Weijun, *Gu Weijun Huiyilu*, vol. 5, p.17.

79. Ibid., p.18.

77. Chen Liwen (Nancy Chen) *Song Ziwen yu Zhanshi Waijiao* (T. V. Soong and Wartime Diplomacy) (Taipei, 1991) p.176.

78. P. van de Messerssche, *A Life to Treasure: The Authorized Biography of Han Lih-wu* (London, 1987) p.40; Han Lih-wu, *The Reminiscences of Mr Han Lih-wu* (Taipei, 1990) p.19.

79. PRO FO371/31664, Seymour to Eden no. 1678, 15 December 1942.

80. *Wellington Koo Papers*, Box 55, Sino–British Treaty 1942–4, Soong to Seymour, 11 January 1943.

81. Ibid., Seymour to Soong, 21 January 1943.

82. Lowe, *Great Britain and the Origins of the Pacific War*, p.159.

Chapter 3

1. John W. Garver, 'China's Wartime Diplomacy', in Hsiung and Levine

(eds) *China's Bitter Victory: The War with Japan 1937–1945* (New York, 1992) p.10.

2. Gu Weijun, *Gu Weijun Huiyilu* (Memoirs of Wellington Koo) vol. 5 (Beijing, 1987) p.176.

3. Earl of Avon, *The Eden Memoirs: The Reckoning* (London, 1965) p.375.

4. Gu Weijun, *Gu Weijun Huiyilu*, vol. 5, p.24.

5. *Waijiaobu 323* (archives of the ROC Foreign Ministry in Taipei) Executive Yuan to Foreign Ministry, order 1774, 24 March 1943.

6. Gu Weijun, *Gu Weijun Huiyilu*, vol. 5, p.232.

7. *Waijiaobu 323*, Executive Yuan to Foreign Ministry, order 1774, 24 March 1943.

8. Chiang Kai-shek, *Zongzi*, vol. 4 ('China's Destiny', March 1943) p.76.

9. Wu Guozhen, *Wu Guozhen Zhuan* (Biography of K. C. Wu) (Taipei, 1995) p.397.

10. Gu Weijun, *Gu Weijun Huiyilu*, vol. 5, p.171.

11. Ho Fengshan, *Waijiao Shengya Sishi Nian* (Forty Years in the Diplomatic Service) (Hong Kong, 1990) pp.178, 186.

12. *Waijiaobu 312.72*, Liang to Guo, letter 1/1907, 26 September 1944.

13. *Waijiaobu 312.72*, paper on methods to recover Hong Kong and Kowloon, undated, September 1944.

14. *Waijiobu 312*, draft papers entitled 'Negotiations for the Recovery of the Kowloon Leased Territory', dated August 1945; and 'Recovery of Hong Kong', August 1945.

15. Ch'i, 'The Military Dimension, 1942–1945', p.166.

16. Bai Zhongxi, *The Reminiscences of General Pai Chung-hsi* (original English title, but text in Chinese) (Taipei, 1989) p.347.

17. PRO FO371/46251, Britmis Chungking to War Office no. 200900H, 20 July 1945.

18. Kirby, *The War Against Japan Volume V: The Surrender of Japan* (London, 1969) p.139.

19. Zheng Dongguo, *Wo de Rongma Shengya: Zheng Dongguo Huiyilu* (My Life Soldiering: Memoirs of Zheng Dongguo) (Beijing, 1992) p.365.

20. Kirby, *The War Against Japan Volume V*, p.144.

21. PRO FO371/46251, Seymour to Bevin no. 827, 13 August 1945.

22. Gu Weijun, *Gu Weijun Huiyilu*, vol. 5, p.177.

23. PRO CO825/35/55104, revised draft paper 'British Far Eastern Policy', July 1942; Cranborne to Amery, letter of 20 August 1942.

24. PRO FO371/31777, Cranborne to Eden, letter of 18 August 1942.

25. PRO CO825/42/55104, minutes by Gent, 11 and 14 August 1943.

26. PRO CO825/42/55104/2, Gent's memo 'Future Status of Hong Kong', 21 July 1943.

27. PRO CO825/42/55104, Minutes by Secretary of State, 23 August 1943.

28. PRO FO371/35824, Clarke's minutes, 3 September 1943.

29. PRO CO825/42/55104, Monsoon's minutes, 12 November 1943.

30. PRO CO825/35/55104/7, Gent's memo, 19 June 1943.

31. PRO CO825/42/55104/2, Gent's minutes, 29 December 1943.

32. Ch'i, 'The Military Dimension, 1942–1945', p.165.

33. PRO CO825/42/55104/2, Ruston's minutes, 6 November 1944.
34. PRO CO537/4805, 'Summary of Assurances given by HMG since 1942 about the Future of Hong Kong'.
35. Quoted in Xiang Lanxin, *Recasting the Imperial Far East: Britain and America in China, 1945–1950* (New York, 1995) p.17.
36. On planning for reform, see Steve Tsang, *Democracy Shelved: Great Britain, China, and Attempts at Constitutional Reform in Hong Kong, 1945–1952* (Hong Kong, 1988) pp.12–24.
37. PRO FO371/46251, Sterndale-Bennett's minutes of 25 July 1945.
38. PRO HS1/133, SOE cipher telegram to Melbourne 986, 16 May 1945.
39. Ibid.
40. Charles Cruickshank, *SOE in the Far East* (Oxford, 1986) pp.156–8.
41. PRO HS1/133, SOE memo 132D/L, Melbourne to London, 23 May 1945.
42. PRO HS1/171, Minutes of a discussion at the Colonial Office on 10 August 1944.
43. Edwin Ride, *British Army Aid Group: Hong Kong Resistance 1942–1945* (Hong Kong, 1981) pp.271–2.
44. PRO FO371/46251, Sterndale-Bennett's minutes, 25 July 1945.
45. PRO HS1/171, Notes of a meeting in the Colonial Office on 23 July 1945.
46. Ibid.
47. PRO HS1/171, Britmis Chungking to War Office, 200900H, 20 July 1945.
48. Aron Shai, *Britain and China, 1941–47* (London and Basingstoke, 1984) p.100.
49. PRO HS1/171, Britmis Chungking to War Office, 200900H, 20 July 1945.
50. PRO HS1/171, Notes of meeting in the Colonial Office on 23 July 1945.
51. Chan Lau Kit-ching, 'The Hong Kong Question during the Pacific War (1941–45)', *Journal of Imperial and Commonwealth History*, vol. 3, no. 1, October 1973, p.72.
52. PRO CO129/591/16, Gent's minutes, 4 August 1945.
53. PRO HS1/171, Foreign Office to Chungking 859, 11 August 1945.
54. PRO HS1/171, Britmis Chungking to War Office, 200900H, 20 July 1945.
55. PRO HS1/171, Rait's minute to DDMI (P/W) 19 August 1944.
56. PRO FO371/46251, 'The Political Issues between Great Britain and China regarding Hong Kong', 7 July 1945.
57. Ibid.
58. PRO FO371/46251, undated note, 'Arrangements for the Administration of Hong Kong in the Event of its Liberation by Regular Chinese Forces', *c.* late July 1945.
59. Kirby, *The War Against Japan Volume V*, p.491.
60. Xie Yongguang, *Xianggang Zhanhou Fengyunlu* (Record of the Volatile Postwar Years in Hong Kong) (Hong Kong, 1996) p.30.

61. Shih Chueh, *The Reminiscences of General Shih Chueh* (Taipei, 1986) p.197.
62. PRO FO371/46252, Sterndale-Bennett's top secret minutes, 14 August 1945.
63. PRO FO371/46252, Sterndale-Bennett's minutes, 14 August 1945.
64. PRO FO371/46252, Foreign Office to Chungking 916, 18 August 1945.
65. PRO FO371/46252, Chingking to Foreign Office 857, 16 August 1945.
66. *Waijiaobu 323*, Foreign Ministry note on the handling of the Japanese surrender in Hong Kong, undated *c.* early September 1945.
67. *Waijiaobu 323*, Foreign Minister to British Ambassador, 17 August 1945.
68. Mao Zedong, *Mao Zedong Xuanji* (Selected Works of Mao Zedong) (Beijing, 1960) vol. 4, pp.1035–7.
69. Ibid., p.1028.
70. *Dongjiang Zongdui Shi* (A History of the East River Column) (Waiyang, Guangdong, 1985) pp.149–50.
71. PRO CO129/591/18, MACHIN to AMSSO TW1688, 26 August 1945.
72. *Dongjiang Zongdui Shi*, p.151.
72. Chiang's diary entry of 25 April 1945. Cited in Huang Renyu, *Zong Da Lishi de Jiaodu du Jiang Jeshi Riji* (Studying the Diaries of Chiang Kai-shek in the Perspective of Macro-History) (Taipei, 1994) p.429.
74. *Wellington Koo Papers*, Box 55, Folder 12b, London Embassy to Chiang, telegram of 13 August 1945.
75. Kirby, *The War Against Japan Volume V*, p.145.
76. PRO FO371/46252, Chungking to Foreign Office, 865, 17 August 1945.
77. PRO CO129/591/18, MACHIN to AMSSO, TW1688, 26 August 1945.
78. PRO CO129/591/18, Gater to General Ismay, letter of 25 August 1945; PRO FO371/46253, Sterndale-Bennett's minutes of 1 September 1945.
79. PRO FO371/46253, Sterndale-Bennett's minutes of 27 August 1945.
80. PRO FO371/46253, Foreign Office to Chungking 1002, 28 August 1945.
81. PRO FO371/46253, Sterndale-Bennett's minutes of 27 August 1945.
82. PRO CO537/4805, 'Summary of Assurances Given by HMG since 1942 about the Future of Hong Kong'.
83. FRUS 1945, vol. VII, pp.501–2 (Hurley to Secretary of State, telegram of 16 August 1945).
84. PRO FO371/46252, Prime Minister to President Truman, 18 August 1945.
85. H. S. Truman, *Memoirs of Harry S. Truman Volume II: Years of Trial and Hope* (New York, 1956) pp.61–2.
86. *Waijiaobu 323*, Hurley to Chiang, 22 August 1945.
87. *Waijiaobu 323* Foreign Ministry note on arrangements for the Japanese surrender in Hong Kong, undated *c.* September 1945.
88. *Waijioubu 312/72*, Note on the handling of the Japanese surrender in Hong Kong, 9 October [1946].
89. *Wellington Koo Papers*, Box 55, Folder 12b, Foreign Ministry to London Embassy, telegram 273, 25–6 August 1945.

90. Xie Yongguang, *Xianggang Zhanhou Fengyunlu*, p.37.
91. PRO FO371/46253, Chungking to Foreign Office 958, 27 August 1945.
92. PRO FO371/46253, Sterndale-Bennett's minutes, 31 August 1945.
93. PRO FO371/46253, Sterndale-Bennett's minutes, 27 August 1945.
94. PRO FO371/46253, Chungking to Foreign Office 973, 29 August 1945.
95. PRO FO371/46253, Chungking to Foreign Office 987, 30 August 1945.
96. *Waijioubu 312/72*, Note on the handling of the Japanese surrender in Hong Kong, 9 October [1946].
97. Tsang, *Democracy Shelved*, p.19.
98. *Franklin Gimson Papers*, 'Hong Kong Reclaimed', pp.169–76, Hung On-to Memorial Library, Hong Kong University.
99. G. B. Endacott and Alan Birch, *Hong Kong Eclipse* (Hong Kong, 1978) p.259.
100. PRO CO129/591/18, 'War Diary: 29th August to 16th September 1945'.

Chapter 4

1. Tsang, *Democracy Shelved*, p. 27.
2. PRO FO371/46258, Commander in Chief, Hong Kong to Cabinet Office IZ10440, 12 November 1945.
3. PRO CO129/594/4, speech by Young, 1 May 1946.
4. Tsang, *Democracy Shelved*, p.186.
5. PRO FO371/53632, Foreign Secretary's minutes to Prime Minister dated 8 March 1946; and PRO FO371/53633, Prime Minister's minute to Foreign Secretary dated 9 March 1946.
6. PRO CO537/5400, Minutes of 9th Meeting on 12 July 1950.
7. G. B. Endacott, *A History of Hong Kong* (Hong Kong, 1964) p.289; Hong Kong Government, *The Government and the People* (Hong Kong, 1962) p.132.
8. Alexander Grantham, *Via Ports: From Hong Kong to Hong Kong* (Hong Kong, 1965) p.172.
9. For a full treatment of the reform attempts between 1946 and 1952, see Tsang, *Democracy Shelved*.
10. PRO CO537/1656, Minutes by Smith, 19 January 1946.
11. PRO CO537/1650, Gent's minutes (for Gater) 21 September 1945.
12. Ibid.
13. First draft in PRO CO129/592/8, 'Status of Hong Kong', August 1945.
14. PRO FO371/46257, GEN77/47, 23 October 1945.
15. PRO FO371/46257, Kitson's minutes, undated, *c.* early November 1945.
16. PRO FO371/53632, Sterndale-Bennett's minutes of 29 January 1946.
17. PRO FO371/53632, 'The Future of Hong Kong', 28 February 1946.
18. Keswick's original proposals are in PRO FO371/46259, 'Notes on Future of Hong Kong', 3 November 1945.
19. PRO FO371/53632, 'The Future of Hong Kong', 28 February 1946.
20. PRO FO371/53632, Sterndale-Bennett's minutes of 2 March 1946.
21. PRO FO371/53632, Sargent's minutes of 19 March 1946.
22. Ibid., and undated minutes by Bevin.

23. PRO FO371/53635, 'The Future of Hong Kong', 18 July 1946.

24. PRO FO371/53637, Lloyd to Dening, letter of 22 August 1946.

25. PRO FO371/53637, Dening to Lloyd, letter of 9 September 1946.

26. PRO CO537/3325, 'China: Annual Report for 1947' by Ambassador Stevenson.

27. PRO FO371/63388, Dening's minutes of 10 May 1947.

28. *Waijiaobu 323*, Copy of Pan's telegram of 21 September [1945].

29. Ibid., Foreign Ministry to Executive Yuan 10479, 31 October 1945.

30. *Waijiaobu 312.72*, paper on questions relating to recovery of Hong Kong and Kowloon, undated *c.* October 1946.

31. *Guofengbu 062.23/5000.4*, Vol. 2, Xu Yongzhang to Chiang, submission of 18 December 1946 (ROC Foreign Ministry, Taipei).

32. A large number of them are filed in *Waijiaobu 312.72*.

33. *Wellington Koo Papers*, Box 55, folder 12b, Waijiaobu to London Embassy, telegram 273, 25–6 August 1945. English translation in PRO CO129/592/8, Extract from President Chiang's address, 25 August 1945.

34. Steven I. Levine, *Anvil of Victory: The Communist Revolution in Manchuria, 1945–1948* (New York, 1987) p.38.

35. *Waijiaobu 323*, Intelligence 243, 28 December 1945.

36. PRO FO371/53635, Annex 1 to 'The Future of Hong Kong', 18 July 1946.

37. *Wellington Koo Papers*, Box 55, Folder 12b, London Embassy to Foreign Ministry telegram 661, 29 June 1946.

38. *Waijiaobu 317.72*, Foreign Ministry submission to Chiang, 15 November 1946.

39. PRO CO537/2193, Governor of Hong Kong to Colonial Office, savingrams dated 5 February 1947 and 16 September 1947.

40. *Waijiaobu 313.72*, vol. 1, Foreign Ministry to London Embassy, telegram 2320, 13 January 1948 (original in English); Foreign Ministry to Commissioner in Hong Kong telegram 170, 20 December 1947.

41. *Waijiaobu 313.72*, vol. 4, Executive Yuan to Foreign Ministry, instruction of 17 February 1948.

42. For the military dimension of the Chinese Civil War, see E. R. Hooton, *The Greatest Tumult: The Chinese Civil War 1936–49* (London and Oxford, 1991); for the political dimension, see Suzanne Pepper, *Civil War in China: The Political Struggle, 1945–1949* (Berkeley, 1978).

43. James Reardon-Anderson, *Yenan and the Great Powers: The Origins of Chinese Communist Foreign Policy 1944–1946* (New York, 1980) pp. 2–3.

44. Edgar Snow, *Red Star Over China* (Harmondsworth, 1972) pp.128–9.

45. Frank Hsiao and Lawrence Sullivan, 'The Chinese Communist Party and the Status of Taiwan', *Pacific Affairs*, vol. 52, no. 3, 1979, p.465.

46. Mao, *Mao Zedong Waijiao Wenxuan*, pp.55–62.

47. Mao Zedong, *Mao Zedong Wenji* (Collected Writings of Mao Zedong) (Beijing, 1996) vol. 5, p.194.

48. Ibid., p.231.

49. Chen Jian, *China's Road to the Korean War: The Making of the Sino–American Confrontation* (New York, 1994) p.29.

50. An example of such Western accounts is Ronald C. Keith, *The Diplomacy of Zhou Enlai* (Basingstoke, 1989).
51. Mao Zedong, *Mao Zedong Junshi Wenxuan* (Selected Writings on Military Affairs by Mao Zedong) (Beijing, 1981) p.319.
52. Mao Zedong, *Jianguo Yilai Mao Zedong Wengao* (Collected Writings of Mao Zedong since the Founding of the Republic) (Beijing, 1987) vol. 1, p.193.
53. Chen, *China's Road to the Korean War*, p.20.
54. James Tuck-hong Tang, *Britain's Encounter with Revolutionary China, 1949–54* (Basingstoke, 1992) pp.72–3. Mao's conditions are in Mao, *Mao Waijiao Wenxuan*, p.129.
55. Mao, *Jianguo Yilai Mao Zedong Wengao*, p.253.
56. *China's Foreign Relations: A Chronology of Events (1949–1988)* (Beijing, 1989) p.492.
57. Robert Boardman, *Britain and the People's Republic of China 1949–1974* (London and Basingstoke, 1976) p.136.
58. *Renmin Ribao* (People's Daily) (Beijing) 1 October 1982.
59. *Renmin Ribao*, 8 March, 1963.
60. *Xianggang yu Zhongguo: Lishi Wenxian Ziliao Huibian*, vol. 1, p.279 (Huang Hua's memo to the UN, 10 March 1972).
61. Mao, *Mao Zedong Wenji*, vol. 4, p.207.
62. PRO FO371/63318, Boyce (Peking) to Chancery (Nanking) 30 December 1946. Xiang Lanxin has described Harmon as a 'British intelligence officer who had personal connections with the Communist leaders'. The original source describes him, a retired colonel, as 'the only British news correspondent stationed' in Beijing who went to Yenan for a visit for the first time. The available official PRC source also refers to him as a visiting British journalist. Xiang's citation and quotation are both partly inaccurate. See, Xiang, *Recasting the Imperial Far East*, p.101.
63. PRO CAB129/35, CP(49)120, 23 May 1949.
64. Xu Jiatun, *Xu Jiatun Xianggang Huiyilu* (Xu Jiatun's Memoirs of Hong Kong) (Taipei, 1993) p.67. The bureau was located in Hong Kong at different times before the Pacific war. See, Deng Maomao, *My Father Deng Xiaoping* (New York, 1995) p.143.
65. Zeng, *Zeng Sheng Huiyilu*, p.569.
66. Gary Wayne Catron, *China and Hong Kong, 1945–1967* (Harvard University, unpublished Ph.D. thesis, 1971) p.70.
67. PRO CAB129/32, Appendix to CP(49)39, 4 March 1949 (translation of a communist document captured in Hong Kong).
68. PRO FO371/75779, Enclosure to Heathcote-Smith to Lamb, 2 December 1948. Qiao is identified as Chiao Mu in this document.
69. Ibid.
70. Goncharov, Lewis and Xue Litai, *Uncertain Partners*, p.40.
71. Zeng, *Zeng Sheng Huiyilu*, pp.570–1.
72. Xu, *Xu Jiatun Xianggang Huiyilu*, vol. 2, pp.473–4.

73. PRO CO537/6798, Colonial Political Intelligence Summary 1951, no. 3, March 1951.

74. Zhou Enlai, *Zhou Enlai Waijiao Wenxuan* (Beijing, 1994) p.83.

75. Mao's words quoted in Joseph Y. S. Cheng, *Hong Kong: In Search of a Future* (Hong Kong, 1984) p.61.

76. Liang Shangyuan, *Zhonggong zai Xianggang* (The Chinese Communists in Hong Kong) (Hong Kong, 1989) p.138.

77. Kevin Rafferty, *City on the Rocks: Hong Kong's Uncertain Future* (London, 1989) p.411.

78. PRO CAB129/31, CP(48)299, 9 December 1948.

79. Qiang Zhai, *The Dragon, the Lion, and the Eagle: Chinese–British–American Relations, 1949–1958* (Kent, Ohio, 1994) pp.30–1.

80. Translation of one such document can be found in PRO CAB129/32, Appendix to CP(49)39, 4 March 1949.

81. Feng Zhong-ping, *The British Government's China Policy 1945–1950* (Keele, Staffordshire, 1994) p.105.

82. PRO CAB129/31, CP(48)299, 9 December 1948.

83. PRO FO371/75877, Draft paper for JIC Committee 'Communist Political Intentions towards Hong Kong', undated, July 1949.

84. PRO CAB129/33, CP(49)52, 5 March 1949.

85. A detailed analysis of Britain's defence plan is in Zeng Ruisheng (Steve Tsang) 'Yingguo Fangwai Xianggang Zhengce de Yanbian' (The Evolution of Britain's Policy to Defend Hong Kong) *Guang Jiao Jing* (The Wide Angle) no. 200, 1989, pp.68–80.

86. Malcolm H. Murfett, *Hostage on the Yangtze: Britain, China, and the Amethyst Crisis of 1949* (Annapolis, Maryland, 1991) pp.72–5.

87. After the escape of HMS *Amethyst*, the incident came to be told as a story of British gallantry and valour.

88. PRO CAB128/15, CM30(49)4, 28 April 1949.

89. Mao, *Mao Zedong Wenji*, vol. 5, p.286.

90. Ibid., p.302.

91. PRO DEFE6/10, JP(49)97(Final) 14 September 1949.

92. PRO CAB128/16, CM54(49)2, 29 August 1949.

93. PRO CAB128/15, CM33(49)2, 9 May 1949.

94. *Arthur Creech-Jones Papers*, Box 57, file 1, CP(49)177, RHL, 19 August 1949.

95. PRO DEFE6/10, JP(49)118(Final) 16 December 1949.

96. *Creech-Jones Papers*, Box 57, file 1, CP(49)177, 19 August 1949.

97. PRO CAB128/16, CM54(49)2, 29 August 1949.

98. See Edwin W. Martin, *Divided Counsel: The Anglo-American Response to Communist Victory in China* (Lexington, Kentucky, 1986).

99. *Harry S. Truman Papers*, Truman Library, President's Secretary's Files Box 257, NSC, CIA Reports — ORE 1949, ORE78–49 of 4 October 1949, 2.

100. *Truman Papers*, President's Secretary's Files Box 206, [NSC] Meeting 47, 20 October 1949; 'NSC55/2 A Report to the National Security Council by the Secretary of Defence', 17 October 1949.

101. *Truman Papers*, President's Secretary's Files Box 206, NSC Meeting 47, Memorandum for the Secretary of Defense, 15 July 1949.
102. *Truman Papers*, President's Secretary's Files Box 206, NSC Meeting 47, Memorandum for the Executive Secretary NSC, 17 October 1949.
103. *Dwight Eisenhower Papers*, White House Office: Special Assistance to NSC: Policy Papers Box 28, NSC6007/1-HK, 'US Policy on Hong Kong (NSC6007/1)', 11 June 1960, 2.
104. Nancy B. Tucker, *Taiwan, Hong Kong and the United States, 1945–1992: Uncertain Friendships* (New York, 1994) p.214.
105. PRO CO1030/1415, JP(58)164(A)(Preliminary Draft) 5 February 1959.
106. PRO FO371/120926, Murray's minutes of 12 March 1956.
107. PRO CO537/5628, Paskin's minutes, 11 March 1950.
108. PRO CO537/5307, Colonial Political Intelligence Summary no. 8, August 1950.
109. PRO CO1030/825, Dalton to Johnson, 28 March 1957.
110. PRO CO1030/825, Ashton's minutes of 18 October 1957.
111. Chinese statement reproduced in Cheng, *Hong Kong in Search of a Future*, p.54.
112. For a detailed analysis, see Steve Tsang, 'Strategy for Survival: The Cold War and Hong Kong's Policy towards Kuomintang and Chinese Communist Activities in the 1950s', *Journal of Imperial and Commonwealth History*, vol. 25, no. 2, May 1997, pp.294–317.
113. PRO CO537/5628, Grantham to Griffiths, no. 230, 5 March 1950.
114. PRO CO1030/430, Hong Kong Governor to Colonial Office, no. 70, 24 January 1958.
115. Sung, *The China–Hong Kong Connection: The Key to China's Open Door Policy* (Cambridge, 1991) p.5.
116. Yu Teh-pei, 'Economic Links among Hong Kong, PRC, and ROC: With Special Reference to Trade', in Jurgen Domes and Yu-ming Shaw (eds) *Hong Kong: A Chinese and International Concern* (Boulder and London, 1988) pp.114–15.
117. David Bonavia, *Hong Kong 1997* (Hong Kong, 1984) pp.78–80.
118. Y. C. Yao, 'Hong Kong's Role in Financing China's Modernization', in A. J. Youngson (ed.) *China and Hong Kong: The Economic Nexus* (Hong Kong, 1983) p.58.
119. Y. C. Yao, 'Banking and Currency in the Special Economic Zones: Problems and Prospects', in Y. C. Yao and C. K. Leung (eds) *China's Special Economic Zones* (Hong Kong, 1986) p.169.

Chapter 5

1. Noel Barber, *The Fall of Shanghai* (New York, 1979) p.229.
2. Beverley Hooper, *China Stands Up: Ending the Western Presence 1948–1950* (Sydney, 1986) p.108.
3. Aron Shai, *The Fate of British and French Firms in China, 1949–54: Imperialism Imprisoned* (Basingstoke, 1996) p.21.
4. PRO CAB129/35, CP(49)120, 23 May 1949.

5. The four were Mao's wife Qiang Qing, Zhang Chunqiao, Wang Hongwen and Yao Wenyuan.

6. Far Eastern Economic Review, *1968 Yearbook* (Hong Kong, 1968) p. 166.

7. Robert Cottrell, *The End of Hong Kong: The Secret Diplomacy of Imperial Retreat* (London, 1993) p.36.

8. Far Eastern Economic Review, *Asia 1979 Yearbook* (Hong Kong, 1979) p.179.

9. Mark Roberti, *The Fall of Hong Kong: Britain's Betrayal and China's Triumph* (New York and London, 1994) p.10. Royle was a member of Edward Heath's Conservative government, which had by then been replaced by James Callaghan's Labour government.

10. Cottrell, *The End of Hong Kong*, p.49.

11. Percy Cradock, *Experiences of China* (London, 1994) p.165.

12. Ibid., p.166.

13. Tsang, *A Documentary History of Hong Kong*, pp.8–9.

14. Grantham, *Via Ports*, p.107.

15. Hong Kong Government, *A Draft Agreement between the Government of the United Kingdom of Great Britain and Northern Ireland and the Government of the People's Republic of China on the Future of Hong Kong* (Hong Kong, 1984) p.2.

16. Andrew Freris, *The Financial Markets of Hong Kong* (London and New York, 1991) p.48.

17. Frank King, *The Hong Kong Bank in the Period of Development and Nationalism*, 1941–1984 (Cambridge, 1991) p.875.

18. Cradock, *Experiences of China*, p.165.

19. Xu, *Xu Jiatun Xianggang Huiyilu*, vol. 1, pp.82–3.

20. Ruan Ming, *Deng Xiaoping: Chronicle of an Empire* (Boulder, 1994) pp.56–9.

21. Han Nianlong (ed.) *Diplomacy of Contemporary China* (Hong Kong, 1990) p.464.

22. Cottrell, *The End of Hong Kong*, pp.54–6; Roberti, *The Fall of Hong Kong*, p.23.

23. The scholarly accounts include James Tang and Frank Ching, 'The MacLehose–Youde Years: Balancing the "Three-Legged Stool" 1971–86', in K. Chan (ed.) *Precarious Balance: Hong Kong Between China and Britain, 1842–1922* (New York, 1994); Ian Scott, *Political Change and the Crisis of Legitimacy in Hong Kong* (Hong Kong, 1989) p.167; and Michael Yahuda, *Hong Kong: China's Challenge* (London and New York, 1996) p.64.

24. *Daily Information Bulletin* (Hong Kong) Supplement, 6 April 1979.

25. See for example, *South China Morning Post* (Hong Kong) 7 April 1979.

26. The timing was confirmed by Foreign Minister Wu Xuejian in 1984. *Xianggang Wenti Wenjian Xuanji* (Selected Documents on the Hong Kong Question) (Beijing, 1995) pp.17–18.

27. Deng Xiaoping, *Deng Xiaoping Lun Tongyi Zhanxian* (Deng Xiaoping on the United Front) (Beijing, 1991) p.150.

28. Lee Lai To, *The Reunification of China: PRC–Taiwan Relations in Flux* (New York, 1991) p.61.
29. Guo Limin (ed.) *Zhonggong du Tai Zhengze Zhiliao Xuanji: 1949–1991* (Selected Material on the Chinese Communist Policy towards Taiwan) vol. 1 (Taipei, 1992) p.413.
30. Zhongguo Xinwen She (ed.) *Liaogong zai Renjian* (The Life of Mr Liao) (Hong Kong, 1984) p.23.
31. Xu, *Xu Jiatun Xianggang Huiyilu*, vol. 1, p.16.
32. Sima Yi, *Ronyao Quangui Deng Xiaoping de Xianggang Qiantu Tanpan* (Negotiations for Hong Kong's Future for which all the Glories belong to Deng Xiaoping) (Hong Kong, 1984) p.2.
33. This section on the resistance within the Chinese leadership is based on the doctoral research of Eugene Qian at Oxford University.
34. *Xianggang Wenti Wenjian Xuanji*, pp.2–3.
35. Cradock, *Experiences of China*, p.170.
36. Ibid., p.172.
37. Rafferty, *City on the Rocks*, pp.438–40.
38. For an analysis of the united front, see Lyman P. Van Slyke, *Enemies and Friends: The United Front in Chinese Communist History* (Stanford, 1967).
39. Analysis on the drafting of the 12 points is based on the doctoral research of Eugene Qian, University of Oxford.
40. Richard Evans, *Deng Xiaoping and the Making of Modern China* (London, 1993) p.267.
41. Margaret Thatcher, *The Downing Street Years* (London, 1993) p.259.
42. Cradock, *Experiences of China*, p.175.
43. Hugo Young, *One of Us* (London, 1990) p.292.
44. Cradock, *Experiences of China*, pp.177–8.
45. Thatcher, *The Downing Street Years*, p.259.
46. Deng Xiaoping, *Deng Xiaoping Wenxuan* (Selected Works of Deng Xiaoping) vol. 3 (Beijing, 1993) p.12.
47. Ibid., p.14.
48. Ibid., p.60.
49. Thatcher, *The Downing Street Years*, pp.260–2.
50. Han, *Diplomacy of Contemporary China*, pp.464–5.
51. Cradock, *Experiences of China*, p.180.
52. Cottrell, *The End of Hong Kong*, p.86.
53. Hong Kong Government, *Hong Kong 1983* (Hong Kong, 1983) p.46.
54. Hong Kong Government, *Draft Agreement on Hong Kong's Future*, p.3.
55. Hungdah Chiu, *The People's Republic of China and the Law of Treaties* (Cambridge, Massachusetts, 1972) p.30.
56. Cradock, *Experiences of China*, pp.184–5.
57. *Beijing Review*, no. 52 (Beijing, 27 December 1982) p.16.
58. Cradock, *Experiences of China*, p.185.
59. Thatcher, *The Downing Street Years*, p.489.
60. *Xin Wan Bao* (New Evening News) (Hong Kong) 13 May 1982.
61. Xu, *Xu Jiatun Xianggang Huiyilu*, vol. 1, pp.86–7.

62. *Pai Shing*, 16 July 1982, p.4.
63. Ibid., pp 7–8.
64. Thatcher, *The Downing Street Years*, p.491.
65. Xu, *Xu Jiatun Xianggang Huiyilu*, pp.89–92.
66. The two are Sir Quo-wei Lee and Lydia (now Baroness) Dunn.
67. Dick Wilson, *Hong Kong! Hong Kong!* (London, 1990) p.207.
68. *Pai Shing*, 1 July 1984, p.3.
69. Deng, *Deng Xiaoping Wenxuan*, vol. 3, p.60.
70. Roberti, *The Fall of Hong Kong*, p.79.
71. Paul H. Kreisberg, 'China's Negotiating Behavior', in T. W. Robinson and D. Shambaugh (eds) *Chinese Foreign Policy: Theory and Practice* (Oxford, 1994) p.454.
72. Geoffrey Howe, *Conflict of Loyalty* (London, 1995) p.366.
73. *Financial Times* (London) 16 September 1983.
74. Ibid.
75. Thatcher, *The Downing Street Years*, pp.489–90.
76. *Wen Hui Pao* (Hong Kong) 21 September 1983.
77. *Ming Pao* (Hong Kong) 2 October 1983.
78. Thatcher, *The Downing Street Years*, p.490.
79. Cradock, *Experiences of China*, p.192.
80. Ibid., p.197.
81. Ibid.
82. Evans, *Deng Xiaoping and the Making of Modern China*, p.268.
83. Howe, *Conflict of Loyalty*, pp.374–5.
84. Deng, *Deng Xiaoping Wenxuan*, vol. 3, pp.67–8.
85. Xu, *Xu Jiatun Xianggang Huiyilu*, pp.111–12.
86. *Pai Shing*, 16 August 1984, p.14.
87. Cradock, *Experiences of China*, p.198.
88. Ibid., pp.198–202.
89. Xu, *Xu Jiatun Xianggang Huiyilu*, pp.112–14.
90. Howe, *Conflict of Loyalty*, pp.375–7.
91. *Ming Pao*, 26 May 1984.
92. Hong Kong Government, *Draft Sino-British Agreement on Hong Kong*, p.13.
93. Ibid., pp.11–13.
94. *Hong Kong: Arrangements for Testing the Acceptability in Hong Kong of the Draft Agreement on the Future of the Territory* (London, 1984) pp.18–25.

Chapter 6

1. Hong Kong Government, *Draft Agreement on Hong Kong's Future*, p.15.
2. Tsang, *A Documentary History of Hong Kong*, pp.11.
3. Ian Scott, 'Political Transformation in Hong Kong: From Colony to Colony', in R. Y. W Kwok and A. Y. So (eds) *The Hong Kong–Guangdong Link: Partnership in Flux* (Hong Kong, 1995) pp.193–4.
4. *Draft Agreement on Hong Kong's Future*, p.7.

5. For a fuller analysis of how the alignment of power changed, see Steve Tsang, 'Realignment of Power: The Politics of Transition and Reform in Hong Kong', in P. K. Li (ed.) *Political Order and Power Transition in Hong Kong* (Hong Kong, 1997).
6. House of Commons, *Parliamentary Debates*, vol. 69, no. 22, 6 December (London, 1984) p.405.
7. Ibid., no. 23, p.470.
8. House of Lords, *Parliamentary Debates,* vol. 458, no. 17, 10 December (London, 1984) p.85.
9. *Cheng Bao* (Hong Kong) 22 November 1985.
10. Ibid.; and Xu, *Xu Jiatun Xianggang Huiyilu*, vol. 1, pp.172–4.
11. House of Commons, *Parliamentary Debates*, vol. 69, no. 22, 6 December 1984, p.391.
12. Hong Kong Government, *Draft Agreement on Hong Kong's Future*, p.14.
13. Cradock, *Experiences of China*, p.218.
14. Ibid.
15. For an in-depth analysis, see Steve Tsang, *Democracy Shelved: Great Britain, China, and Attempts at Constitutional Reform in Hong Kong, 1945–1952* (Hong Kong, 1988).
16. PRO FO371/63318, Boyce (Peking) to Chancery (Nanking) 30 December 1946.
17. PRO FO371/99251, Oakeshott's minutes of 31 March 1952.
18. For Sun's kipnapping, see J. Y. Wong, *The Origins of an Heroic Image: Sun Yatsen in London, 1896-1897* (Hong Kong, 1986).
19. PRO CO1030/595, 'Note by Lt. Col. K. Cantlie on his interviews with Chou En-lai in Peking on 30 January 58'.
20. PRO CO1030/595, Colonial Office to Hong Kong 107, 3 February 1958.
21. See for example, PRO CO1030/595, Summary of Talk between Chou and Wilson, 25 February 1958.
22. PRO CO1030/595, Peking to Foreign Office, telegrams 518 and 519, 28 August 1958.
23. Hong Kong Government, *Hong Kong Annual Report 1952* (Hong Kong, 1953) pp.11–14.
24. *Zhongguo Minzhu Lundan* (The Chinese Democratic Forum) vol. 2, no. 8, 15 April 1966, p.11.
25. Scott, *Political Change and the Crisis of Legitimacy in Hong Kong*, p.104.
26. Hong Kong Government, *The City District Officer Scheme: Report by the Secretary for Chinese Affairs* (Hong Kong, 1969) p.3.
27. Hong Kong Government, *District Administration in Hong Kong* (Hong Kong, 1981) p.4.
28. Ambrose King, 'Administrative Absorption of Politics in Hong Kong: Emphasis on the Grass Roots Level', *Asian Survey*, vol. 15, no. 5 (May 1975) pp.422–39.
29. Lau Siu-kai, 'Colonial Rule, Transfer of Sovereignty and the Problem of Political Leaders in Hong Kong', *Journal of Commonwealth and Comparative Politics*, vol. 30, no. 2 (July 1992) p.225.
30. Tsang, *A Documentary History of Hong Kong*, pp.53–6.

31. Ramon Myers (ed.) *Two Societies in Opposition: The Republic of China and the People's Republic of China* (Stanford: Hoover Institution Press, 1991) p.xviii.

32. James Hayes, *Friends and Teachers: Hong Kong and its People 1953–87* (Hong Kong, 1996) p.281.

33. *Guancha Xianggang: Xianggang Guangchashe Yanlunji* (Observing Hong Kong: A Collection of Writings by the Hong Kong Observers) (Hong Kong, 1982) pp.41–8.

34. *Ming Pao*, editorials of 31 August 1982 and 9 September 1983.

35. *Qishi Niandai* (The Seventies) no. 142, January 1981, pp.67–9.

36. *Pai Shing*, 1 January 1983, p.10.

37. See *Qishi Niandai*, no. 152, September 1982, special issue on the 1997 question.

38. *Pai Shing*, 1 January 1986, p.10.

39. Tsang, *A Documentary History of Hong Kong*, pp.121–2.

40. Hong Kong Government, *Green Paper: The Further Development of Representative Government in Hong Kong* (Hong Kong, 1984) p.4.

41. Ibid., p.3.

42. Hong Kong Government, *Hong Kong 1982* (Hong Kong, 1982) p.241.

43. Hong Kong Government, *Green Paper of 1984*, p.3.

44. Hong Kong Government, *White Paper: The Further Development of Representative Government in Hong Kong* (Hong Kong, 1984) pp.14–55.

45. Xu, *Xu Jiatun Xianggang Huiyilu*, vol. 1, p.173.

46. Ibid., p.172.

47. *Cheng Bao*, 22 November 1985.

48. *Jibenfa: Xianggang Weilai de Gouhua* (The Basic Law: Blueprint for the Future of Hong Kong) (Hong Kong, 1986) p.117 (Record of Xu Jiatun's press interview on 21 November 1985).

49. Dennis Chang, 'How China Sees It', in William McGurn (ed.) *Basic Law, Basic Questions* (Hong Kong, 1988) p.138.

50. Xu, *Xu Jiatun Xianggang Huiyilu*, vol. 1, p.177.

51. Edward Youde, *The Chairman's Lecture: The Political and Commercial Prospects for Hong Kong* (London, 1985) p.5.

52. Roberti, *The Fall of Hong Kong*, pp.161–4

53. Hong Kong Government, *Green Paper: The 1987 Review of Developments in Representative Government* (Hong Kong, 1987).

54. Hong Kong Government, *White Paper: The Development of Representative Government: The Way Forward* (Hong Kong, 1988) p.4.

55. *Independent*, 11 February 1988.

56. Hong Kong Government, *Public Response to Green Paper: The 1987 Review of Developments in Representative Government — Report of the Survey Office Part I* (Hong Kong, 1987) p.52.

57. Ibid., p.57.

58. Hong Kong Government, *White Paper of 1984*, p.8.

59. Hong Kong Government, *White Paper of 1988*, p.8.

60. *Independent*, 11 February 1988.

61. Lau Siu-kai, 'Institutions Without Leaders: The Hong Kong Chinese View of Political Leadership', *Pacific Affairs*, vol. 63, no. 2 (1990) p.191.
62. Tsang, *A Documentary History of Hong Kong*, p.227.

Chapter 7

1. For a detailed analysis, see Steve Tsang, 'Maximum Flexibility, Rigid Framework: China's Policy Towards Hong Kong and Its Implications', *Journal of International Affairs*, vol. 49, no. 2 (Winter 1996) pp.413–31.
2. Tse-tsung, *The May Fourth Movement*, pp.92–4.
3. For the PRC's approach to end the Western presence, see Beverley Hooper, *China Stands Up* (Sydney, 1986).
4. Xianggang Wenhuibao (ed.) *Jibenfa de Dansheng* (The Birth of the Basic Law) (Hong Kong, 1990) p.59.
5. Ibid., pp.58–9.
6. K. P. Lane, *Sovereignty and Status Quo: The Historical Roots of China's Hong Kong Policy* (Boulder, 1990) p.6.
7. Ezra Vogel, *One Step Ahead in China: Guangdong Under Reform* (Cambridge, Massachusetts, 1989) p.63.
8. Ibid, p.67.
9. Hong Kong Government, *Hong Kong 1989* (Hong Kong, 1989) p.61.
10. Sung, *The China–Hong Kong Connection*, p.173.
11. Cheng Lisheng, *Deng Xiaoping 'Yiguo Liangzhi' Sixiang Yanjiu* (An Analysis of Deng Xiaoping's Idea of 'One Country, Two Systems') (Shenyang, 1992) pp.87–8.
12. The following five paragraphs are based substantially on part of my article 'Maximum Flexibility, Rigid Framework', pp.421–3.
13. Quoted in Zhao Quansheng, *Interpreting Chinese Foreign Policy* (Hong Kong, 1996) p.238.
14. Deng Xiaoping, *Deng Xiaoping Lun Xianggang Wenti* (Deng Xiaoping on the Problem of Hong Kong) (Hong Kong, 1993) p.6.
15. Deng, *Deng Xiaoping Lun Tongyi Zhanxian*, pp.278–9.
16. Deng, *Deng Xiaoping Lun Xianggang Wenti*, p.14.
17. Cheng, *Deng Xiaoping 'Yiguo Liangzhi' Sixiang Yanjiu*, p.178.
18. Deng, *Deng Xiaoping Wenxuan*, vol. 3, p.221.
19. Ibid.
20. Ibid., pp.154–5.
21. Ibid., p.156.
22. Harry Harding, *Organizing China: The Problem of Bureaucracy 1949–1976* (Stanford, 1981) p.1.
23. Xu, *Xu Jiatun Xianggang Huiyilu*, vol. 2, pp.432–3.
24. Norman Miners, *The Government and Politics of Hong Kong* (Hong Kong, 1991) pp.68–9.
25. Wu Kangmin, *Renda Huiyilu* (Memoirs of the National People's Congress) (Hong Kong, 1990) pp.97, 152.
26. Xu, *Xu Jiatun Xianggang Huiyilu*, vol. 1, p.17.

27. A. D. Barnett, *The Making of Foreign Policy in China* (London, 1985) p.45.
28. Carol Lee Hamrin, 'The Party Leadership System', in Kenneth Lieberthal and David Lampton (eds) *Bureaucracy, Politics, and Decision Making in Post-Mao China* (Berkeley, 1992) p.115.
29. Ibid., p.44.
30. Ye Lei, 'Xianggang Xinhuashe fazhan shi' (A History of the Evolution of the Xinhua News Agency in Hong Kong) in Liang Shangyuan, *Zhonggong zai Xianggang* (The Chinese Communists in Hong Kong) (Hong Kong, 1989) p.189.
31. Cradock, *Experiences of China*, p.193.
32. Long Xin, *Xianggang de Lingyige Zhengfu* (The Other Government of Hong Kong) (Hong Kong, n.d.) pp.11–12.
33. Kenneth Lieberthal and Michael Oksenberg, *Policy Making in China: Leaders, Structures, and Process* (Princeton, 1988) p.143.
34. Xu, *Xu Jiatun Xianggang Huiyilu*, vol. 1, p.310.
35. Ibid., pp.12, 15–16.
36. John Burns, 'The Role of the New China News Agency', *Hong Kong and China in Transition* (Canada and Hong Kong Papers No. 3) (Toronto, 1994) p.39.
37. Qian Yuanle, *Xinhuashe Tousshi* (Seeing Through the Xinhua News Agency) (Hong Kong, 1987) p.106.
38. The following four paragraphs are based substantially on my article 'Maximum Flexibility, Rigid Framework', pp.416–17.
39. CO537/4824, Grantham to Creech-Jones 311, 1 April 1949.
40. John Burns, 'The Structure of Communist Party Control in Hong Kong', *Asian Survey*, vol. 30, no. 8, August 1990, p.752.
41. Xu, *Xu Jiatun Xianggang Huiyilu*, vol. 1, p.53.
42. For a more detailed explanation of the concept of *xitong* in PRC politics, see Kenneth Lieberthal, *Governing China: From Revolution Through Reform* (New York, 1995) pp.194–5.
43. Xu, *Xu Jiatun Xianggang Huiyilu*, vol. 1, pp.68–70.
44. For a perceptive and detailed analysis of the origins and meaning of the united front, see Van Slyke, *Enemies and Friends*.
45. *Dangdai* (Contemporary) 7 April 1990, p.35; Xu, *Xu Jiatun Xianggang Huiyilu*, vol. 1, p.300.
46. Ming Chan and Tuen-yu Lau, 'Dilemma of the Communist Press in a Pluralistic Society', *Asian Survey*, vol. 30, no. 8, August 1990, pp.742–4.
47. Liu Huiqing, *Liu Huiqing Miandui Xianggang* (Emily Lau Facing Hong Kong) (Hong Kong, 1991) p.287.
48. Wilson, *Hong Kong*, p.207.
49. Qian Yuanle, *Xinhuashe Tousshi*, p.159.
50. Ibid., p.69.
51. Burns, 'The Structure of Communist Party Control in Hong Kong', p.755.
52. Xu, *Xu Jiatun Xianggang Huiyilu*, vol. 1, p.72.
53. Ibid., p.54.

54. Ibid., vol. 2, p.426.
55. Wu Kangmin, *Renda Huiyilu*, pp.152–6.
56. Hong Kong Government, *Draft of Sino–British Agreement on Hong Kong*, p.13.
57. Hong Kong Government, *The Basic Law of the Hong Kong Special Administrative Region of the People's Republic of China* (Hong Kong, 1990) p.5.
58. Xianggang Wenhuibao, *Jibenfa de Dansheng*, p.205.
59. By the time the committee had completed its task in 1990, the number of its Hong Kong drafters had fallen to 18, for one had died, two had resigned and two had been expelled. Three mainland Chinese drafters had also died in the meantime.
60. Xu, *Xu Jiatun Xianggang Huiyilu*, vol. 1, pp.156–8.
61. Xianggang Wenhuibao, *Jibenfa de Dansheng*, pp.22–3.
62. I have been unable to ascertain whether or not they were card carrying members of the Communist Party.
63. Xu, *Xu Jiatun Xianggang Huiyilu*, vol. 1, p.161.
64. Ibid., p.157.
65. Ibid., pp.160–1.
66. Chinese Government, *Jibenfa: Xianggang Weilai de Gouhua*, p.91.
67. Ibid., p.111.
68. *Pai Shing*, 16 December 1985, pp.6–8, 58.
69. Xu, *Xu Jiatun Xianggang Huiyilu*, vol. 1, p.164.
70. M. K. Chan, 'Democracy Derailed: Realpolitik in the Making of the Hong Kong Basic Law, 1985–90', in M. K. Chan and David Clark (eds) *The Hong Kong Basic Law* (Hong Kong, 1991) p.8.
71. Stuart Schram, *The Political Thought of Mao Tse-tung* (New York, 1969) pp.316–17.
72. Based on the doctoral research of Eugene Qian at Oxford University.
73. For a detailed analysis of commander–commissar relations, see Hsiao-shih Cheng, *Party–Military Relations in the PRC and Taiwan* (Boulder, 1990).
74. Xianggang Wenhuibao, *Jibenfa de Dansheng*, p.231.
75. *Pai Shing*, 1 December 1988, pp.3–5; Xu, *Xu Jiatun Xianggang Huiyilu*, vol. 2, pp.211–12.
76. Lo Shiu-hing, *The Politics of Democratization in Hong Kong* (Basingstoke, 1997) p.121.
77. *Pai Shing*, 16 December 1988, pp.9–16.
78. Lo, *The Politics of Democratization in Hong Kong*, pp.214–15.
79. Hong Kong Government, *The Basic Law*, p.5; *Beijing Review*, 27 December 1982, p.16.
80. *Beijing Review*, 27 December 1982, p.10.
81. Ibid.
82. Andrew Nathan, 'Political Rights in Chinese Constitutions', in Randle Edwards, Louis Henkin and Andrew Nathan (eds) *Human Rights in Contemporary China* (New York, 1986) p.121.

83. Xiao Weiyun (ed.) *Yiguo Liangzhi yu Xianggang Tebie Xingzhengqu Jibenfa* (One Country Two Systems and the Basic Law for the Hong Kong Special Administrative Region) (Hong Kong, 1990) pp.8–13.

Chapter 8

1. Immanuel Hsu, *China Without Mao: The Search for a New Order* (Oxford, 1990) pp.92–4.
2. Franz Michael, 'China and the Crisis of Communism', in George Hicks (ed.) *The Broken Mirror: China after Tiananmen* (Harlow, 1990) p.449.
3. Hicks (ed.) *The Broken Mirror*, p.x.
4. Li Binyan, *China's Crisis, China's Hope* (Cambridge, Massachusetts, 1990) pp.53–5.
5. Cheng, Chu-yuan, *Behind the Tiananmen Massacre: Social, Political, and Economic Ferment in China* (Boulder, 1990) pp.29–32.
6. Minzhu Han, *Cries for Democracy: Writings and Speeches from the 1989 Chinese Democracy Movement* (Princeton, 1990) p.5.
7. Lowell Dittmer, *China Under Reform* (Boulder, 1994) pp.98–9, 146.
8. Han, *Cries for Democracy*, pp.8–9.
9. Lucian Pye, 'Tiananmen and Chinese Political Culture', *Asian Survey*, vol. 30, no. 4, April 1990, p.333.
10. Joseph Esherick and Jeffrey Wasserstrom, 'Acting out Democracy: Political Theater in Modern China', in Jeffrey Wasserstrom and Elizabeth Perry (eds) *Popular Protest and Political Culture in Modern China* (Boulder, 1994) pp.36–8.
11. Pye, Tiananmen and Chinese Political Culture, p.338.
12. Michael Fathers and Andrew Higgins, *Tiananmen: The Rape of Peking* (London, 1989) pp.68–9.
13. Melanie Manion, 'Introduction: Reluctant Duelists: The Logic of the 1989 Protests and Massacre', in Michael Oksenberg, Lawrence Sullivan and Marc Lambert (eds) *Beijing Spring, 1989: Confrontation and Conflict The Basic Documents* (New York, 1990) pp.xxvi–xxvii.
14. Deng, *Deng Xiaoping Wenxuan*, vol. 3, p.303.
15. Chen Xitong, 'Report on Checking the Turmoil and Quelling the Counter-Revolutionary Rebellion', supplement in *Beijing Review*, 17–23 July 1989, p.I.
16. Oksenberg el al (eds) *Beijing Spring, 1989*, pp.320–7.
17. Xu, *Xu Jiatun Xianggang Huiyilu*, vol. 2, pp.376–7.
18. Siu-kai Lau, 'Public Attitude Towards Sino–British Relations in the Late Transitional Period in Hong Kong' (abstract in English; paper in Chinese) in One Country Two Systems Economic Institute (ed.) *Hong Kong in Transition* (Hong Kong, 1993) pp.421–2.
19. Joseph Cheng, 'Prospect for Democracy in Hong Kong', in George Hicks (ed.) *The Broken Mirror: China after Tiananmen* (Harlow, 1990) p.278.
20. Xiaobo Liu, 'That Holy Word, "Revolution"', in Wasserstrom and Perry (eds) *Popular Protest and Political Culture in Modern China*, pp.314–5.

21. Wong, Jan, *Red China Blues* (Toronto, 1997) p.235.

22. Fathers and Higgins, *Tiananmen*, p.65.

23. Quoted in Geremie Barme, 'Totalitarian Nostalgia: Chinese Utopias, Future Imperfect', paper presented at the 'China Facing the Challenges of Modernization' Conference at Universidad Autónoma de Madrid, 2–3 October 1995, p.9. Chai's comments were recorded on tape during an interview with Philip Cunningham.

24. Ibid., p.10.

25. Wong, *Red China Blues*, pp.235–6.

26. Cheng, *Behind the Tiananmen Massacre*, p.204. Hong Kong's pro-democracy activists claimed a turn out of one million. The Hong Kong police's estimate was half a million.

27. Xu, *Xu Jiatun Xianggang Huiyilu*, vol. 2, pp.368–9.

28. *Xin Bao* (Hong Kong Economic Journal) (Hong Kong) 5 June 1989.

29. Ibid.

30. CO1030/383, Annex to OAG, HK to Secretary of State, savingram 1744, 10 October 1956.

31. Steve Tsang, 'Identity Crisis in Hong Kong', *Hong Kong Monitor*, September 1990, p.11.

32. Siu-kai Lau and Hsin-chi Kuan, *The Ethos of the Hong Kong Chinese* (Hong Kong, 1988) p.178.

33. Steve Tsang, 'Political Probems Facing the Hong Kong Civil Service in Transition', *Hong Kong Public Administration*, vol. 3, no. 1, March 1994, p.138.

34. Hugh Baker, 'Life in the Cities: The Emergence of Hong Kong Man', *The China Quarterly*, no. 95, September 1983, p.478.

35. *Dongfang Ribao* (The Oriental Daily) (Hong Kong) 5 June 1989; and *Xin Bao*, 6 June 1989.

36. *Pai Shing*, 1 July 1989, p.51; Ming-kuan Lee, 'Community and Identity in Transition in Hong Kong', in Reginald Kwok and Alvin So (eds) *The Hong Kong-Guangdong Link: Partnership in Flux* (Hong Kong, 1995) p.312

37. *South China Morning Post* (Hong Kong) 12 June 1989.

38. Foreign Affairs Committee, *Second Report on Hong Kong* (Session 1988–9) (London, 1989) p.vii.

39. Ibid., p.xii.

40. Ibid., p.viii.

41. Miners, *The Government and Politics of Hong Kong* (fifth edition) p.39.

42. Ibid.

43. William Shawcross, *Kowtow!* (London, 1989) pp.37–8.

44. *Pai Shing*, 16 June 1989, pp.12–13. The remaining members of Hong Kong's population were not born there and therefore are not British subjects, except for those who have become naturalized.

45. Steve Tsang, 'A Future Built on Hope: How the Foreign Affairs Committee Sees It', *Hong Kong Monitor*, September 1989, p.4.

46. *Pai Shing*, 1 July 1989, p.53.

47. Bernard Corry, *The Corry Report* (Hong Kong, 1989) p.50.

48. *Far Eastern Economic Review*, 22 June 1989, p.14.
49. *Independent*, 5 April 1990.
50. *Guardian*, 5 April 1990.
51. Thatcher, *The Downing Street Years*, p.495.
52. *Far Eastern Economic Review*, 8 June 1989, p.18.
53. Ibid.
54. Thatcher, *Downing Street Years*, p.495.
55. Ibid.
56. Foreign Affairs Committee, *Second Report on Hong Kong*, pp.xiii–xiv.
57. Cradock, *Experiences of China*, p.231.
58. Ibid.
59. Tsang, *A Documentary History of Hong Kong*, p.97 (British Foreign Secretary Hurd to Chinese Foreign Minister Qian, message of 12 February 1990).
60. Hong Kong Government, *Draft Agreement on Hong Kong's Future*, p.23.
61. Hong Kong Government, *An Introduction to Hong Kong Bill of Rights Ordinance* (Hong Kong, undated, 1991) p.3.
62. 'China Sticks to HK, Macao Policy', *Beijing Review*, 3–9 July 1989, p.6.
63. Wu Xiongcheng, 'The International Climate and the June Rebellion', *Beijing Review*, 11–17 September 1989, p.9.
64. 'China Sticks to HK, Macao Policy', p.6.
65. Chen Xitong, 'Report on Checking the Turmoil', pp.ii, vi, xii, xvi.
66. Cradock, *Experiences of China*, p.229.
67. Ibid., p.230. For a critical analysis of the Hong Kong government's policy towards subversion against the PRC in an earlier time, see Tsang, 'Strategy for Survival', pp.294–317.
68. Xu, *Xu Jiatun Xianggang Huiyilu*, vol. 2, pp.385.
69. Ibid., pp.384–5.
70. Cradock, *Experiences of China*, p.232.
71. *Xin Bao*, 13 May 1990.
72. Xu, *Xu Jiatun Xianggang Huiyilu*, vol. 2, p.395–6.
73. *Renmin Ribao*, 21 July 1989.
74. For details, see Ming Chan and David Clark (eds) *The Hong Kong Basic Law: Blueprint for 'Stability and Prosperity' under Chinese Sovereignty* (Hong Kong, 1991) pp.21–9.
75. Cradock, *Experiences of China*, pp.228–33.
76. Hong Kong Government, *Hong Kong 1990* (Hong Kong, 1990) p.5.
77. Cradock, *Experiences of China*, p.246.
78. Norman Miners, *The Government and Politics of Hong Kong* (fourteenth edition) (Hong Kong, 1986) pp.32–4.
79. Joan Leung, 'Summary Findings and Implications', in Rowena Kwok, Joan Leung and Ian Scott (eds) *Votes Without Power: The Hong Kong Legislative Council Elections 1991* (Hong Kong, 1992) p.145.
80. Leung Sai-wing, 'The "China Factor" in the 1991 Legislative Council Election', in Siu-kai Lau and Kin-sheun Louie (eds) *Hong Kong Tried Democracy: The 1991 Elections in Hong Kong* (Hong Kong, 1993) pp.187–8.

81. Ian Scott, 'An Overview of the Hong Kong Legislative Council Elections of 1991', in Kwok, Leung and Scott (eds) *Votes Without Power*, p.5.

82. The Hong Kong government's official figure is 39.15 per cent, but two independent studies suggest this figure is incorrect. According to them, either between 45.5 and 51.8 per cent voted or 48 per cent. Robert Chung, 'What Went Wrong with the Turnout Rate?', unpublished paper, cited in Kwok, Leung and Scott (eds) *Votes Without Power*, p.8; and Kin-sheun Louie et al., 'Who Voted in the 1991 Elections?', in Lau and Louie (eds) *Hong Kong Tried Democracy*, p.34.

83. Steve Tsang, 'A Triumph for Democracy?', *Hong Kong Monitor*, December 1991, p.1.

84. Hong Kong Government, *Hong Kong 1991* (Hong Kong, 1991) p.21.

85. Cradock, *Experiences of China*, p.237.

86. Deng, *Deng Xiaoping Wenxuan*, vol. 3, p.68.

87. Liao Guangsheng, *Xianggang Minzhuhua de Kunjing* (The Impossible Situation for Democratization in Hong Kong) (Taipei, 1996) p.91.

88. Ibid., p.104.

89. Ian Scott, 'Political Transformation in Hong Kong', p.216.

90. Cradock, *Experiences of China*, p.239.

91. *South China Morning Post*, 9 February 1990.

92. *Independent*, 5 July 1991.

93. Cradock, *Experiences of China*, p.241.

94. *Documents on the Prime Minister's Visit to Peking, 2–4 September 1991* (London, undated, 1991) Memorandum of Understanding

95. Scott, 'Political Transformation in Hong Kong', p.218.

Chapter 9

1. *Independent*, 3 January 1992.

2. Major's short spell as foreign secretary in the summer of 1989 coincided with the period when Sino–British relations were put on hold.

3. Liao, *Xianggang Minzhuhua de Kunjing*, p.92.

4. If the idea to replace the governor had come from within the diplomatic service, it would not have forced one of its own, who had not let the side down, to retire prematurely.

5. Tim Heald, *Beating Retreat: Hong Kong Under the Last Governor* (London, 1997) pp.4–5.

6. Ibid., p.6.

7. Frank Ching, 'A Discredited Past? One Hong Kong View on Lord Wilson', *Hong Kong Monitor*, December 1992, p.5.

8. Frank Ching, 'Toward Colonial Sunset: The Wilson Regime, 1987–92', in Chan (ed.) *Precarious Balance*, p.192.

9. Heald, *Beating Retreat*, p.316.

10. Emily Lau, ' "Dear Governor": An Elected Lady Offers Some Advice', *Hong Kong Monitor*, September 1992, p.7.

11. Liao, *Xianggang Minzhuhua de Kunjing*, p.204.

12. Chris Patten, *Our Next Five Years: The Agenda for Hong Kong* (Hong Kong, 1992) pp.32–3. Patten avoids mentioning that such an overlap is inherent in the British parliamentary system.

13. Ibid., pp.34–5.

14. Ibid., pp.35–6.

15. Ibid., p.37.

16. Ibid., p.38.

17. Hong Kong Government, *The Basic Law*, p.66.

18. Ibid., p.66.

19. Patten, *Our Next Five Years*, p.41.

20. Ibid., p.39.

21. Douglas Hurd, 'Governor Patten Unveils a Bold Blueprint for Hong Kong's Future', *Hong Kong Monitor*, December 1992, p.2.

22. Patten, *Our Next Five Years*, p.36.

23. Ibid., p.37.

24. Cradock, *Experiences of China*, p.245.

25. One can see the increase from 15 to 18, for the draft Basic Law at that time sanctioned 15 directly elected seats before 1997.

26. *Wen Hui Pao*, 24 October 1992.

27. *Wen Hui Pao*, 3 December 1992.

28. *Renmin Ribao*, 22 October 1992.

29. *Wen Hui Pao*, 24 October 1992.

30. Wang Hongxu, *Qishi Niandai Yilai de Zhongying Guanxi* (Sino–British Relations Since the 1970s) (Harbin, 1996) p.243. Strictly speaking, by the Chinese calculation, the number concerned should be 39, not 40.

31. Wang, *Qishi Niandai Yilai de Zhongying Guanxi*, p.243.

32. Lai Qizhi, *Peng Dingkang Zhenggai Fangan Mianmianguan* (Looking at the Patten Plan from Many Different Aspects) (Hong Kong, 1993) appendix.

33. Chris Patten, *Hong Kong: Today's Success, Tomorrow's Challenges* (Hong Kong, 1993) p.37.

34. *Wen Hui Pao*, 27 December 1992.

35. Wang, *Qishi Niandai Yilai de Zhongying Guanxi*, p.245; and *Renmin Ribao*, 22 October 1992.

36. *Renmin Ribao*, 24 October 1992.

37. Deng, *Deng Xiaoping Wenxuan*, vol. 3, p.75.

38. Nicholas Kristof and Sheryl WuDunn, *China Wakes: The Struggle for the Soul of a Rising Power* (London, 1994) p.405.

39. *Wen Hui Pao*, 28 January 1993.

40. Wang, *Qishi Niandai Yilai de Zhongying Guanxi*, p.245.

41. Roger Buckley, *Hong Kong: The Road to 1997* (Cambridge, 1997) p.145.

42. Wang, *Qishi Niandai Yilai de Zhongying Guanxi*, pp.252–5.

43. Lai, *Peng Dingkang Zhenggai Fangan Mianmianguan*, p.18.

44. *Wen Hui Pao*, 14 March 1992.

45. Patten, *Hong Kong: Today's Success, Tomorrow's Challenges*, p.40.

46. Ibid.

47. UK Government, *Representative Government in Hong Kong* (Com 2432) (London, 1994) p.10.
48. Ibid., pp.39–40.
49. Ibid., p.42.
50. Ibid., p.16.
51. *Renmin Ribao*, 3 December 1993.
52. *Renmin Ribao*, 16 December 1993.
53. UK Government, *Representative Government in Hong Kong*, p.14.
54. Ibid., pp.24–5.
55. Percy Cradock, 'Losing the Plot in Hong Kong', *Prospect*, April 1997, p.23.
56. *Wen Hui Pao*, 24 October 1992.
57. K. K. Leung, 'The Basic Law and the Problem of Political Transition', in Stephen Cheung and Stephen Sze (eds) *The Other Hong Kong Report 1995* (Hong Kong, 1995) p.40.
58. Hong Kong Government, *The Basic Law*, p.65.
59. Liao, *Xianggang Minzhuhua de Kunjing*, p.228.
60. Xu Simin, *Guoshi Gangshi Hua Sannian* (Speaking about the Affairs of the Country and Hong Kong in the Last Three Years) (Hong Kong, 1996) p.30.
61. Wang, *Qishi Niandai Yilai de Zhongying Guanxi*, p.264.
62. Ibid., p.268.
63. Quoted in Li Yi, *Xianggang Yijiujiuqi* (Hong Kong 1997) (Taipei, 1996) p.67.
64. Li, *Xianggang Yijiujiuqi*, p.68.
65. Buckley, *Hong Kong: The Road to 1997*, p.176.
66. BBC, *Summary of World Broadcasts (SWB)* FE/2796/F/1, Xinhua report, 12 December 1996.
67. Hong Kong Government, *The Basic Law*, p.65.
68. BBC, *SWB*, FE/2802/F/1, Xinhua news agency report of 21 December 1996.
69. Ibid.
70. *Xianggang Shang Bao* (Hong Kong Commercial News) (Hong Kong) 22 December 1996.
71. BBC, *SWB*, FE/2796/F/1, Xinhua report, 12 December 1996.
72. *Far Eastern Economic Review*, 9 January 1997, p.22.
73. BBC, *SWB*, FE/2801/F2, Zhongguo Tongxun She report, 19 December 1996.
74. BBC, *SWB*, FE/2798/F/1, Xinhua report, 16 December 1996. For Tung's business reliance on the PRC, see Leng Xia and Wang Tong, *Sheizhu Xiangjiang* (Who Will Be in Charge in Hong Kong?) (Hong Kong, 1996) pp.23–6.
75. *Far Eastern Economic Review*, 13 March 1997, pp.25–6.
76. This information comes from a source close to the PRC establishment in Hong Kong. Prominent Hong Kong citizens' membership of the Communist Party is usually treated as a PRC state secret.
77. *Dateline Hong Kong* (Hong Kong) 1997 issue 2, undated, March 1997.

Chapter 10

1. For a fuller explanation of 'peaceful transformation' see the section 'The International Dimension' below.

2. This and the following two paragraphs are substantially the same as part of my article, 'Maximum Flexibility, Rigid Framework', pp.431–2.

References

PRIMARY SOURCES

Butler Library, Columbia University
Wellington Koo Papers, Boxes 55 and 56

Eisenhower Library, Abilene, Kansas
Dwight Eisenhower Papers

Hung On-to Memorial Library, Hong Kong University
Franklin Gimson Papers, 'Hong Kong Reclaimed'

Ministry of Defence (Taipei)
Guofengbu 062.23/5000.4

Ministry of Foreign Affairs (Taipei)
Waijiaobu 312, 313, 323

Public Record Office (PRO) Kew Gardens, London
Cabinet Office (CAB) 65; 128; 129
Colonial Office (CO) 19; 129; 537; 825; 882; 1030
Foreign Office (FO) 17; 371
Ministry of Defence (DEFE) 6/10, JP(49)
Special Operations Executive (HS) 1/133; 1/171

Rhodes House Library, Oxford (RHL)
Arthur Creech-Jones Papers

Truman Library, Independence, Missouri
Harry S. Truman Papers

PRINTED DOCUMENTS

Chinese Documents

China's Foreign Relations: A Chronology of Events, 1949–1988 (Beijing, 1989)

Jibenfa: Xianggang Weilai de Gouhua (The Basic Law: Blueprint for the Future of Hong Kong) (Hong Kong, 1986)

The Basic Law of the Hong Kong Special Administrative Region of the People's Republic of China (Hong Kong, 1990)

White Paper: The Development of Representative Government: The Way Forward (Hong Kong, 1988)

Xianggang Wenti Wenjian Xuanji (Selected Documents on the Hong Kong Question) (Beijing, 1995)

Xianggang yu Zhongguo: Lishi Wenxian Ziliao Huibian (Hong Kong and China: Collected Historical Writings) (Hong Kong, 1984)

Zhonghua Minguo Zhongyao Shiliao Chubian: Duijih Gangzhan Shichi (A First Selection of Important Historical Material of the Republic of China: The Period of the War of Resistance against Japan)

Hong Kong Government

A Draft Agreement between the Government of the United Kingdom of Great Britain and Northern Ireland and the Government of the People's Republic of China on the Future of Hong Kong (Hong Kong, 1984)

An Introduction to Hong Kong Bill of Rights Ordinance (Hong Kong, undated, 1991)

District Administration in Hong Kong (Hong Kong, 1981)

Green Paper: The Further Development of Representative Government in Hong Kong (Hong Kong, 1984)

Green Paper: The 1987 Review of Developments in Representative Government (Hong Kong, 1987)

Hong Kong Annual Report 1952 (Hong Kong, 1953)

Hong Kong 1982 (Hong Kong, 1982)

Hong Kong 1983 (Hong Kong, 1983)

Hong Kong 1989 (Hong Kong, 1989)

Hong Kong 1990 (Hong Kong, 1990)

Hong Kong 1991 (Hong Kong, 1991)

Patten, Chris, Our Next Five Years: The Agenda for Hong Kong (Hong Kong, 1992)

— *Hong Kong: Today's Success, Tomorrow's Challenges* (Hong Kong, 1993)

Public Response to Green Paper: The 1987 Review of Developments in Representative Government — *Report of the Survey Office Part I* (Hong Kong, 1987)

The City District Officer Scheme: Report by the Secretary for Chinese Affairs (Hong Kong, 1969)

The Government and the People (Hong Kong, 1962)

White Paper: The Further Development of Representative Government in Hong Kong (Hong Kong, 1984)

UK Government

Documents on the Prime Minister's Visit to Peking, 2–4 September 1991 (London, undated, 1991) Memorandum of Understanding

Foreign Affairs Committee, *Second Report on Hong Kong* (Session 1988–9) (London, 1989)

Hong Kong: Arrangements for Testing the Acceptability in Hong Kong of the Draft Agreement on the Future of the Territory (London, 1984)

House of Commons, *Parliamentary Debates* (London, 1984)

House of Lords, *House of Lords Debates*, 56 (1898)

— *Parliamentary Debates* (London, 1984)

Representative Government in Hong Kong (Com 2432) (London, 1994)

Newspapers and Journals

BBC, *Summary of World Broadcasts* (Reading)

Beijing Review (Beijing)

Cheng Bao (Hong Kong)

Daily Information Bulletin (Hong Kong)

Dateline Hong Kong (Hong Kong)

Dongfang Ribao (The Oriental Daily) (Hong Kong)

Far Eastern Economic Review (Hong Kong)

Financial Times (London)

Guardian (London)

Hong Kong Monitor (London)

Independent (London)

Ming Pao (Hong Kong)

Pai Shing (bimonthly, Hong Kong)

Qishi Niandai (The Seventies) (Hong Kong)

Renmin Ribao (People's Daily) (Beijing)

South China Morning Post (Hong Kong)

Wen Hui Pao (Hong Kong)

Xianggang Shang Bao (Hong Kong Commercial News) (Hong Kong)

Xin Bao (Hong Kong Economic Journal) (Hong Kong)

Xin Wan Bao (New Evening News) (Hong Kong)

Zhongguo Minzhu Lundan (The Chinese Democratic Forum) (Hong Kong)

SECONDARY SOURCES

Books and Articles (in Chinese)

Anon, *Dongjiang Zongdui Shi* (A History of the East River Column) (Waiyang, Guangdong, 1985)

Anon, *Guancha Xianggang: Xianggang Guangchashe Yanlunji* (Observing Hong Kong: A Collection of Writings by the Hong Kong Observers) (Hong Kong, 1982)

Bai Zhongxi, *The Reminiscences of General Pai Chung-hsi* (original English title, but text in Chinese) (Taipei, 1989)

Chen Liwen (Nancy Chen) *Song Ziwen yu Zhanshi Waijiao* (T. V. Soong and Wartime Diplomacy) (Taipei, 1991)

Cheng Lisheng, *Deng Xiaoping 'Yiguo Liangzhi' Sixiang Yanjiu* (An Analysis of Deng Xiaoping's Idea of 'One Country, Two Systems') (Shenyang, 1992)

Deng Xiaoping, *Deng Xiaoping Lun Tongyi Zhanxian* (Deng Xiaoping on the United Front) (Beijing, 1991)

— *Deng Xiaoping Wenxuan* (Selected Works of Deng Xiaoping) vol. 3 (Beijing, 1993)

— *Deng Xiaoping lun Xianggang Wenti* (Deng Xiaoping on the Problem of Hong Kong) (Hong Kong, 1993)

Gu Weijun, *Gu Weijun Huiyilu* (Memoirs of Wellington Koo) vol. 5 (Beijing, 1987)

Guo Limin (ed.) *Zhonggong du Tai Zhengze Zhiliao Xuanji: 1949–1991* (Selected Material on the Chinese Communist Policy Towards Taiwan) vol. 1 (Taipei, 1992)

Ho Fengshan, *Waijiao Shengya Sishi Nian* (Forty Years in the Diplomatic Service) (Hong Kong, 1990)

Huang Renyu, *Zong Da Lishi de Jiaodu du Jiang Jeshi Riji* (Studying the Diaries of Chiang Kai-shek in the Perspective of Macro-History) (Taipei, 1994)

Jiang Jieshi, *Zongtong Jianggong Sixiang yanlun Zongzi* (Collected Works of President Chiang Kai-shek) (Taipei, 1984) vol. 4 (*China's Destiny*, March 1943)

— *Zongtong Jianggong Sixiang yanlun Zongzi* (Collected Works of President Chiang Kai-shek) vol. 36 (Taipei, 1984)

Lai Qizhi, *Peng Dingkang Zhenggai Fangan Mianmianguan* (Looking at the Patten Plan from Many Different Aspects) (Hong Kong, 1993)

Lau Siu-kai, 'Public Attitude Towards Sino–British Relations in the Late Transitional Period in Hong Kong' (abstract in English; paper in Chinese) in One Country Two Systems Economic Institute (ed.) *Hong Kong in Transition* (Hong Kong, 1993)

Leng Xia and Wang Tong, *Sheizhu Xiangjiang* (Who Will Be in Charge in Hong Kong?) (Hong Kong, 1996)

Li Dongfang, *Xishuo Kangzhan* (Explaining the War of Resistance in Detail) (Taipei, Yuanliu Chubenshe, 1995)

Li Yi, *Xianggang Yijiujiuqi* (Hong Kong 1997) (Taipei, 1996)

Liang Binghua, *Chengzhai yu Zhongying Waijiao* (The Fort and Sino–British Diplomacy) (Hong Kong, 1995)

Liang Shangyuan, *Zhonggong zai Xianggang* (The Chinese Communists in Hong Kong) (Hong Kong, 1989)

Liao Guangsheng, *Xianggang Minzhuhua de Kunjing* (The Impossible Situation for Democratization in Hong Kong) (Taipei, 1996)

Liu Huiqing, *Liu Huiqing Miandui Xianggang* (Emily Lau Facing Hong Kong) (Hong Kong, 1991)

Long Xin, *Xianggang de Lingyige Zhengfu* (The Other Government of Hong Kong) (Hong Kong, n.d.)

Mao Zedong, *Jianguo Yilai Mao Zedong Wengao* (Collected Writings of Mao Zedong since the Founding of the Republic) vol. 1 (Beijing, 1987)

— *Mao Zedong Junshi Wenxuan* (Selected Writings on Military Affairs by Mao Zedong) (Beijing, 1981)

— *Mao Zedong Waijiao Wenxuan* (Mao Zedong's Selected Writings on Foreign Affairs) (Beijing, 1995)

— *Mao Zedong Wenji* (Collected Writings of Mao Zedong) (Beijing, 1996) vols 4 and 5

— *Mao Zedong Xuanji* (Selected Works of Mao Zedong) (Beijing, 1960) vol. 4

Qian Yuanle, *Xinhuashe Tousshi* (Seeing Through the Xinhua News Agency) (Hong Kong, 1987)

Sima Yi, *Ronyao Quangui Deng Xiaoping de Xianggang Qiantu Tanpan* (Negotiations for Hong Kong's Future for which all the Glories belong to Deng Xiaoping) (Hong Kong, 1984)

Wang Fu, *Jihjun Qinhua Zhanzheng 1931–1945* (The Japanese Army's Aggressive War Against China) (Shenyang, 1990) vol. 3

Wang Hongxu, *Qishi Niandai Yilai de Zhongying Guanxi* (Sino–British Relations Since the 1970s) (Harbin, 1996)

Wu Guozhen, *Wu Guozhen Zhuan* (Biography of K. C. Wu) (Taipei, 1995)

Wu Kangmin, *Renda Huiyilu* (Memoirs of the National People's Congress) (Hong Kong, 1990)

Xianggang Wenhuibao (ed.) *Jibenfa de Dansheng* (The Birth of the Basic Law) (Hong Kong, 1990)

Xiao Weiyun (ed.) *Yiguo Liangzhi yu Xianggang Tebie Xingzhengqu Jibenfa* (One Country Two Systems and the Basic Law for the Hong Kong Special Administrative Region) (Hong Kong, 1990)

Xie Yongguang, *Xianggang Zhanhou Fengyunlu* (Record of the Volatile Postwar Years in Hong Kong) (Hong Kong, 1996)

Xu Jiatun, *Xu Jiatun Xianggang Huiyilu* (Xu Jiatun's Memoirs of Hong Kong) (Taipei, 1993) vols. 1 and 2

Xu Kangming, *Zhonghuo Yuanzhengjun Zhanshi* (A History of the Battles of the Chinese Expeditionary Force) (Beijing, 1995)

Xu Simin, *Guoshi Gangshi Hua Sannian* (Speaking about the Affairs of the Country and Hong Kong in the Last Three Years) (Hong Kong, 1996)

Ye Lei, 'Xianggang Xinhuashe fazhan shi' (A History of the Evolution of the Xinhua News Agency in Hong Kong) in Liang Shangyuan, *Zhonggong zai Xianggang* (The Chinese Communists in Hong Kong) (Hong Kong, 1989)

Yu Shengwu and Liu Cunkuan (eds) *Shijiu Shiji de Xianggang* (Nineteenth Century Hong Kong) (Beijing, 1994)

Zeng Ruisheng (Steve Tsang) 'Yingguo Fangwai Xianggang Zhengce de Yanbian' (The Evolution of Britain's Policy to Defend Hong Kong) *Guang Jiao Jing* (The Wide Angle) no. 200, 1989

Zeng Sheng, *Zheng Sheng Huiyilu* (Memoirs of [General] Zeng Sheng) (Beijing, 1991)

Zheng Dongguo, *Wo de Rongma Shengya: Zheng Dongguo Huiyilu* (My Life Soldiering: Memoirs of Zheng Dongguo) (Beijing, 1992)

Zhongguo Xinwen She (ed.) *Liaogong zai Renjian* (The Life of Mr Liang) (Hong Kong, 1984)

Zhou Enlai, *Zhou Enlai Waijiao Wenxuan* (Beijing, 1994)

Books and Articles (in English)

Atwell, Pamela, *British Mandarins and Chinese Reformers: The British Administration of Weihaiwei (1898–1930)* (Hong Kong, 1985)

Avon, Earl of, *The Eden Memoirs: The Reckoning* (London, 1965)

Baker, Hugh, 'Life in the Cities: The Emergence of Hong Kong Man', *The China Quarterly*, No. 95, September 1983, p.478.

Barber, Noel, *The Fall of Shanghai* (New York: 1979)

Barme, Geremie, 'Totalitarian Nostalgia: Chinese Utopias, Future Imperfect', paper presented at the 'China Facing the Challenges of Modernization' Conference at Universidad Autónoma de Madrid, 2–3 October 1995

Barnett, A. D., *The Making of Foreign Policy in China* (London, 1985)

Boardman, Robert, *Britain and the People's Republic of China 1949–1974* (London and Basingstoke, 1976)

Bonavia, David, *Hong Kong 1997* (Hong Kong, 1984)

Brice, Martin H., *The Royal Navy and the Sino–Japanese Incident 1937–41* (London, 1973)

Bruce, Philip, *Second to None: The Story of the Hong Kong Volunteers* (Hong Kong, 1991)

Buckley, Roger, *Hong Kong: The Road to 1997* (Cambridge, 1997)

Burns, John, 'The Structure of Communist Party Control in Hong Kong', *Asian Survey*, vol. 30, no. 8 (August 1990)

— 'The Role of the New China News Agency', in *Hong Kong and China in Transition* (Canada and Hong Kong Papers No. 3) (Toronto, 1994)

Catron, Gary Wayne, *China and Hong Kong, 1945–1967* (Harvard University, unpublished Ph.D. thesis, 1971)

Chan, M. K., 'Democracy Derailed: Realpolitik in the Making of the Hong Kong Basic Law, 1985–90', in M. K. Chan and David Clark (eds) *The Hong Kong Basic Law* (Hong Kong, 1991)

— (ed.) *Precarious Balance: Hong Kong Between China and Britain, 1842–1922* (New York, 1994)

Chan, M. K. and David Clark (eds) *The Hong Kong Basic Law* (Hong Kong, 1991)

Chan, Ming and Tuen-yu Lau, 'Dilemma of the Communist Press in a Pluralistic Society', *Asian Survey*, vol. 30, no. 8 (August 1990)

Chan Lau Kit-ching, 'The Hong Kong Question during the Pacific War (1941–45)', *Journal of Imperial and Commonwealth History*, vol. 3, no. 1, October 1973

— *China, Britain and Hong Kong 1895–1945* (Hong Kong, 1990)

Chang, Dennis, 'How China Sees It', in William McGurn (ed.) *Basic Law, Basic Questions* (Hong Kong, 1988)

Chen Jian, *China's Road to the Korean War: The Making of the Sino–American Confrontation* (New York, 1994)

Chen Xitong, 'Report on Checking the Turmoil and Quelling the Counter-Revolutionary Rebellion', supplement in *Beijing Review*, 17–23 July 1989

Cheng, Chu-yuan, *Behind the Tiananmen Massacre: Social, Political, and Economic Ferment in China* (Boulder, 1990)

Cheng Hsiao-shih, *Party–Military Relations in the PRC and Taiwan* (Boulder, 1990)

Cheng, Joseph Y. S., *Hong Kong: In Search of a Future* (Hong Kong, 1984)

— 'Prospect for Democracy in Hong Kong', in George Hicks (ed.) *The Broken Mirror: China after Tiananmen* (Harlow, 1990)

Cheung, Stephen and Stephen Sze (eds) *The Other Hong Kong Report 1995* (Hong Kong, 1995)

Ch'i Hsi-sheng, *Nationalist China at War: Military Defeats and Political Collapse, 1937–45* (Ann Arbor, 1982)

— 'The Military Dimension, 1942–1945', in James Hsiung and Steven Levine (eds) *China's Bitter Victory: The War with Japan 1937–1945* (New York, 1992)

Ching, Frank, 'A Discredited Past? One Hong Kong View on Lord Wilson', *Hong Kong Monitor*, December 1992

— 'Toward Colonial Sunset: The Wilson Regime, 1987–92', in Ming K. Chan (ed.) *Precarious Balance: Hong Kong Between China and Britain, 1842–1922* (New York, 1994)

Chiu Hungdah, *The People's Republic of China and the Law of Treaties* (Cambridge, Massachusetts, 1972)

Chou Tse-tsung, *The May Fourth Movement: Intellectual Revolution in Modern China* (Stanford, 1967)

Churchill, Winston S., *The Second World War Volume III: The Grand Alliance* (London, 1950)

Corry, Bernard, *The Corry Report* (Hong Kong, 1989)

Cottrell, Robert, *The End of Hong Kong: The Secret Diplomacy of Imperial Retreat* (London, 1993)

Cradock, Percy, *Experiences of China* (London, 1994)

— 'Losing the Plot in Hong Kong', *Prospect*, April 1997

Cruickshank, Charles, *SOE in the Far East* (Oxford, 1986)

Deng Maomao, *My Father Deng Xiaoping* (New York, 1995)

Dilks, David (ed.) *Retreat from Power: Studies in Britain's Foreign Policy of the Twentieth Century. Volume One 1906–1939* (London and Basingstoke, 1981)

Dittmer, Lowell, *China Under Reform* (Boulder, 1994)

Domes, Jurgen and Yu-ming Shaw (eds) *Hong Kong: A Chinese and International Concern* (Boulder and London, 1988)

Edwards, Randle, Louis Henkin and Andrew Nathan (eds) *Human Rights in Contemporary China* (New York, 1986)

Endacott, G. B., *A History of Hong Kong* (Hong Kong, 1964)

Endacott, G. B. and Alan Birch, *Hong Kong Eclipse* (Hong Kong, 1978)

Esherick, Joseph W., *The Origins of the Boxer Uprising* (Berkeley, 1987)

Esherick, Joseph and Jeffrey Wasserstrom, 'Acting out Democracy: Political Theater in Modern China', in Jeffrey Wasserstrom and Elizabeth Perry (eds) *Popular Protest and Political Culture in Modern China* (Boulder, 1994)

Evans, Richard, *Deng Xiaoping and the Making of Modern China* (London, 1993)

Far Eastern Economic Review, *1968 Yearbook* (Hong Kong, 1968)

— *Asia 1979 Yearbook* (Hong Kong, 1979)

Fathers, Michael and Andrew Higgins, *Tiananmen: The Rape of Peking* (London, 1989)

Feng Zhong-ping, *The British Government's China Policy 1945–1950* (Keele, Staffordshire, 1994)

Freris, Andrew, *The Financial Markets of Hong Kong* (London and New York, 1991)

FRUS, *Foreign Relations of the United States*, vol. VII (Washington, 1969)

Fung, Edmund S. K., *The Diplomacy of Imperial Retreat: Britain's South China Policy, 1924–1931* (Hong Kong, 1991)

Garver, John W., 'China's Wartime Diplomacy', in James Hsiung and Steven Levine (eds) *China's Bitter Victory: The War with Japan 1937–1945* (New York, 1992)

Gilbert, Martin, *Road to Victory: Winston S. Churchill 1941–1945* (London, 1986)

Goncharov, S. N., J. W. Lewis and Xue Litai, *Uncertain Partners: Stalin, Mao, and the Korean War* (Stanford, 1993)

Goto-Shibata, Harumi, *Japan and Britain in Shanghai 1925–31* (Basingstoke, 1995)

Grantham, Alexander, *Via Ports: From Hong Kong to Hong Kong* (Hong Kong, 1965)

Hamrin, Carol Lee, 'The Party Leadership System', in Kenneth Lieberthal and David Lampton (eds) *Bureaucracy, Politics, and Decision Making in Post-Mao China* (Berkeley, 1992)

Han, Minzhu, *Cries for Democracy: Writings and Speeches from the 1989 Chinese Democracy Movement* (Princeton, 1990)

Han Lih-wu, *The Reminiscences of Mr Han Lih-wu* (Taipei, 1990)

Han Nianlong (ed.) *Diplomacy of Contemporary China* (Hong Kong, 1990)

Harding, Harry, *Organizing China: The Problem of Bureaucracy 1949–1976* (Stanford, 1981)

Hayes, James, *Friends and Teachers: Hong Kong and its People 1953–87* (Hong Kong, 1996)

Heald, Tim, *Beating Retreat: Hong Kong Under the Last Governor* (London, 1997)

Hicks, George (ed.) *The Broken Mirror: China after Tiananmen* (Harlow, 1990)

Hooper, Beverley, *China Stands Up: Ending the Western Presence 1948–1950* (Sydney, 1986)

Hooton, E. R., *The Greatest Tumult: The Chinese Civil War 1936–49* (London and Oxford, 1991)

Howard, Michael, 'British Military Preparations for the Second World War', in David Dilks (ed.) *Retreat from Power: Studies in Britain's Foreign Policy of the Twentieth Century Volume One 1906–1939* (London and Basingstoke, 1981)

Howe, Geoffrey, *Conflict of Loyalty* (London, 1995)

Hsiao, Frank and Lawrence Sullivan, 'The Chinese Communist Party and the Status of Taiwan', *Pacific Affairs*, vol. 52, no. 3, 1979

Hsiung, James and Steven Levine (eds) *China's Bitter Victory: The War with Japan 1937–1945* (New York, 1992)

Hsu, Immanuel, *China Without Mao: The Search for a New Order* (second edition) (Oxford, 1990)

Hurd, Douglas, 'Governor Patten Unveils a Bold Blueprint for Hong Kong's Future', *Hong Kong Monitor*, December 1992

Jordan, Donald A., *The Northern Expedition: China's National Revolution of 1926–1928* (Honolulu, 1976)

Joseph, Philip, *Foreign Diplomacy in China 1894–1900* (New York, 1971)

Keith, Ronald C., *The Diplomacy of Zhou Enlai* (Basingstoke, 1989)

King, Ambrose, 'Administrative Absorption of Politics in Hong Kong: Emphasis on the Grass Roots Level', *Asian Survey*, vol. 15, no. 5, May 1975

King, Frank, *The Hong Kong Bank in the Period of Development and Nationalism, 1941–1984* (Cambridge, 1991)

Kirby, S. Woodburn, *The War Against Japan Volume I: The Loss of Singapore* (London, 1957)

— *The War Against Japan Volume V: The Surrender of Japan* (London, 1969)

Kreisberg, Paul H., 'China's Negotiating Behavior', in T. W. Robinson and D. Shambaugh (eds) *Chinese Foreign Policy: Theory and Practice* (Oxford, 1994)

Kristof, Nicholas and Sheryl WuDunn, *China Wakes: The Struggle for the Soul of a Rising Power* (London, 1994)

Kwok, Rowena, Joan Leung and Ian Scott (eds) *Votes Without Power: The Hong Kong Legislative Council Elections 1991* (Hong Kong, 1992)

Kwok, R. Y. W and A. Y. So (eds) *The Hong Kong–Guangdong Link: Partnership in Flux* (Hong Kong, 1995)

Lau, Emily, ' "Dear Governor": An Elected Lady Offers Some Advice', *Hong Kong Monitor*, September 1992

Lau Siu-kai, 'Institutions Without Leaders: The Hong Kong Chinese View of Political Leadership', *Pacific Affairs*, vol. 63, no. 2, 1990

— 'Colonial Rule, Transfer of Sovereignty and the Problem of Political Leaders in Hong Kong', *Journal of Commonwealth and Comparative Politics*, vol. 30, no. 2, July 1992

Lau Siu-kai and Hsin-chi Kuan, *The Ethos of the Hong Kong Chinese* (Hong Kong, 1988)

Lau Siu-kai and Kin-sheun Louie (eds) *Hong Kong Tried Democracy: The 1991 Elections in Hong Kong* (Hong Kong, 1993)

Lee Lai To, *The Reunification of China: PRC–Taiwan Relations in Flux* (New York, 1991)

Leung, Joan, 'Summary Findings and Implications', in Rowena Kwok, Joan Leung and Ian Scott (eds) *Votes Without Power: The Hong Kong Legislative Council Elections 1991* (Hong Kong, 1992)

Leung, K. K., 'The Basic Law and the Problem of Political Transition', in Stephen Cheung and Stephen Sze (eds) *The Other Hong Kong Report 1995* (Hong Kong, 1995)

Leung Sai-wing, 'The "China Factor" in the 1991 Legislative Council Election', in Siu-kai Lau and Kin-sheun Louie (eds) *Hong Kong Tried Democracy: The 1991 Elections in Hong Kong* (Hong Kong, 1993)

Levine, Steven I., *Anvil of Victory: The Communist Revolution in Manchuria, 1945–1948* (New York, 1987)

Li Binyan, *China's Crisis, China's Hope* (Cambridge, Massachusetts, 1990)

Lieberthal, Kenneth, *Governing China: From Revolution Through Reform* (New York, 1995)

Lieberthal, Kenneth and David Lampton (eds) *Bureaucracy, Politics, and Decision Making in Post-Mao China* (Berkeley, 1992)

Lieberthal, Kenneth and Michael Oksenberg, *Policy Making in China: Leaders, Structures, and Process* (Princeton, 1988)

Lindsay, Oliver, *The Lasting Honour: The Fall of Hong Kong 1941* (London, 1978)

Liu Xiaobo, 'That Holy Word, "Revolution"', in Jeffrey Wasserstrom and Elizabeth Perry (eds) *Popular Protest and Political Culture in Modern China* (Boulder, 1994)

Lo Shiu-hing, *The Politics of Democratization in Hong Kong* (Basingstoke, 1997)

Louie Kin-sheun et al., 'Who Voted in the 1991 Elections?', in Siu-kai Lau and Kin-sheun Louie (eds) *Hong Kong Tried Democracy: The 1991 Elections in Hong Kong* (Hong Kong, 1993)

Lowe, Peter, *Great Britain and the Origins of the Pacific War: A Study of British Policy in East Asia 1937–1941* (Oxford, 1977)

McGurn, William (ed.) *Basic Law, Basic Questions* (Hong Kong, 1988)

Manion, Melanie, 'Introduction: Reluctant Duelists: The Logic of the 1989 Protests and Massacre', in Michael Oksenberg, Lawrence Sullivan and Marc Lambert (eds) *Beijing Spring, 1989: Confrontation and Conflict The Basic Documents* (New York, 1990)

Martin, Edwin W., *Divided Counsel: The Anglo-American Response to Communist Victory in China* (Lexington, Kentucky, 1986)

Michael, Franz, 'China and the Crisis of Communism', in George Hicks (ed.) *The Broken Mirror: China after Tiananmen* (Harlow, 1990)

Miners, Norman, *Hong Kong Under Imperial Rule, 1912–1941* (Hong Kong, 1987)

— *The Government and Politics of Hong Kong* (fourth and fifth editions) (Hong Kong, 1986 and 1991)

Ming Chan and David Clark (eds) *The Hong Kong Basic Law: Blueprint for 'Stability and Prosperity' under Chinese Sovereignty* (Hong Kong, 1991)

Ming Chan and Tuen-yu Lau, 'Dilemma of the Communist Press in a Pluralistic Society', *Asian Survey*, vol. 30, no. 8, August 1990

Murfett, Malcolm H., *Hostage on the Yangtze: Britain, China, and the Amethyst Crisis of 1949* (Annapolis, Maryland, 1991)

Myers, Ramon (ed.) *Two Societies in Opposition: The Republic of China and the People's Republic of China* (Stanford: Hoover Institution Press, 1991)

Nathan, Andrew, 'Political Rights in Chinese Constitutions', in Randle Edwards, Louis Henkin and Andrew Nathan (eds) *Human Rights in Contemporary China* (New York, 1986)

Oksenberg, Michael, Lawrence Sullivan and Marc Lambert (eds) *Beijing Spring, 1989: Confrontation and Conflict The Basic Documents* (New York, 1990)

One Country Two Systems Economic Institute (ed.) *Hong Kong in Transition* (Hong Kong, 1993)

Pepper, Suzanne, *Civil War in China: The Political Struggle, 1945–1949* (Berkeley, 1978)

Pye, Lucian, 'Tiananmen and Chinese Political Culture', *Asian Survey*, vol. 30, no. 4, April 1990

Qiang Zhai, *The Dragon, the Lion, and the Eagle: Chinese–British–American Relations, 1949–1958* (Kent, Ohio, 1994)

Rafferty, Kevin, *City on the Rocks: Hong Kong's Uncertain Future* (revised and updated edition) (London, 1989)

Reardon-Anderson, James, *Yenan and the Great Powers: The Origins of Chinese Communist Foreign Policy 1944–1946* (New York, 1980)

Ride, Edwin, *British Army Aid Group: Hong Kong Resistance 1942–1945* (Hong Kong, 1981)

Roberti, Mark, *The Fall of Hong Kong: Britain's Betrayal and China's Triumph* (New York and London, 1994)

Robinson, Ronald and John Gallagher, *Africa and the Victorians: The Official Mind of Imperialism* (second edition) (London and Basingstoke, 1981)

Robinson, T. W. and D. Shambaugh (eds) *Chinese Foreign Policy: Theory and Practice* (Oxford, 1994)

Ruan Ming, *Deng Xiaoping: Chronicle of an Empire* (Boulder, 1994)

Schiffrin, H. Z., *Sun Yat-sen and the Origins of the Chinese Revolution* (Berkeley, 1970)

Schram, Stuart, *The Political Thought of Mao Tse-tung* (revised and enlarged edition) (New York, 1969)

Schrecker, John E., *Imperialism and Chinese Nationalism: Germany in Shantung* (Cambridge, Massachusetts, 1971)

Scott, Ian, Political *Change and the Crisis of Legitimacy in Hong Kong* (Hong Kong, 1989)

— 'An Overview of the Hong Kong Legislative Council Elections of 1991', in Rowena Kwok, Joan Leung and Ian Scott (eds) *Votes Without Power: The Hong Kong Legislative Council Elections 1991* (Hong Kong, 1992)

— 'Political Transformation in Hong Kong: From Colony to Colony', in R. Y. W Kwok and A. Y. So (eds) *The Hong Kong–Guangdong Link: Partnership in Flux* (New York, 1995)

Shai, Aron, *Origins of the War in the East: Britain, China and Japan 1937-39* (London, 1976)

— *Britain and China, 1941–47* (London and Basingstoke, 1984)

— *The Fate of British and French Firms in China, 1949–54: Imperialism Imprisoned* (Basingstoke, 1996)

Shawcross, William, *Kowtow!* (London, 1989)

Shih Chueh, *The Reminiscences of General Shih Chueh* (Taipei, 1986)

Snow, Edgar, *Red Star Over China* (revised and enlarged edition) (Harmondsworth, 1972)

Sung Yun-wing, *The China–Hong Kong Connection: The Key to China's Open Door Policy* (Cambridge, 1991)

Tang, James Tuck-hong, *Britain's Encounter with Revolutionary China, 1949–54* (Basingstoke, 1992)

Tang, James and Frank Ching, 'The MacLehose–Youde Years: Balancing the "Three-Legged Stool" 1971–86', in Ming K. Chan (ed.) *Precarious Balance: Hong Kong Between China and Britain, 1842–1922* (New York, 1994)

Teichman, Sir Eric, *Affairs of China* (London, 1938)

Thatcher, Margaret, *The Downing Street Years* (London, 1993)

Thorne, Christopher, *Allies of a Kind: The United States, Britain and the War against Japan, 1941–1945* (Oxford, 1978)

Truman, H. S., *Memoirs of Harry S. Truman Volume II: Years of Trial and Hope* (New York, 1956)

Tsang, Steve, *Democracy Shelved: Great Britain, China, and Attempts at Constitutional Reform in Hong Kong, 1945–1952* (Hong Kong, 1988)

— 'A Future Built on Hope: How the Foreign Affairs Committee Sees It', *Hong Kong Monitor*, September 1989

— 'Identity Crisis in Hong Kong', *Hong Kong Monitor*, September 1990

— 'A Triumph for Democracy?', *Hong Kong Monitor*, December 1991

— (ed.) *A Documentary History of Hong Kong: Government and Politics* (Hong Kong, 1995)

— 'Maximum Flexibility, Rigid Framework: China's Policy Towards Hong Kong and Its Implications', *Journal of International Affairs*, vol. 49, no. 2, Winter 1996

— 'Realignment of Power: The Politics of Transition and Reform in Hong Kong', in P. K. Li (ed.) *Political Order and Power Transition in Hong Kong* (Hong Kong, 1997)

— 'Strategy for Survival: The Cold War and Hong Kong's Policy Towards Kuomintang and Chinese Communist Activities in the 1950s', *Journal of Imperial and Commonwealth History*, vol. 25, no. 2, May 1997

Tuchman, Barbara, *Sand Against the Wind: Stillwell and the American Experience in China 1911–45* (London, 1985)

Tucker, Nancy B., *Taiwan, Hong Kong and the United States, 1945–1992: Uncertain Friendships* (New York, 1994) van de Messerssche, P., *A Life to Treasure: The Authorized Biography of Han Lih-wu* (London, 1987)

Van Slyke, Lyman P., *Enemies and Friends: The United Front in Chinese Communist History* (Stanford, 1967)

Vogel, Ezra, *One Step Ahead in China: Guangdong Under Reform* (Cambridge, Massachusetts, 1989)

Wasserstrom, Jeffrey and Elizabeth Perry (eds) *Popular Protest and Political Culture in Modern China* (Boulder, 1994)

Welsh, Frank, *A History of Hong Kong* (London, 1993)

Wesley-Smith, Peter, *Unequal Treaty 1897–1997: China, Great Britain and Hong Kong's New Territories* (Hong Kong, 1983)

Wilbur, Martin, *Sun Yat-sen: Frustrated Patriot* (New York, 1976)

— *The Nationalist Revolution in China, 1923–1928* (Cambridge, 1983)

Wilgus, Mary H., *Sir Claude MacDonald, the Open Door, and British Informal Empire in China, 1895–1900* (New York and London, 1987)

Wilson, Dick, *Hong Kong! Hong Kong!* (London, 1990)

Wong, J. Y., *The Origins of an Heroic Image: Sun Yatsen in London, 1896-1897* (Hong Kong, 1986)

Wong, Jan, *Red China Blues* (Toronto, 1997)

Wright, Mary C., *China in Revolution: The First Phase* (New Haven and London, 1968)

Wu Xiongcheng, 'The International Climate and the June Rebellion', *Beijing Review*, 11–17 September 1989

Xiang Lanxin, *Recasting the Imperial Far East: Britain and America in China, 1945–1950* (New York, 1995)

Yahuda, Michael, *Hong Kong: China's Challenge* (London and New York, 1996)

Yao, Y. C., 'Hong Kong's Role in Financing China's Modernization', in A. J. Youngson (ed.) *China and Hong Kong: The Economic Nexus* (Hong Kong, 1983)

— 'Banking and Currency in the Special Economic Zones: Problems and Prospects', in Y. C. Yao and C. K. Leung (eds) *China's Special Economic Zones* (Hong Kong, 1986)

Yao, Y. C. and C. K. Leung (eds) *China's Special Economic Zones* (Hong Kong, 1986)

Youde, Edward, *The Chairman's Lecture: The Political and Commercial Prospects for Hong Kong* (London, 1985)

Young, Hugo, *One of Us* (London, 1990)

Young, L. K., *British Policy in China 1895–1902* (Oxford, 1970)

Youngson, A. J. (ed.) *China and Hong Kong: The Economic Nexus* (Hong Kong, 1983)

Yu Teh-pei, 'Economic Links among Hong Kong, PRC, and ROC: With Special Reference to Trade', in Jurgen Domes and Yu-ming Shaw (eds) *Hong Kong: A Chinese and International Concern* (Boulder and London, 1988)

Zhang Yongjin, *China in the International System, 1918–20: The Middle Kingdom at the Periphery* (Basingstoke, 1991)

Zhao Quansheng, *Interpreting Chinese Foreign Policy* (Hong Kong, 1996)

Index